TUFFERS' CRICKET HALL OF FAME

My willow-wielding idols, ball-twirling legends . . .
and other random icons

TUFFERS' CRICKET HALL OF FAME

PHIL TUFNELL

My willow-wielding idols, ball-twirling legends . . .
and other random icons

with Justyn Barnes

HEADLINE

First published in Great Britain in 2017
by HEADLINE PUBLISHING GROUP

1

Cataloguing in Publication Data is available from the British Library

Hardback ISBN 978 1 4722 2939 7

Typeset in 10.5/16 pt Bliss by Jouve (UK), Milton Keynes

Printed and bound by CPI Group (UK) Ltd, Croydon, CR0 4YY

HEADLINE PUBLISHING GROUP
An Hachette UK Company
Carmelite House
50 Victoria Embankment
London EC4Y 0DZ

www.headline.co.uk
www.hachette.co.uk

CONTENTS

INTRODUCTION

As a sporty young kid in the mid-Seventies, it was football in the winter and cricket in the summer – watching and playing. During the school summer holidays, my mum would often drop me round at my mate's house in the morning and we'd spend the day watching the Test match on telly. We'd get orange squash and biscuits and settle down in the living room to watch Geoff Boycott blocking the arse out of it against the Aussie quicks or West Indies' battery of fast bowlers for hours on end. At lunchtime, we'd eat a sandwich, go out in the back garden to try to imitate what we'd seen, then it was back to the living room ready for the afternoon session. We might get the old cricket dice game of Owzthat! going on the carpet, but always keeping half an eye on the screen. More practice in the garden at the tea interval, watch some more Test match and about half five, mum would come and me pick me up and take me home for my tea.

Other days, my mate might come over to ours instead, but the routine was much the same and this happened most days through the summer when a Test match was on telly. It's funny looking back, because we were enthralled by it and yet, compared to today's Test cricket, there were so few attacking shots played. Boycs stroking a technically perfect off drive past mid-off for four might be as good as it got in some sessions.

Televised cricket was free childcare for our parents and Geoff Boycott was basically my babysitter. Halcyon days.

That's how my love of the game began to grow, and all these years later, having played cricket and gone on to talk about it for a living, it's fun to be asked to select my all-time cricket heroes. But with so many wonderful players to choose from, where do I start? Childhood heroes, perhaps? Hmm. Who did I have posters of on my bedroom wall? Well, I always had Arsenal pictures growing up – they were my team. Charlie George, Liam Brady and the annual team photo from *Shoot!* magazine. Then there was Scooby Doo. Debbie Harry. The Sex Pistols, when I got into punk. Linda Lusardi, when I got a bit older. I also had a poster of a Lamborghini Countach – that was my first dream car. Then again, I remember watching James May drive it on *Top Gear* years later. It had been his childhood ambition to drive it, too, but he discovered it was a heap of junk. The brakes were rubbish, the windows didn't open, you couldn't see out of the back window, the gearbox was crap, no air conditioning . . . Both our dreams were shattered. Never meet your heroes, even if it is a car.

I also loved motorbikes and had posters of Evel Knievel and

Barry Sheene. To me, Barry Sheene was glamour. He broke just about every bone in his body, but he always seemed to have the pretty girls around him. I started getting into riding bikes myself when I was 12 or 13. I had all sorts – a Yamaha 'Fizzy' (FS1E), granddad bikes, the ones you see cabbies doing 'The Knowledge' on ... anything cheap. My mate Ian Chambers down the road would soup them up and me and my mates would go riding them in the woods.

But, no, I don't recall having any posters of cricketers. I loved playing and watching the game, I supported Middlesex and England, but, for some reason, I must have preferred looking at a photo of Linda Lusardi to Graham Gooch and his gorgeous handlebar 'tache.

Oh well, in the course of my playing career and then working as a commentator, I have played against, watched and talked to many potential Hall of Famers. And along the way I've heard lots of tales about players who've made a memorable contribution to cricket – sometimes not in the way they planned, but often all the better and/or funnier for that. This book also gives me the chance to seek out lesser-known cricketers, characters from county, club, village and schools cricket, who have done extraordinary things. Or failed heroically – to me, heroic failure can be as entertaining as a match-winning century or eight-fer, so why not celebrate that, too? I might even show some love for umpires, not something I was prone to do in my playing days.

So what are the exact criteria for earning a place in the Tuffers HoF? Don't know yet, but I can figure it out as I go along. That's how I approached my cricket career and life in general, and – apart from the odd catastrophe – that seems to have worked out alright.

A polite warning, though: I'm the gatekeeper here and if a player's name is not on the list, they're not coming in. You'll probably (definitely) scream about some great players I omit, but it's only my personal choice. Some players might be brilliant, but their story doesn't move me, excite me or tug at the heartstrings like others do. Even if you disagree with some of my selections, hopefully together we'll enjoy reliving historic cricket moments together, learn a few little-known nuggets about even the best-known superstars, and dig up plenty of amusing anecdotes along the way. Let's get stuck in . . .

1

DOUBLE ACTS

Lillian Marsh

Strange to say it considering he was an Aussie, but Dennis Lillee was my first cricket hero; the first bloke who really captured my imagination for cricket. He had that long run-up, open shirt, necklace bobbing around as he ran in, big handlebar moustache. He bowled fast and aggressively, drank beer and had an attitude that excited me. He looked like someone you'd fancy on your side in a punch-up in a pub. As a kid trying to bowl fast in the garden, I didn't want to bowl like Mike Hendrick; I wanted to be Dennis Lillee.

His attitude was a bit more me than buttoned-up English cricketers, like this is war rather than a jolly old game of cricket on the playing fields of Eton. Famously, when Dennis visited Buckingham Palace in 1972, he greeted the Queen with a 'G'day'. And when he met her again at the Centenary Test in Melbourne in 1977, he asked Her Maj for her autograph. I liked that. I later got to meet him a couple of times myself, which was a great thrill.

Lillee could walk into any cricket hall of fame on his own, but over his career he became closely linked to two team-mates – Jeff Thomson and Rodney Marsh – so much so that people mashed their names together to become 'Lillian Thomson' and 'Lillian Marsh'. They were both lovely girls.

His fast-bowling affair with Thomson was terrifying for batsmen, but I want to pay tribute to his cricketing marriage with his moustachioed mate Marsh. Both retired from Test cricket in the same game (along with Greg Chappell) and Lillee ended up with 355 Test wickets, Marsh with 355 Test dismissals – both world records at the time.

Of those 355 wickets, 95 were 'c Marsh b Lillee' which appeared so often in the scorebook, it became a cliché. As they both played for Western Australia together from the late Sixties, they jointly achieved 200-plus 'c Marsh b Lillee' dismissals during their whole careers.

'It is Dennis who deserves most credit,' Marsh said about their partnership. 'It is he, after all, who deceives the bat. I'm the "straight man" of the duo, if you like. I merely accept what comes my way.'

In contrast to the image I had of Lillee as a tinny-swilling Aussie, he was actually the straight man off the pitch in his younger days, and they didn't really hit it off. Marsh was 19, a couple of years older, and, as Lillee puts it, 'a scruffy, overweight, beer-swilling intellectual, a pianist and a good singer. He wasn't my sort of person. He probably thought I was a bit of a nerd while he was a typical cricketer of that era, enjoying a drink and having a great time.'

They only really started to bond when Lillee made his Test debut against England in the Sixth Ashes Test at Adelaide in 1971. Marsh was the only other Western Australian player in the side and they went out for a few drinks after the match. Before then, Marsh (and Aussie captain Ian Chappell) had thought it was weird for a fast bowler not to drink, so their night out helped to break down some barriers. I'm sure the five-fer Lillee took in the first innings helped too.

Unlike Lillee, Marsh, who'd made his own Test debut in the First Test, had not got off to a flyer. Indeed, considering the amount of byes he leaked during the series, it could well have been bye-bye Rodney from the Australia team, if it hadn't been for his powerful lower-order batting. Unimpressed Aussie fans had nicknamed him 'Iron Gloves', but the catcalls only spurred him on to improve, by watching and learning from his opposite number, the great Alan Knott (more on him later . . .). And learn he did. Eleven years later, Marsh passed Knotty's world record of 269 Test dismissals (and in 22 fewer Tests than it took Knott), showing how far he had come from his tin-pan-hands days. The victim of Marsh's record-breaking dismissal, at Headingley in 1981, was Ian Botham and the bowler was Dennis Lillee, of course.

Knott sent Marshy a bottle of champagne to mark his achievement, along with a note: 'Congratulations. Well deserved. I hope you don't drop this one.'

On the 1972 England tour, when Lillee was bowling at his fastest, Marsh recalls times when he was quicker than anyone he'd ever seen and the ball actually hurt when it hit his gloves. A serious stress fracture of the back stopped Lillee bowling for almost a whole season in 1973/74. On his return after rehab, he had to slow down a little bit, but Marsh reckoned the injury ultimately benefited him. From just relying on sheer pace and more pace, Lillee developed greater control of swing and seam, and the ability to bowl a fantastic leg-cutter that would earn him many more Test wickets. Batsmen rarely had a clue what he was going to bowl, but Marsh played with him for so long that they had an almost telepathic understanding.

'I know from the way he runs up – the angle, the speed, where he hits the crease – where the ball is going to be,' he said. 'I can see the way his mind is working and I can virtually bowl his over for him, ball by ball.'

They might have been in sync on the pitch, but Lillee never got near Marsh's epic capacity for boozing. Famously, before an Ashes tour, Marsh decided he was going to try and beat Doug Walters' record of drinking 44 cans of beer on the flight over. Many different versions of the events that followed have been told over the years – Lillee himself has told a couple of different ones, and people have variously claimed this happened in 1977 (when Lillee was injured and unavailable for selection) or in 1983 (which would have been difficult as the Ashes series was in Australia that year!).

Anyway, never let the facts get in the way of a good drinking story; and as Graeme Wood plays a minor role in it, and he was in the Aussie squad in 1981, let's go with that year. From what I can gather, Lillee didn't want his mate Marshy to get into trouble with the team management, so he took him on a drinking binge the night before with the idea that he would then be too hungover to go ahead with his record attempt. They each had eight rums on their flight from Perth to Melbourne to meet up with the team, then Marsh got straight on the beer at the hotel. He was still going when Lillee went to bed at 2am.

When Dennis rang Rod's room the next morning, he expected him to be in a right state, but Rod said he was fine, and actually he was just going to have lunch and a few beers with the local boys who'd turned up ready for the afternoon flight to England. Good work.

By the time Dennis arrived at the restaurant, beer was flowing and Marshy was getting stuck in again.

They flew to Sydney first, where Marsh met up with current record holder Doug Walters and had a couple more beers, and then some more with various dignitaries. By the time they got on the plane bound for England, Dennis was certain that Marsh, with the amount he'd drunk already, had given up on the whole record attempt idea, but he was very wrong.

Marsh had tinnies lined up, scorers to keep an official tally, pace-setters to help him on his way and all the air stewards primed to maintain a constant supply of beer. They were doing the flight in three legs – Sydney to Singapore, Singapore to Bahrain, Bahrain to London – so Marsh had worked out that he 'only' needed to drink 15 cans a leg.

All in all, Marsh had an impressively professional approach to the task in hand, with the sort of attention to detail you see from analysts with laptops before Test matches these days. The drinks the previous night and morning had just been a warm-up jog around the boundary for Marsh, and as the plane took off, he went about it with great gusto.

While Lillee slept the whole way between Singapore and Bahrain, Marsh kept up a strong pace and was still going when Lillee woke up. By the time, the plane was making its approach to London, Marsh had consumed his 43rd tinny (we're talking Aussie 'stubbies' here, so each can was about two-thirds of a pint). As he slowly drained the 44th, he suddenly faltered.

'I can't make it,' he told his team-mates.

'Bullshit', they replied helpfully and tipped his head back to force-feed him the record-breaking 45th can as they landed at Heathrow.

Marsh was paralytic – it was the only time anyone had ever seen him drunk, and it had taken approximately 30 pints (plus all those warm-ups) to get him there. That is some engine he had.

A relatively sober Lillee and team-mate Graeme Wood helped him stagger off the plane, only to be snapped by the waiting press photographers. The next day's papers ran the picture with stories about 'their' drinking session, which left Lillee a bit miffed as he hadn't touched a drop since Singapore.

Lillee and Marsh would spend a lot of time together on tours and they had plenty of jolly japes along the way. One of Lillee's favourite wheezes was to offer local drivers of taxis or the team bus advice on how to manoeuvre out of tight situations on the road.

'You're all-clear this side, driver,' he'd say before banging his hand loudly on the side of the vehicle and giving it a big 'Oooh' and then stepping out to inspect the 'damage'.

One night, when a taxi driver was driving Lillee, Marsh and co through the gates of the residence of the governor of Barbados to drop them off at a function, Lillee yelled, 'Look out for the dog!' then banged on the side of the car.

The driver screeched to a halt, and Lillee leapt out, making whimpering noises as he picked up the imaginary dog and carried it into a neighbouring garden. The taxi driver stayed behind the wheel in shock, and when Lillee returned he passed on the sad news that the dog had expired. As the taxi set off up the drive, Lillee continued the wind-up – 'It was a beautiful little dog, too. The governor will be furious . . .'

The poor driver dropped them off and didn't wait for the fare.

The pair of them fell victim to pranks themselves, like the time when Rod and him were roomies at a dodgy hotel called Hottel (yes, double 't') Ripple in Faisalabad in 1977. The en-suite toilet consisted of a hole in the concrete floor. As both boys were nursing dodgy knees, they didn't fancy squatting over that, so they asked the hotel to sort out an alternative, which they did . . . a big box with a hole in it to put over the hole in the floor.

Three days later, they noticed there was a terrible stink in the room (over and above the normal smell of the Hottel, which wasn't the most hygienic place in the world). Turned out one of their team-mates had moved the box slightly which meant Dennis and Rod's number two's hadn't been hitting the target and were still teetering on the edge . . .

Touring isn't all shits and giggles though, especially when you lose and opposition fans are giving you gyp, and neither Lillee nor Marsh were ones to back down from a confrontation. For instance, feelings were running high after the Fourth Test at Edgbaston in the 1981 Ashes series. Australia had collapsed when needing just 151 to win in their second innings, thanks, of course, to a remarkable spell of bowling by Ian Botham when he took five for one in 28 balls, including Marsh's own wicket. The grizzly Aussie called it 'one of the most shameful batting collapses in cricket history' and admitted that he cried in the pavilion afterwards.

To make matters worse, the Aussie players then had to run the gauntlet of hundreds of jeering England fans to reach the team coach which was a couple of hundred metres from the pavilion. When Marsh made it to the coach, he realised he'd left something in the dressing room, so he had to go back which meant another dose of abuse going there and back.

So by the time he took his seat on the coach and opened a tinny, he was not in the best of moods. Then the team physio pointed out of the window, 'Hey, have a look at this guy.'

There was an England supporter leaning over a high fence, gesturing and making some uncomplimentary comments. After a very bad day, Marshy had had enough. He abandoned his beer, slipped past the Australian management, off the coach and marched up to the bloke who was shouting, 'You Australians are a load of rubbish – the whole lot of you . . .', then looking at Marsh, 'Yes, and you're one of them, Lillee – you're nothing but a load of rubbish.'

Lillee? The man was obviously no cricket expert, mistaking the six-foot-tall Lillee with Marsh who's no more than five foot eight. Marsh's lack of height saved the guy though, because the Aussie keeper tried but couldn't jump high enough to grab him.

Marsh proceeded to call him a lot worse things than 'rubbish'.

'I'll sue you, Lillee,' yelled the bloke in response.

'You'll get your chance to sue me if you jump the fence and come over here,' said Marshy, enjoying the idea that if he did thump the England fan, his mate Dennis might get the blame.

It turned out that the England fan was called Peter Jennings and when he wasn't busy abusing Aussies, his day job was working as the Bishop of Birmingham's press advisor.

Even though he was the one who started it, Jennings kicked up a fuss about Marsh's behaviour (he must have realised afterwards that he'd mixed up the two moustachioed men) and it made a juicy front-page headline for the *Sun* the next day: BISHOP'S AIDE CLAIM: 'TEST STAR HIT ME.'

'It was disgusting. I was attacked and faced a barrage of four-letter words,' Jennings was quoted as saying, while the Australian tour manager denied that Marsh ever threw a punch.

Marsh got loads of mail about it and, apparently, most England fans who wrote to him were on his side, seeing that Jennings had behaved like a bit of a tit. Someone did write challenging him to a fight outside the Oval after the final Test though. Marsh didn't read that letter until two weeks after he got back to Oz. 'I'm no great pugilist, and my hands are much too valuable to risk in a punch-up anyway,' he said later. If he had read it in time, he could always have sent his big mate Dennis out to fight for him instead, and hope his opponent was as clueless as the Bishop's press guy.

The item which Marsh had gone back for in the Edgbaston dressing room was an envelope of photos a press photographer had given him of his world record-breaking catch off Lillee to dismiss Botham in the first innings at Headingley. While that new landmark made the sports news, it was bets struck by Lillee and Marsh during England's second innings there that made tabloid headlines.

On the fourth day, with England in deep trouble, the latest betting odds flashed up on the scoreboard: 500–1 for an England win. Dennis couldn't believe such long odds were available for a two-horse race, and spent the lunch break trying to persuade his team-mates to lump on with him. He wanted to put £50 on himself just in case England did the unthinkable, but everyone, including his mate Marshy, thought it was a daft bet because England were running out of wickets in their second innings and still needed quite a few runs to even make Australia bat again.

In the end, Lillee decided to just stick a tenner on and sent the team bus driver to place the bet. As they walked out for the afternoon session, Marsh caved in and called out to the driver to put a fiver on for him too. The bus driver thought it was such a ridiculous waste of money that he nearly didn't put the bets on, but in the end thought he'd better do what he'd been asked.

Then, of course, Beefy scored that brilliant 149 not out, England set a target of 130, and Bob Willis scorched through the Aussie batting line-up to earn a famous victory – and an infamous betting win for Lillee and Marsh.

Their bets were controversial then and would get you banned these days, but Lillee claims he 'forgot all about the bet and got on with the game' and it's unthinkable that fierce competitors like him and Marsh would ever ease up just to nick a few quid. The drinks were on them as the Aussies drowned their sorrows after the match, too.

The Fabulous Bajan Boys

When I think of opening batting partnerships, the first one that comes to my mind is Desmond Haynes and Gordon Greenidge, *aka* 'the Fabulous Bajan Boys'. Of course, there have been some other great opening pairs, but I just loved their Caribbean style and flair. As a kid watching Test matches on telly when the great West Indies sides toured England, Desi and Gordon would often be the ones who got the party started for the West Indian fans in the crowd. A few flashes of the blade, balls hit on the up racing to the boundary, the sound of tin cans bashed together and conch shells being blown by the Windies faithful, fans dancing around then leaping over the advertising boards to throw the balls back . . . all that appealed to me. In a different way to the Aussies, I found the Caribbean style of cricket more inspiring than the traditional English ways, and the West Indies team that Haynes and Greenidge played for was Caribbean cricket at its best.

If he hadn't become a destructive opening batsman, Greenidge might have been a preacher. Having moved from sunny Barbados to England as a 14-year-old, he was going to church three times a week and was thinking about it. He didn't really want to become a cricketer and reckoned he wasn't good enough to be any more than a 'reasonable weekend club player'.

As a West Indian immigrant in the Sixties, he endured a lot of racism and, ironically, racial stereotyping may have kickstarted his cricket career. He reckoned that he only got selected for Berkshire Schools because 'I was from Barbados and *had* to be good at cricket'.

He started to enjoy his cricket more, but he still didn't have any plans to become a pro. 'I had a good eye for the ball and liked hitting it hard and often, yet I cannot honestly remember getting many runs.'

Come on, Gordon – have a bit of belief, son!

The story goes that John Arlott spotted his potential, though, and recommended him to Hampshire (Greenidge never knew if that was true), and it was there that he learnt how to build big innings.

He formed an awesome opening partnership with South African legend Barry Richards, and Ray Illingworth tried to persuade 21-year-old Gordon to make himself available for selection for the England team. Unluckily for us, he decided to go back to the Windies and soon got in their side to begin another fine partnership, with Roy Fredericks.

During their 1976 tour of England, the one before which England skipper Tony Greig promised to make the Windies 'grovel' (oops), he scored over 2,000 runs at an average of 55 in conditions he was so familiar with.

West Indian fans back home didn't warm to him, though, thinking of him as 'an English player' who just happened to be born in Barbados. It took a long time for him to earn their affection, whereas Desi had it instantly when he made the Test team in 1978 (four years after Gordon) because he was Barbados born and bred.

Like a lot of good sporting duos, the two boys were quite different characters. Greenidge was more serious, a bit of loner in the corner of the dressing room with his kit meticulously laid out. Desi, as I discovered when I had the pleasure of playing with him at Middlesex, was a sunny sort of person who'd brighten up your day – he wore a necklace with the words 'Live, Love, Laugh' and that was how he lived.

Mind you, when it came to cricket, both of them were perfectionists and could kill you with a stare. Desi may have seemed less intense, but Gordon claimed that Desi was the more likely of the two of them to have a tantrum back in the West Indies dressing room after getting out. At Middlesex I don't remember him having tantrums as such over his batting, but if the team wasn't performing, he would speak up and everyone listened because we respected him so much.

They were not particularly close friends away from cricket – Gordon was more of a family man, Desi more sociable – but communication was key to their success out in the middle.

'We'd talk about how each of us felt he was playing,' said

Greenidge. 'Was I coming out far enough? Was he going back enough? At times you do get distracted during an innings, so it was good to have someone there to remind you of the job in hand, to get you back in line ... The understanding was so good that we had no need to call for singles, merely a more or less perfected understanding of when either of us wanted to run – and we always got in with plenty of time to spare.'

I saw that with Desi and Mike Roseberry, his opening partner at Middlesex in my time. They'd sneak singles because there was no call. Usually a fielder hears the call of 'yes' and that helps you react quicker. On the first morning of a county cricket match, Desi and Mike could rack up 20-odd runs while the oppo were rubbing the sleep out of their eyes. Obviously, that would never have happened on my watch – when I was fielding, I was like a coiled spring ...

West Indies skipper Clive Lloyd rated Roy Fredericks highly, but as a partnership he said there was no comparison between him and Greenidge and Greenidge – Haynes; the latter duo was the best. They laid the foundations for West Indies to make a good total that set up their battery of fast bowlers to rip into the opposition. For example, over a five-match Test series against Australia in 1984, they averaged 136 runs per opening stand. And in their most productive run, the Greenidge – Haynes opening combo helped West Indies to 21 wins and just one defeat.

If one or other of them lost their wicket early, that would only inspire the other to go on and make a score – of 16 Test centuries scored by Desi with Greenidge as his opening partner, seven arrived after his mate was dismissed for single figures, and Desi scored less than 10 runs for six of Greenidge's 14 hundreds when they opened together.

Indeed, Greenidge's most iconic innings, against England in the Second Test at Lord's in 1984, was compiled mostly without his mate at the other end. For once, England were on top against the Windies, declared on the fifth day and set what they thought was an unreachable target of 342 to give their bowlers a chance to go for the win. Desi was out early, run out for 17, but Gordon boshed 214 not out in partnership with Larry Gomes to get the required runs in just 66 overs. That sort of run rate in Test cricket was so rare back then.

That day, Graeme Fowler was fielding at backward point for England while Allan Lamb was at cover. 'Greenidge was giving himself room and smacking it past us for four,' Graeme recalled. 'The closer we got, the harder he would hit it to one side or the other – he was playing games with us.'

Greenidge was a fearsome cutter and also puller of the ball, while Desi was particularly strong off his legs and a powerful driver. They were both aggressive players – Greenidge more so – but they both also knew how to judge the pace of an innings. One of the things that struck me watching Desi bat for Middlesex was that he left the ball as well as anyone. He knew where his off-stump was and didn't flash away outside off early on. He'd grind down the opening bowlers, then he'd marmalise them.

Haynes always looked up to Greenidge as the senior partner. 'Gordon was a marvellous influence,' he said. 'I learnt so much from the way he built an innings, and from our conversations about bowlers. Just watching him from the other end was a lesson. You looked across at Gordon and said, "Man, that's a true pro." I was perfectly happy, and proud, to be second fiddle to him.'

The respect cut both ways though. Their old team-mate Courtney Walsh observed how they played for each other: 'If Desi saw Gordon was going well he would give him the strike, and vice versa. They had a great understanding, as could be seen in their running between the wickets and in their instinctive summing up of opposing bowling, each taking the bowling they preferred. They were the ideal partnership.'

Session bowlers

As for Courtney Walsh and his partner in bowling terrorism, Curtly Ambrose (now, Sir Curtly, I should say), what a pair they were. As well as being quick and intimidating, they just seem to bowl for ever. Our quick bowlers were off for a rest after five or six overs, whereas they just seemed to bowl for sessions. When we played West Indies, it often seemed like it was our batters against those two.

Ask Mark Ramprakash. When he first came on the Test scene in England's 1991 series against West Indies, all I can remember him doing was batting against Ambrose and Walsh. He kept on making starts, 20 or 30 runs, battling away out there for an hour or two, but couldn't see them off.

These boys kept on charging in and hardly ever got injured. Walsh in particular just kept going and going. Once he started bowling, it seemed like he never took his jumper from the umpire.

As a kid, Courtney used to switch between bowling leg-spin and fast. When he was 16, he actually took all ten wickets in an innings of a school match, five bowling pace and five bowling spin, so he was obviously a decent leggie. People told him he could make better use of his height if he bowled quick, but even when he started playing for Jamaica at 18 he still wanted to bowl spin. It was only when he realised another guy was ahead of him in the pecking order for Jamaica that he focused on pace. I wish he hadn't.

As a fast bowler, Walsh earned his stripes in the West Indies team down the pecking order behind Michael Holding, Malcolm Marshall and Joel Garner, so he'd often be the one bowling into the wind. He did that without complaining and never lost that work ethic when he became one of the top dogs.

The most amazing example of that was against the Aussies in Perth 1997, when he tore a hamstring and the team doctor thought his game was over. Instead, he went out the next day, staggered in off a shorter run and bowled 20 overs in a row to help his team win the match. He couldn't walk for the next fortnight, but that shows how strong he was mentally.

Curtly made the Windies squad soon after Walsh, but with little first-class experience behind him. He dreamt of being an NBA basketball player as a kid and even in his early twenties he didn't really like cricket. His mum was a cricket fan, though, hence his full name, Curtly Elconn Lynwall Ambrose, with 'Lynwall' a tribute to legendary Australian fast bowler Ray Lindwall.

In 1986, aged 23, he got sent over to England to play in the Liverpool & District League, as part of the Viv Richards Scholarship scheme, to get experience. Leaving the Caribbean to live in cold England wasn't much fun for Curtly, and when he wasn't playing he didn't want to leave the house. But I doubt playing against Curtly was much fun for the amateur batsmen around Liverpool either. Imagine rolling up at the ground for a nice game of cricket, probably with no helmet and a skinful on board from the night before, only to find yourself spending your leisure time fending off life-threatening deliveries from Curtly Ambrose on a lively track in Bootle.

'Alright, Curtly, calm down, calm down . . .'

He took 84 wickets that year, then took over a hundred wickets the following season playing in the Lancashire League.

By the time Ambrose and Walsh were established as the team's opening bowlers, the Windies no longer had that battery of four fast bowlers, so more depended on them. There were other quick bowlers around like Patrick Patterson, who was also very scary, but they seemed like a relief in comparison because they tended to bowl a few more loose ones.

'I watched what happened when the Marshall – Garner – Holding trio ran the show,' recalled Walsh. 'In the course of time we were able to run our own show.'

Walsh and Ambrose's bowling never seemed to leave a good area – always a nasty just-short-of-a-length delivery rearing up at you, unless they were deliberately dropping in a bouncer or a yorker. I seriously can't remember Ambrose getting driven through mid-off – he must have been once or twice, but I can't remember it.

At Sabina Park in 1994, Courtney bowled an over to Michael Atherton that Athers reckons was 'one of the quickest and most hostile' he'd ever faced. Courtney bowled 14 overs on the bounce and effectively won the Test match for the Windies.

That was my first tour of the Caribbean, and I wasn't picked for the first three Tests, which on the plus side was six less times I'd potentially have to face those two. It really was Ambrose and Walsh who were the difference between the two teams in that series.

They liked to team up and put everything into getting the opposition's star batsman and skipper out early, in the hope that it would trigger a collapse. Against us that worked a treat a few times. A classic example was Graeme Hick, who came into the England team after scoring a mountain of runs in Zimbabwe and was being hailed by the English media as 'the new Bradman'. The Windies reckoned they had better batsmen than Hicky, and Ambrose and Walsh made it their personal missions to prove it. They saw his vulnerability to the short ball and just peppered him.

Neither Ambrose nor Walsh sledged batsmen; they simply gave you the death stare and let their evil bowling do the talking for them. Ambrose's silence was particularly intimidating. Unlike Courtney, who captained the team and was more demonstrative and talkative on the pitch, Curtly would just glare down at you from a great height. He never seemed to say much off the pitch either. He now claims he never actually said the legendary phrase 'Curtly talks to no man' when asked for an interview, but it's true that he rarely said anything to the media in his career and that added to his mysterious, menacing persona. Personally, I never even attempted to socialise with Curtly after a game – I was too scared.

'Courtney is different from me: he can tolerate a lot more nonsense,' said Ambrose. 'It doesn't take me long to explode if something bothers me.

'We were (and still are) like brothers – really close. There was never any rivalry between us – ever. If it was his day to take wickets, then my job was to just keep the pressure on at the other end. If it was my day, he would do the same thing.'

It was Courtney who convinced Curtly to carry on to do a final tour of England, when he was ready to quit, so he'd join him in the 400 wickets club (only Kapil Dev, Richard Hadlee, Wasim Akram and Walsh were in it at the time).

'There are few people in this world who are able to convince me to do something that I don't want to do, but Courtney did it, and I'm pleased he did.'

Apart from his bowling, Walsh fancied himself as a good batsman. He wasn't. Mind you, he did once smash me all over the place. I'd actually forgotten that until I mentioned in a *Test Match Special* commentary that no one had ever hit me for two sixes in an over. Our ace stats man Andy Samson, who seems able to access every random statistic on his database in seconds, tapped away on his laptop and piped up that in fact Courtney had hit me for three sixes in five balls at Bridgetown in 1994. That was slightly embarrassing.

I played against Courtney a couple of years ago in a six-a-side benefit game in Shenley. He's in his fifties now and was bowling off a five- or six-pace run-up. And he was suffering really badly with hayfever that day. The conditions were ideal, therefore, for me to attempt a lifetime first. When I went out to bat, I thought to myself, 'Right, this is it, I'm actually going to try and hit Courtney Walsh on the legside.'

I was desperate to do it, so at least I could say I'd done it once in my career. Now, finally, this was my time to shine. Of course, it took a huge mental adjustment after all those years of stepping away to leg to get out of the way of his missiles. As Courtney lolloped in and gently rolled his arm over, I leapt across to the offside and managed to connect, sending the ball to a spot never previously marked on a Tufnell 'wagon wheel' against his bowling.

Courtney immediately realised the epic significance of this moment. 'My God, Tuffers, man – for the first time in 30 years, you've got behind the line and hit me to leg,' he laughed, giving me a high-five as I ran past.

The toe-breakers

Walsh and Ambrose were awesome, top-notch Tuffers HoF material. Imagine, then, another bowler that Sir Curtly thought was 'possibly the greatest', saying, 'He could swing the ball, he could seam the ball off the pitch, he could bowl at high pace when he wanted to. He had it all . . . I've seen him do things with a cricket ball that mere mortals like myself couldn't do.'

He was talking about Pakistan's Wasim Akram, one half of my next duo with Waqar Younis. Having faced Wasim's bowling – usually, not for very long – I can vouch for Curtly's opinion of him. And Waqar? He was quite good, too.

Wasim came into the Pakistan side in 1985 and Waqar followed in 1989, just as the great Imran Khan, who'd been Pakistan's only real strike bowler for many years, was exiting the scene.

In Pakistan, there was no first-class cricket structure, so it wasn't as if they could play the equivalent of county cricket and get noticed. It was pure luck that Imran saw them playing in regional cricket, spotted their potential and gave them a chance to play at international level. He helped them both develop, giving them advice on everything from fitness, to their run-up and how to win the psychological battle with batsmen.

On the tour of Sri Lanka in 1986, after Wasim had been hacked around the ground in a one-day game in Kandy, Imran took him aside and gave him a lesson in how to bowl the yorker. He got him to put one stump in the ground, aim at the top of it and bowl the ball at top pace – he told him it had to be an 'effort ball' to get the ball under the bat. The next one-dayer in Colombo, Wasim took four wickets, including three with yorkers. He was a quick learner.

Imran advised Wasim on how to smooth out his run-up, which was too long and stuttering, and also how to bowl reverse swing. When Wasim was selected to join the Pakistan Under-19s in 1984, the great batsman Javed Miandad happened to have a net when he was bowling and couldn't believe how naturally talented Wasim was – 'he had wonderful command of line and length and he was very sharp to go with it.' Javed was captaining the full Pakistan team while Imran was injured, and picked Wasim for their next tour of New Zealand and he soon became a key player.

Waqar made his debut for Pakistan in the Sharjah Champions Trophy in October 1989, aged 17, but people questioned his age because he had the powerful physique of someone at least half a dozen years older.

Wasim had first seen Waqar bowl when he joined the United Bank squad, which Waqar was a part of, for some bowling practice: 'I saw this guy sprinting in and bowling very quick on a green wicket; I didn't immediately realise he was Waqar, as I didn't know him by sight. I had heard of his reputation for being erratic, but on this day he was bowling really well, and I was very impressed.'

The next day, Wasim was round at Imran's house watching a local cup game on TV that Waqar was playing in. Wasim told Imran to look out for this kid he'd seen. Imran was so impressed after watching three overs on telly, he dashed down to the ground in Lahore to watch the rest of his spell. Imran spoke to the selectors and the next day Waqar was called up to the senior Pakistan squad for Sharjah.

In his first match on a lifeless pitch, he only managed four overs before getting cramp in the sweltering heat, but in that short time he bowled even faster than Curtly Ambrose and Ian Bishop and had the Windies batsmen hopping about.

'Like me, Waqar seemed to come from nowhere,' recalled Wasim, 'but he was a much more rounded bowler than I was when he came into the Pakistan side. He had it all – reverse swing, great pace, the yorker, and a strong physique.'

Imran knew that if he nurtured Waqar's talent, he'd found a strike partner for Wasim. So it was that a terrifying fast-bowling double act was born.

Sure enough, Waqar soon harnessed his ridiculous pace and late swing with control. When he joined Surrey, he was a danger to all county batsmen's feet with his vicious late-inswinging yorker. It was either somehow get your bat down on the ball, see your stumps splattered or get your toe crushed and be given out lbw. In my case, the first scenario was unlikely; the lbw part of the third option was impossible because my feet were about a yard outside leg stump by the time he bowled (although Waqar would sometimes chase you with the yorker and try to squelch your toes anyway); and option two was inevitable sooner rather than later. A lot better batsmen than me got 'Waqared'.

Where Younis and Akram differed from the great West Indian fast bowlers of the 1980s and '90s was their mastery of reverse swing that made them lethal even on slow wickets. Both preferred to bowl with the older ball when it started reversing, and they'd pitch the ball up much further, bowling mostly at the stumps, using the bouncer as a shock tactic. That put a different kind of pressure on the batsmen because they had to play at so many deliveries. They got lots more wickets clean bowled or lbw. You needed to go out there with steel-capped Doc Martens boots as well as a helmet.

Waqar came in off this long run-up and delivered the ball with a big leap in the air and a slinging action that made the ball skid – his stock ball was an outswinger and then he bowled the occasional inswinger which he learnt by watching videos of Imran in slow motion.

Wasim had a more relaxed-looking, short run-up, then this amazing whipping arm and wrist action that generated incredible pace when he wanted it, and the ability to move the ball both ways. He said that Imran also taught him how to recognise when batsmen were afraid of him, but I doubt he would have needed Imran to tell him I was bricking it whenever I had to face him.

Wasim might have had more natural cricketing talent, but Waqar was naturally the stronger and more athletic of the pair and his competitive fire pushed him on to be as good as Wasim. 'If Wasim takes a wicket, then I think I'm going to get one as well; if he takes two, then I think I'll take two,' he said.

For all the help and guidance he'd given them, Wasim and Waqar didn't appreciate it when in a book in 1993, the retired Imran admitted using a bottle top to scuff up a ball to make it swing while playing for Sussex. Immediately, the finger of suspicion pointed at Wasim and Waqar who were busy ploughing through batting line-ups with their lethal reverse swing, but they furiously denied ball-tampering allegations.

English bowlers were, literally, behind the curve on this new technique of reverse swing. In the 1992 England v Pakistan series, Wasim and Waqar destroyed England on mostly dry, flat pitches – Wasim reckoned England hadn't done their homework because preparing pitches like that was playing to Pakistan's strength. Prepping pitches that benefited the opposition was a recurring problem when I was playing; thankfully, we seem to have stopped doing that now.

At the end of the series, there were veiled accusations of cheating from England team manager Mickey Stewart. But neither match referees saw that Waqar and Wasim had done anything wrong. Wasim, for his part, said that he'd shown his Lancashire team-mates how to bowl reverse swing years before but no one had bothered to practise and learn how to do it. Hmm, they might have missed a trick there.

Anyhow, this new style of bowling made for exciting cricket – because the ball was being pitched up rather than jagged in short at the their ribs, batsmen had the chance to drive the ball if Wasim and Waqar veered off line or length. The problem for England was that too often they got it absolutely right and sent stumps cartwheeling out of the ground or the batsman hobbling back to the pavilion, out lbw and with a broken toe.

Wasim took 82 wickets on that tour in total (and that was after missing some early games and the First Test with a stress fracture of the shin), and he and Waqar shared 43 wickets out of 71 taken by Pakistan in the Test series.

They preferred the Readers ball for reverse swing because there is too much lacquer on a Duke's and it doesn't scuff up. In that series, Pakistan won the toss for choice of balls in Tests and ODIs so often that the Readers ball was used eight times and the Duke just two. So that helped them, but Geoff Boycott summed it up best when he said, 'Wasim and Waqar could bowl out our lot with an orange, because they are great bowlers.'

c Jayawardene b Muralitharan

Now to the most successful bowler–fielder combo in cricket history – Muttiah Muralitharan and Mahela Jayawardene.

Statistics show the incredible effect 'Murali' had on the Sri Lankan international team. Before him, their Test wickets cost just under 40 runs apiece on average. In 132 Tests with Murali in the team, when he averaged 22.67 per wicket, with a strike rate of a wicket every nine overs, the team's average runs per wicket fell to approximately 31 runs. That meant the opposition were averaging 100 runs less per innings. That is the definition of 'influential'.

Funny to think then that on his first tour to England with Sri Lanka in 1991, Murali didn't take a single wicket in three first-class matches and didn't get selected to play in the one Test of the tour at Lord's (he ended up having to wait until his 103rd Test match for his maiden Test appearance at the Home of Cricket). After that barren tour he got the hang of international cricket, bagging 800 Test wickets and another 534 in ODIs. Not jealous. Much.

An effortlessly elegant batsman, Jayawardene was the first Sri Lankan player to score over 10,000 runs in both Test and ODI formats. He picked the length of a delivery early, timed the ball beautifully, and was a great player of spin bowling, which must have helped him when he was fielding at slip for Murali, who had so many variations.

In fact, Jayawardene deserves a spot among my 'Masters in the field' (see page 42), because he was excellent not only in the slips but anywhere inside the inner ring with a laser throwing arm that bagged him many run – outs in ODI cricket.

Of Jayawardene's 205 catches in Test matches, 77 of them were off the bowling of Muralitharan – by far the largest number of dismissals for any fielder – bowler combination other than wicket-keepers.

They started as they meant to go on in Jayawardene's debut Test against India in Colombo, August 1997, where the first 'c Jayawardene b Muralitharan' victim was none other than Sachin Tendulkar.

Jayawardene took six catches in a Test match on two occasions, including the Second Test against Pakistan in Peshawar in their 1999/2000 series when he had three catches in each innings, all six off Muralitharan's bowling.

It was fitting that Jayawardene was the safe pair of hands to help Murali reach two of his many career landmarks. In May 2004, in Harare, it was Jayawardene who took the bat-pad catch off Mluleki Nkala to give Murali his 520th Test match wicket, overtaking Courtney Walsh's 519 and making him Test cricket's highest wicket-taker at the time. Then there was Murali's dramatic bid to reach 800 Test wickets in his final Test match versus India at Galle in 2010.

Aged 38, he needed eight wickets to reach 800 going into the game, a tall order for most mortals. He got a five-fer in the first innings, got another two in the second, but nearly ran out of wickets in trying to get his 800th. In fact, he himself nearly scuppered his own chances by almost running out India's last-wicket pair twice. Instead, after wheeling away for a few tense overs, Murali finally found the edge of Pragyan Ojha's bat and his mate Jayawardene nabbed the catch.

Eight hundred Test wickets. Wow. That record may stand for ever and Jayawardene, who was Murali's skipper from late 2005 through to his retirement from Test cricket, can take some credit for him taking such a silly amount of wickets. When Jayawardene took over the captaincy, he reckoned Murali only attacked when he was in control, so he encouraged him to be more aggressive.

'I wanted to use him in a different way [from previous captains],' he recalled. 'I wanted to create opportunities for him rather than us sitting and waiting for an opening to happen.' Murali was 'a bit stubborn' and took some persuading, but he eventually took a more proactive approach and made even more world-class batsmen suffer.

Murali was always grateful for Jayawardene's guidance and his skills as a fielder. 'Mahela was very good with the strategy side of things and setting fields . . . he gave all his players a lot of confidence,' he said. 'He started off at short leg, and he took a lot of catches there as well, before moving into slip. I preferred him at slip because he had very fast reflexes, a good technique and good hands. I think taking slip catches off spinners is one of the hardest things, but he was the best at that.'

Deadly duo

Kent's St Lawrence Ground in Canterbury had three stands named after outstanding individuals from the club's history – Frank Woolley, Colin Cowdrey and Les Ames. Then, in 2011, the Annexe Stand was redeveloped and renamed after a legendary Kent and England double act: Derek Underwood and Alan Knott.

Older fans sitting in the Underwood & Knott Stand today will have fond memories of watching Knotty standing up to keep wicket to his Kent team-mate 'Deadly' Derek Underwood who bowled a lot quicker than the average spinner. It took exceptional agility and hand-to-eye coordination to do that, especially on the old uncovered wickets where one delivery might whistle through past the batsman's bootstraps and the next one rear up off a good length.

In the 72 Tests they played together, there were 27 'c Knott b Underwood' dismissals, and for Kent the total was 198.

I have vague memories of watching the pair of them on telly playing for England when I was a boy, and maybe Underwood's bowling style rubbed off on me a bit because there were some similarities between our bowling actions, even though his stock ball was a lot quicker than mine. He tended to bowl cutters rather than spinners, getting his movement off the pitch by dragging his bowling hand across the ball, rather than giving it a tweak with his wrist and fingers.

Like me, Underwood also started out as a kid wanting to be a fast bowler, which led to his long run-up. Knott started keeping wicket to Underwood for Kent Schools and even as a fast bowler Knott says he was freakishly accurate.

When Underwood realised that he wasn't quick enough to be a fast bowler in adult cricket, he adapted his style but kept quite a long run-up which marked him out from conventional spinners.

Jim Laker reckoned that a young spinner should learn how to spin the ball first and worry about accuracy later, but Underwood did the opposite. According to Knott, when Underwood first made the Kent county side, he barely got any spin on the ball, relying on changes of flight and pace to get his wickets. Back then, he was bowling over the wicket, but changed to round the wicket to give him the chance to get lbw decisions with balls that pitched in line and straightened.

Knotty always thought that his extra speed compared to a normal spinner was his trump card. 'If only the occasional delivery moves, it deviates so quickly that it can have any batsman in trouble ... it only need one ball to go like that and the batsman feels that he must play slightly outside the line.'

Underwood's run-up was mostly obscured from the batsman by the umpire, so that added to the problems when he finally appeared and delivered the ball. Not easy for the wicket-keeper either, but Knotty reckoned he learnt to read each and every one of Underwood's variations over the years so he was more ready than the batsmen.

According to Knott, Deadly didn't bowl ten long hops or full tosses in his whole career – incredible for a 'slow bowler'. 'If you could back anyone to pitch a ball on a 50p piece, then Derek would be my favourite,' he said.

When fully covered pitches were introduced in 1981, many people thought it would do for Underwood. But Deadly proved everyone wrong, as he continued to bamboozle batsmen with subtle changes of pace, direction and flight – so much so that the only bowlers in first-class cricket who took more wickets than him over the next two years were Malcolm Marshall and Richard Hadlee . . . and they were quite useful bowlers themselves.

Deadly's record on tour in dry conditions also stands up – he took more than half of his Test wickets overseas, with fifty-plus wickets taken in both Australia (at 31 runs per wicket) and India (at 26).

He could get the best of them out, as well – no one got the great Indian opener Sunil Gavaskar out more times than Under-wood (12 times in the 20 Tests they faced each other) and he also got the prize Australian wicket of Greg Chappell 13 times.

He was a great bowler in the early days of one-day cricket, tying batsman down mid-innings just when they were looking to up the run-rate. It would be interesting to see how he would have fared in the modern one-day and Twenty20 game with fielding restrictions and people swinging their big bats with gay abandon. On dry pitches, he tended to push the ball through flatter because he hated being hit straight back over his head. In the modern-day game, that's an occupational hazard. Like everyone else, he'd have gone for a few more runs, but he was such an intelligent bowler, constantly setting traps for batsmen, that I reckon he'd have pro-duced just as many match-winning performances.

He was a bit of a rabbit with the bat, averaging around ten, but one thing Derek managed which I didn't was to score a first-class century. It took him 591 matches and 618 innings, but he finally managed to reach three figures at the old Central Recreation Ground in Hastings in 1984. He must have been better than me, because that innings started when he went in at number three as nightwatchman, a job I was only asked to do once – also, coinci-dentally, at Hastings, in August 1989, the last first-class game before the ground was bulldozed and replaced by a shopping centre. For the record, I was out second ball for four runs – the first ball, the slips ducked I had such a heave at it. I hadn't really grasped the key requirement of a nightwatchman (i.e. to stay in).

Good to hear that Deadly was old school, too. He liked a cigarette and was no fan of the gym – he kept fit for bowling, simply by bowling and doing it very, very well. My kind of cricketer.

Alan Knott, on the other hand, was one of the most thorough trainers for cricket there has ever been – one of those players I admire, but could never have been like. In those days, you didn't see players doing exercises during a day's play, but Knotty was an exception to the rule. He was constantly doing stretches. Some people thought that was for show, but it was actually because he wasn't the most naturally flexible person and wanted to get the absolute best from himself. Also, I guess it helped him to keep his concentration through a long day in the field.

Although he wasn't quite in Adam Gilchrist's league with the bat, he was very good – you don't make six Test centuries without knowing which end of the bat to hold. A particularly inventive stroke-player against pace bowling, he was a genuine wicket-keeping all-rounder.

Everything Knott did was geared to improve his cricket, whether it was doing extra fitness training with Charlton Athletic FC or playing table tennis to sharpen his reflexes and footwork. He was a total perfectionist and actually relished getting criticism from his captain and team-mates. He liked to know where he was going wrong so he knew what to work on – a great attitude.

He became a Christian halfway through his career and he felt that gave him a more balanced view of the game. He then put more emphasis on trying to give his absolute best at all times rather than worrying about the results, believing that if you try to do the right things, the results will come anyway. Although he wasn't 'one of the lads', no one had a bad word to say about him, and he was known for being a really encouraging and generous team-mate. There's a lovely story about how he grabbed a bail as a souvenir when England won the Ashes in 1977 and rather than keep it for himself, he gave it to Ian Botham, who was playing in only his second Test but had been off the field injured when the game ended.

Top man, and, alongside Derek Underwood, another great double act for my Hall of Fame.

Jimmy and Broady

Finally, a nod to a great modern English duo: James Anderson and Stuart Broad.

Are they the best England opening bowling pair of all time? It's very hard to compare different eras, and good arguments can also be made for the Freddie Trueman – Brian Statham and Ian Botham – Bob Willis combos. What is for certain is that Jimmy and Broady belong right up there at that elite level.

Watching him now, it's hard to believe that Jimmy spent a fair bit of time carrying the drinks early in his England career, and it took him a while to prove he could cut it at Test level. Both he and Stuart, who got his Test debut four-and-a-half years later, were plucked from county cricket, at the age of 20 and 21 respectively, and given the chance to develop their games at international level. They benefited from central contracts and consistent selection policies that just weren't there when I began my international career – if they were dropped, they weren't just banished back to their county and forgotten about. They both had a wobble here or there, but they developed a partnership that has spearheaded England's bowling attack in four Ashes series victories.

Jimmy is such a skilful bowler. He can get the ball to swing late and in either direction just with a slight adjustment of his wrist or fingers and without any noticeable change in his action. He has so many deliveries in his locker, from cutters to reverse-swingers, wobble-seamers to slower balls, and he's mastered all of them. When he's at his best in favourable bowling conditions, the batsmen have no chance, and even on batting-friendly roads, he is very hard to play.

Broady uses his height to hit the seam hard and subtle variations to outfox a batsman. He's very good at working out a batsman's weaknesses and setting traps for them. He's also ultra-competitive, and won't go missing when things are not going so well. 'He is very smart on the field and reads the game really well,' Jimmy has said about his partner. 'The captain needs that and the two of us working together, especially opening the bowling.'

Stuart has talked about how he likes Jimmy fielding next to him at mid-off when he's bowling (and vice versa) so he can get his opinion on what to do next. Because they have confidence in each other's judgement, they'll listen and take note. Sometimes when you're bowling in Test cricket, you can keep doing the same things for too long or try to change things too much in search of a wicket, so it helps to have someone in the same boat on hand to give an opinion.

When one of them is bowling out of his skin, the other will happily slot into the supporting role, trying to keep things tight at the other end to build the pressure on the batsman. A good example of that was at the Lord's Test against New Zealand in 2013, where Jimmy bowled a brilliant spell at the Pavilion End and Stuart backed him up. Ironically, the Kiwis were so preoccupied trying to keep Jimmy out, they felt they had better try to get after Stuart's bowling to get some runs and it was Broady who ended up getting a seven-fer.

They are both lethal bowlers in English conditions, and while their stats aren't so impressive away from home (the less said about the 2016 winter tour of India the better . . .), they have shown themselves able to thrive in different conditions. For instance, Jimmy was key to the Ashes series win Down Under in 2010/11, taking 24 wickets, and in India in 2012, and Stuart has also produced some great performances overseas. At the Wanderers Stadium, Johannesburg, in January 2016, Broady's blistering opening spell in South Africa's second innings where he took five for one in 31 balls, including the vital wickets of Hashim Amla and AB de Villiers, turned what was a finely balanced match into an England win and an unassailable 2–0 lead in the series.

At the time of writing, they stand first (Jimmy) and third

(Stuart) in the list of England's individual all-time Test wicket-takers, and together have proven to be deadly again and again. The 15 wickets they shared in the Headingley Test against Sri Lanka back in summer 2016 took their joint tally in matches they had played together to 646 in 84 matches, putting them well ahead of third-placed Wasim and Waqar (559 wickets in 61 matches together) and, if they both stay fit and hungry for more, Ambrose and Walsh's record of 762 wickets (95 Tests together) might be within reach. It would be great for them and English cricket if they can carry on as they are and get there. I'd love to see them do it.

MASTERS IN THE FIELD

2

A reluctant fielder

It took me a while to understand the power of fielding. As a young-ster starting out, I just thought that if the ball comes your way, you try to stop it or catch it, or have a go at throwing down the stumps if there is a chance of a run-out.

It was only on my first England tour, playing one-day cricket in Australia, that I really grasped just how much it could influence a game. Every time our batsmen took a quick single to Dean Jones or Allan Border at midwicket or cover point, they always hit the stumps. It was never like, 'Oh, that's going to be tight', have a shy at the stumps and miss. Every time they picked it up, they hit the stumps and often it was out. It became a mode of dismissal, rather than something you had to do.

That was amazing to me. Our boys would have a go, and have plenty of near-misses. There'd be 'ahhs' and hands thrown up in the air in anguish as the ball fizzed high and/or wide of the sticks, but the bottom line was we'd usually miss. Border and Jones seemed to hit every time.

I just thought it was luck. We were doing fielding practice every day too, hours of chucking a ball haplessly at the stumps, and yet we'd only have the occasional hit when called upon during a game, while they were doing it all the time. But there must have been more to it than that.

When I started playing, as a rule, players hated fielding. It was boring; it wasn't part of the game. Most people weren't diving around and running after the ball – they didn't want to get their whites dirty.

When it was a fielding day, we loved a bit of rain. Anything to get back to the pavilion. Every team had their own Michael Fish. He'd slip away from fielding practice in the morning to focus on meteorology, checking the weather on Ceefax. And at each ground, we all knew where the weather came from. Some days, you'd look round and your mate was staring up at the sky, miming lassoing the rain clouds in the distance towards the ground. I think Graham Gooch was the first player I knew who actually wanted to get out there and play!

The excellent fielders really stood out because they were the exception to the rule. When I joined Middlesex, Roland Butcher was the main man. He used to just float over the ground in the outfield, had a good arm and he was also a great catcher in the slips. As a young fella, it used to slightly infuriate me how good he was because I'd thought I was a decent fielder until I saw him in action – I was reasonably quick, could run about and had a pretty good arm. The difference was that when I was fielding in the deep, the batsmen ran two unless the ball came straight to me. Roland – and this was towards the back end of his career – was like Thierry Henry to the ball, so the batsmen would only get one . . . and even that might be a struggle.

Watching the great fielders, it dawned on me that you just have to try and be the best fielder you can be, because I was never ever going to be a Roland Butcher or Dean Jones. It was like me saying I'm going to become a 100-metre runner and run against Usain Bolt – the gap in ability was just too vast. I've got ten-to-two feet and Usain has got lot longer legs. And I never had the fast-twitch fibres.

I saw some amazing catches, and I never really knew how they did it. Some fielders just made it look so easy and elegant. If I got it wrong, I'd end up face down in the dirt. Especially as I got older; if I got my legs in the wrong position, I'd end up in a heap.

Also, I just didn't have big enough hands. I'm not saying my hands are Donald-Trump small, but you look at the safe catchers down the years like Freddie Flintoff and they've got huge hands. Freddie's dad Colin's nickname at his local cricket club is 'Colin Big Hands' so it obviously runs in his family – mind you, Colin famously dropped Freddie when he hoisted a huge six into the stand during his century against the Windies at Edgbaston in 2004, so size isn't everything.

The best I could hope for was competence – field tidily, throw accurately and catch as many as I can. And I did take some great catches, just not day in, day out.

To become a great fielder is a matter of talent, hard work and also loving fielding. And I definitely did not love fielding; I was a very reluctant fielder, as an incident during my second Australian tour illustrates.

It was a red-hot day in Brisbane, and after two-and-a-half hours batting in the cauldron, Graham Thorpe had retired to the physio's bed for a lie-down with a severe case of dehydration. He'd spent the last hour of his innings of 89 downing a bottle of water every other over and feeling very faint.

I was sitting in the dressing room next door and discussions were underway between the coach and captain Mike Atherton as to whether Thorpey would be fit to field. I hadn't been picked for the starting XI and I suddenly began to twig that there was a chance I'd be called upon to take Thorpey's place. My slow-twitch fibres started to twitch a bit faster. Leaving the shade of the dressing room and spending hours dashing around after the ball across the Gabba's wide expanses in sweltering heat didn't really appeal to me.

'I should be alright, Gatt's in front of me,' I reassured myself.

Mike Gatting was twelfth man and I was thirteenth, but I didn't want to take any chances, so I went to check up on Thorpey. Well, not so much check up on his welfare as literally try to drag him off his sick bed.

When I walked in, he was swaddled in cold wet towels, ice packs on his head and groaning incoherently. I think he was calling for his mother.

'Get up, you lazy bastard! Get up! You've done this on purpose. I don't want to go out there for fifty overs – it's me day off!'

I had poor old Thorpey by one arm hanging on to the bed, towels falling off his fevered body.

'Waaarrgghh.'

Graham, who barely seemed to know where he was, just about managed to fend me off with the help of the physio.

'I'll never forgive you for this, Gray,' I said as I departed.

Back in the dressing room, conversation was turning to the choice of his replacement. I dropped in my own bits of advice: 'Gatt's got lovely hands, great catcher . . .' I said loudly to no one in particular. 'You can have him at slip.'

The problem was that this was a one-day game and there was a lot of running about, so despite my shortcomings as a fielder, the consensus seemed to be to go with the younger man with longer legs.

I threw out, 'He could narrow the angle at gully.' Desperate times.

Not that I'd given up on Thorpey either and made a quiet exit to offer him more 'encouragement'.

'Where's Phil?' I heard someone say back in the dressing room as I squirted water on Thorpey's face.

'I think he's next door giving Thorpey mouth to mouth!'

My efforts were to no avail so I went out and sulked my way through 50 overs. Fifty overs of fielding in blazing heat, and not even allowed a bowl to break the monotony – poor me. As for Thorpey, his sterling innings proved to be a match-winner, he was named Man of the Match and had to spend four hours in a Brisbane hospital on a saline drip.

Bland revolution

So, no, being a fielder didn't excite me, but watching masters in the field is a different matter. And one fella who I wished I'd seen play live is Bulawayo-born South African international, Colin Bland, whose name crops up in any discussions about the best fielders of all time. He finished his Test match career in 1967 when I was still a little bundle of joy, but ask the older generation who witnessed him in action and he was something special.

Bland was probably the first player ever to attract cricket fans to matches purely to watch a player field. That was certainly the case during South Africa's 1965 tour of England when home supporters flocked to see him patrol the covers.

He had a Test batting average nudging 50 and yet he is remembered much more for his fielding, which gives you an idea of how he revolutionised this aspect of cricket. Bland showed that fielding could change the course of the game.

He took fielding practice very, very seriously, doing his own extra sessions at home on the family farm. There he'd set up one spring-loaded stump in front of a hockey goal, and get members of his family and farm labourers to chuck balls for him to run, pick up and aim to throw down the stump from 30-odd yards away.

Another fielding drill he had was to set up three stumps spaced apart in front of a hockey goal and give himself up to six balls to knock them down. He got so good that he often didn't need all six balls.

Even when he got to international level, none of his team-mates were volunteering to join in with his drills. As I said, until relatively recently in cricket history, players generally didn't pay that much attention to fielding other than pretty straightforward catching practice. For example, I always remember me and Robin Smith – or 'Judge' as we called him because his hair looked like a judge's wig – at Old Trafford before an Ashes Test in 1993. We all traipsed out to warm up before the day's play. The coaches took us for a bit of fielding practice as a team to wake us up, then people broke off to do their own thing. Some of the batters were doing throwdowns, others doing slip catches off the face of the bat. Judgey and I found ourselves at a bit of a loose end.

'Judge,' I said, 'we'd better look like we're doing something.'

So he stood there with his bat in front of him like he was playing French cricket, and I threw the ball to him from about five feet away and he tapped it back to me. It was like a dad teaching a five-year-old how to catch a ball. Absolutely pointless.

Mark and Steve Waugh walked past, looked across and just shook their heads and rolled their eyes at this sorry spectacle. Slightly embarrassed, Judgey and I looked at each other, and without a word sloped back to the sanctuary of the pavilion.

Colin Bland was well ahead of his time. His logic was that he wasn't a bowler, so if he failed with the bat, he could at least make a contribution in the field. It was reckoned he saved the South Africans 30-odd runs per innings which is some contribution. Throw in his half-century batting average and you've got an all-time great non-bowling, batting-fielding all-rounder.

I, on the other hand, probably cost England an average of 10–20 runs per innings, which means that with my batting average over 42 Test matches of five, if I wasn't bowling, I was basically playing for the opposition.

Bland was six foot one and you might imagine that someone of that height might not be the quickest to the low ball. But Bland was a very graceful mover. Playing international hockey previously also must have helped him develop that ability to get down low while running at speed. His throw was not just accurate, it was powerful – he could throw the ball in flat and fast from 80 metres. I would take cricket tales of legendary feats like this with a pinch of salt, but recently I had a chat with an old friend of mine who saw that '65 series live and he confirmed the legend, and more.

Bland worked out that a brilliant piece of fielding could instantly shift the momentum in a game. When nothing much was happening for the bowlers, Bland would occasionally give the wicket-keeper a heads-up and next time the ball came to him, even though there was no chance of a run out, he'd sprint to it and fire it in over the stumps. 'It would wake up all the buggers dozing off – including the fielders,' he said.

During that 1965 tour of England, spectators at Canterbury got a special treat when the start of a match between the tourists and Kent was delayed by drizzling rain. Colin Cowdrey persuaded Bland to give an exhibition of his throwing ability in the meantime. The damp conditions should have made it difficult, but Bland wowed the crowd by hitting the stumps 12 times out of 15 throws. 'They spoilt me by giving me three stumps to aim at,' he said casually afterwards.

If only Jonty had stuck to hockey . . .

In my day, I was unfortunate enough to play against the next South African superstar fielder, Jonty Rhodes. I used to watch Rhodes with a mixture of bafflement and envy about his enthusiasm for fielding.

I couldn't see how he could enjoy it so much. I guess he was so good that he was always looking forward to the next buzz of making a great stop, catch or run-out. He needed to get out more.

Apart from all his physical skills — his speed to the ball, great hands, agility and all that — you could see that he actually loved fielding, which meant he was always alert and ready.

We all wanted something exciting to happen in the field, but he *made* it happen. He was proactive whereas I was reactive. And he was a right pain in the arse to play against.

As a young boy growing up in Hilton, South Africa, with his country excluded from international sport, Jonty first dreamt of becoming a professional footballer in England — he had a poster of his hero, Kevin Keegan, on his bedroom wall. He also had an uncle who lived in Margate and hoped he'd arrange trials for him with professional clubs over here. Unfortunately, his uncle didn't come through.

His PE teacher at Maritzburg College, who was hockey-mad, got him into that game instead. He proved to be brilliant at it, playing for the college's first team when he was just 14. By his final year, he was regarded as one of the best young players in South Africa.

Like Bland, that hockey background, running around half crouched whacking a puck, obviously helped on the cricket field. He'd play hockey in winter and cricket in summer, earning a reputation in schools cricket as a big-scoring batsman and outstanding fielder either close in or in the deep.

With South Africa accepted back into the international sporting fold, Jonty could easily have gone to the 1992 Olympics as a hockey player, but cricket chose him when he was controversially picked for South Africa's 1992 World Cup squad. It was a massive call because big-name veterans Clive Rice and Jimmy Cook were left at home, while this 22-year-old kid, an unproven batsman who at that point had made just one first-class century and didn't bowl, had a seat on the plane to Australia.

It was the first time South Africa had ever chosen a fielder who could bat a bit. Their coach, Mike Procter, admitted that part of the reason for selecting Rhodes was that the team needed to improve their fielding. But he'd also seen the uplifting effect Rhodes' attitude had had on Natal, the team he played for in domestic cricket. 'He was so enthusiastic and so full of life . . . He was something special,' said Procter.

Those who hadn't seen him play before soon realised what Procter meant about Rhodes, when the young South Africa side led by Kepler Wessels (also featuring an unknown fast bowler called Allan Donald) started playing in Oz.

This is the review he got from the *Sydney Morning Herald* writer watching a warm-up game: 'In one over Rhodes will clap his hands at least fifty times, retrieve the ball from the umpire, take it to the bowler, ferry the bowler's jumper back to the umpire, move the bowling mark, sprint to the other end of the ground, encourage everyone and then field virtually any ball on the offside without mistake. And that's when he's not excited.'

Spot on – that was Jonty Rhodes.

He was sensational fielding at point in South Africa's opening World Cup match, a nine-wicket win over the hosts at the SCG. And the photograph of him diving like Superman and crashing through the stumps to run out Pakistan's Inzamam-ul-Haq later in the tournament went global.

Big Inzamam had set off for a run, changed his mind and slipped turning back towards the batting crease. Rather than risk throwing and missing, Rhodes sprinted in from gully with ball in hand, dived headfirst and demolished the stumps, before Inzy could get back.

He winded himself in the process, but the wicket effectively ended Pakistan's hopes of winning the match. Funnily enough, the umpires could easily have given Inzamam not out because they couldn't really see if he'd broken the stumps with the ball – 'You could say it wasn't a very good piece of cricket at all,' Rhodes later admitted, but it sealed his status as a fielding superstar.

Rhodes also got a taste of my dynamite fielding during that tournament. He was batting at four against us in a group match at Melbourne with Kepler Wessels. I'd been placed in the covers, for some reason, and Wessels saw an opportunity to nick some extra singles. During a mid-pitch conference between overs, Rhodes *thought* that he heard his skipper tell him in Afrikaans there is a single every time to the covers.

I don't think word of my fielding skills had reached Jonty before, but he was more concerned with obeying captain's orders, so when Wessels pushed the ball towards me a couple of balls later, he sprinted from the bowler's end without waiting for a call.

Rhodes was already almost down at Wessels' end before the skipper could set off in the forlorn hope of saving his wicket. Naturally, I picked the ball up and threw in one graceful movement and sent middle stump at the non-striker's end cartwheeling out of the ground . . .

. . . well, no, of course I didn't – I fumbled it and Wessels comfortably made his ground.

At the end of the over, Wessels asked Rhodes what he was thinking.

'I thought you said there is *always* one in the covers.'

'No! I said always look out for one in the covers.'

Jonty didn't speak perfect Afrikaans and had misunderstood.

Bit of respect there from Kepler – good to know he realised there wasn't *always* a single available with the 'Cat' patrolling the covers, only some of the time.

Later in that game, Jonty showed how it should be done with a miraculous bit of fielding to dismiss Alex Stewart. Stewie hit a crunching square drive which Rhodes dived to his left to collect then back-flicked the ball to hit the stumps direct at the bowler's end. Ridiculous.

After the tournament, Rhodes humbly claimed he wasn't in the same class as Bland, especially when it came to throwing down the stumps – his lack of confidence in his throwing at one stump was the reason for the way he literally ran out Inzamam. But Bland himself pointed out that modern-day heavy bats meant edges travelled much faster, meaning Rhodes had to dive around more than he did and it's much harder to throw accurately from on the ground.

Rhodes wasn't in Bland's class as a batsman though. In fact, he was once described as 'the worst number five batsmen in world cricket', and his final Test batting average of 35 across 52 Tests was certainly below par. But he worked hard on his batting technique, and averaged 50 in the last few years of his Test career. Add on all the runs he saved just by his mere presence around the bat, let alone the diving stops and catches and miracle run-outs, and he brought plenty to the party, and changed the course of many games.

He was an entertainer and must have been a great man to have on your side when the energy was flagging in the field, because he never switched off. Even on the hard grounds of the sub-continent, he'd dive around to stop balls and make catches, ignoring the burns, bruises and bloodied elbows, and even opposition fans loved it.

Against England, batsmen would get a single to gully all the time, but when we were batting against South Africa and our boys realised the ball was heading in Jonty's direction there, it was immediate panic. Then just when they'd got it drilled into their head not to even begin to attempt a run to Jonty at gully, occasionally he'd swap positions unannounced between balls. Next thing, the batsman drops the ball short on the legside, only to see Jonty steaming in from midwicket.

It gave even the best batsmen even more to think about. Not only did they have to dig out a 90mph yorker from Allan Donald, they had to ask 'Where's Jonty?' Again, that's the power of fielding – when it's done properly.

Rhodes for a day

The nearest I got to experiencing what it's like to be Jonty Rhodes was in that Old Trafford Ashes Test mentioned above. After those intensive few minutes of pit-pat fielding practice with Robin Smith, I found myself at cover point for the start of the Australia innings, demonstrating again how unscientific our fielding game plan was back in the day. Basically, all the good catchers were in the slips and then the old bowlers had to make up the outfield.

Early on, Mark Taylor smashed the ball and I made a great diving stop. Nice round of applause from the crowd and I felt very pleased with myself. But I made the mistake of thinking that my work here is done. I had to stand there for the next four hours and never got hold of another one. Didn't get anywhere near the ball.

After a session and a half, I was knackered. It got to the stage where unless it was hit straight at me, I'd almost be waving the ball on its way. I came off at the end of play covered in mud, with bruised knees, my elbows cut up, and my hands were swollen from the battering they'd taken. Please send me back to my natural habitat at fine leg . . .

Jonty Rhodes modestly described himself as 'a glorified goal-keeper – my goal is a 15-metre arc around cover point . . . and it's much easier than soccer because the shots come from the same place.' I suppose I was bit like a goalkeeper, too, but more a Sunday League keeper who let in 15.

On the gallop with Arkle

Unusually, Rhodes didn't follow the textbook method of walking in as the ball was bowled. He stood absolutely still, feeling that by being stationary and alert he was better able to spring into action. In contrast to Rhodes, my next Hall of Fame nominee, Derek Randall, was always on the move. 'Arkle', as Randall was nicknamed after the great racehorse, would start at deep cover as the bowler began his run-up and almost run in so he was bearing down on the batsman when the ball was delivered, which must have freaked them out.

I can still vividly remember watching his lightning run-out of Rick McCosker at Headingley during the 1977 Ashes on telly. McCosker was backing up at the non-striker's end and Arkle galloped in from mid-on, slid on his knees to pick up the ball and threw down the stumps in the blink of an eye. It was fitting that he also took the catch that won the Ashes that year, which he celebrated by doing a cartwheel.

Then there was a blinder to dismiss Andy Roberts in a one-dayer at the SCG in 1979, diving full-length to his right and behind him to take the catch. The same year he ran out Gordon Greenidge in the first over of the World Cup final.

On another occasion, he got rather over-excited after taking a miraculous full-length diving catch at deep square leg at Lord's, whirled the ball over his shoulder in celebration, released it a bit too late and clonked a spectator straight on the bonce and ironed him out. Never a dull moment with Randall around.

Like Jonty Rhodes, his Test batting average (33 over 47 Tests) was not great for a top-order batsman. Randall was certainly more talented with the willow than Rhodes, but he was a nervous starter. His trademark shuffle across the stumps and tendency to have a nibble outside off-stump could get him in trouble when his timing was a bit off. If he could just get through those first few overs and get settled in, he was alright. Seven hundreds and 12 fifties, which don't come easily at international level, give a hint of his quality.

At his best, he was a very entertaining batter to watch and had the ability to play shots that others couldn't and made them look easy. He was all that and more in the field.

A smallish fella, standing five foot eight, he had long arms, big hands and great agility which all helped him get down to the low balls and pouch high ones out of the sky. He also had huge feet for a little chap, and my *TMS* colleague Vic Marks says that Randall wasn't above using his to his team's advantage: 'It was surprising how often his size 11s just happened to crunch on a length as he was crossing the pitch!'

He must have been a great man to have in your team, even if he wasn't scoring the runs. On the 1976/77 tour of India, he struggled horribly with the bat, but Randall was actually a key part of England's 3–1 series win. Encouraged by skipper Tony Greig, who wanted to find a way to win over the partisan Indian fans, Randall clowned for the crowd, doing cartwheels and borrowing the hat and gun of a policeman patrolling the boundary and marching along in front of them. When oranges were thrown at him, he threw them back, except for one which he peeled and ate. The Indian fans lapped up his antics and it diffused the intimidation factor. Derek Randall really was the clown prince.

Windies wonders

Another fielder I enjoyed watching on TV as a kid was West Indies skipper Clive Lloyd. He was absolutely lethal at cover point, but to look at Clive you wouldn't have picked him as a great fielder, because he was so tall and rather loping. But he had lightning reactions, could get down to the low ball with ease with his long arms and could throw the ball unbelievably powerfully and accurately on the run with seemingly no effort.

The amazing thing was he didn't have the best eyesight. As a kid, he'd tried to break up a fight on the way home from school, and got a ruler in the eye for his troubles. His eye could never be properly fixed so he had to wear glasses. Before he became well-known, Clive reckoned the glasses were an advantage when he wandered out to bat, because the fielders were looking at him wondering who this bloke who couldn't see was . . . until he started carting the bowling all over the place.

Another unlucky incident as a kid nearly cost him his life. Playing cricket in the garden, he climbed over the garden fence to fetch the ball, the fence broke, and a splinter got lodged in his right shin. He got a tetanus infection and he ended up in a coma and in hospital for six weeks.

That wasn't the end of Clive's dramas playing cricket – representing the Rest of the World XI v South Australia in 1971, Clive had another dicey experience while fielding. In making a brilliant attempt to catch Ashley Mallett, he twisted in mid-air and landed heavily. He couldn't move and had to be stretchered off and taken to hospital. X-rays showed he'd cracked his spinal cord and for a while it was touch and go whether he'd ever walk again.

Thankfully, after intensive physio he made a miraculous recovery, and a couple months after his accident he was back prowling the covers again. Me, I'd have been scared to have gone outside my house in case I had another accident.

Lloyd reckons anticipation was the key to his success as a fielder. 'They'd see a gap but I was already on the go, ready to strike,' he said. 'I also had telescopic arms which helped, so the batsman thought the ball was past me, but I'd still get to it.'

As his reputation grew, he'd save runs by his mere presence. David 'Bumble' Lloyd says nobody would take a run to Clive's right hand, but the odd person did try and paid the price. In 1970, playing for Lancashire, he ran out Worcestershire's top New Zealand batsman Glenn Turner on 99 when Turner just needed that single to get a record tenth century in a season. 'It was not a ludicrous run,' said Turner afterwards.

Another great West Indies fielder who I played against towards the back end of his career was Roger Harper. Absolute dynamite, he was. Six foot five inches tall, with an incredible reach, and fast and agile with it. West Indies team-mates called him 'The Greyhound'. Courtney Walsh said, 'Jonty Rhodes is a great fielder but I would've liked to see him play on the same field as Roger when he was at his peak.'

Harper learnt his trade on the bumpy outfields of the Demerara Cricket Club in Guyana, which might explain why, unlike Rhodes, he wasn't one for diving for balls hit along the ground.

'For a catch, yeah, I'd dive left, right and centre,' he recalled. 'I just had the ability to anticipate. For a tall guy, I was quick off the mark. I was pretty flexible. All that and knowing what the bowler was doing and the batsman was doing and then anticipate based on the way the batsman positions himself.'

So anticipation was the key for big Roger, as well as him being another one of those strange people who actually really enjoyed fielding. As a kid, he used to join in the backyard games with his cricket-mad brother and cousins, who were all a few years older than him. The bigger boys didn't give him much chance to bat or bowl, so he tried to field. 'That enjoyment for fielding, finding ways to make it interesting, finding ways to make it fun really meant that I was honing my skills without even realising it,' he said.

Those skills served him well. In an international career from the mid-Eighties to mid-Nineties, he was a steady off-spinner with a good economy rate of just over two in Tests and under four in ODIs, which made him a good foil for West Indies' strike bowlers. He was also a handy lower-order batsman at Test level, but fielding was his exceptional talent.

Playing for the Rest of the World v MCC in an exhibition match at Lord's in 1987, Harper bowled to Graham Gooch who danced down the wicket and drilled the ball just onside of stumps at the non-striker's end. In a millisecond of blurring movement, Harper got down to his right, grabbed the ball and threw down the stumps, leaving poor old Goochy on all fours looking back at his broken stumps in disbelief.

'I had played against Gooch a few times . . . I saw him come down the track and I sort of knew where he was going to hit it, so I was a step ahead,' Roger reckoned. It's one thing anticipating what's going to happen, another to be able to pounce like that, though. It was a stunning bit of fielding.

He took another belter in a one-dayer against England in Perth in January 1987. Fielding at backward point, he took off like an

NBA player going up for a slam dunk to catch a full-blooded cut from Allan Lamb at full-stretch. Goodness knows how high above ground level the ball must have been flying.

Maybe his best catch, though, was against the Aussies in Melbourne in December 1988. On as a substitute fielder, he pouched Dean Jones at third slip, a catch commentator Bill Lawry called 'one of the greatest catches I've ever seen in Test matches' and it was absolute different gravy. Jones, aiming to hit a rare leg-stump half-volley from Curtly Ambrose through midwicket, got the leading edge and the ball skewed away low down to Harper's left. 'I think I froze for a moment,' he remembered. 'I heard an edge and then the next thing I knew I was going for it with my left hand. That was a real reflex catch.'

Roger Harper – handy sub fielder to have in your locker.

Top slips: Beefy and an Aussie

Slip catching like that really blows my mind. I went in the slips a couple of times – when we needed one wicket and we had eight slips and a gully – and, my God, those edges travel fast. It's like being a coconut in a coconut shy. It was more about self-preservation for me rather than going towards the ball to try and catch it.

My favourite slipper of all time to watch was Ian Botham. Beefy's favourite position was second slip, and despite breaking all the technical rules of slip fielding, he was brilliant there.

For a start, he used to stand ridiculously close to the bat – I can only remember one other top slip fielder that ever stood so far up

(Mark Waugh – more of him in a minute . . .). And often, as time went on and he got more and more tuned into the game, Beefy would inch further and further forward. When Mike Brearley was his England captain and standing way behind him at first slip, he would have to tell him to move back a bit. Never one who took kindly to being told what to do, Beefy's first response was to accidentally-on-purpose flick mud off his boots in the direction of his skipper. Brearley used to joke that he spent a lot of his time 'gardening' when Ian was alongside him (well, yards in front of him) in the slips. He put up with the rebellious response though, because Beefy would take his advice and move back after making his muddy protest.

Then there was Beefy's habit of standing half up rather than crouching down. The textbooks say that if you are crouching, you're in position to catch the low edged ball, and it's easier to rise up to catch the high ball than it is to go down for the low ball. Beefy's excuse for not crouching down was that he was tired from bowling – and to be fair, in his prime, he often bowled long spells – but you'd think it would have made him a liability in the slips.

Even worse, he had his hands on his knees as the bowler delivered the ball rather than cupped in front of him. He also admitted that sometimes he was a ball-watcher – following the ball's path from the bowler's arm to batsman – which, again, is a cardinal sin. In theory. Because the ball is travelling so fast, you're supposed to watch the bat and wait for the edges to come.

I wonder if standing up so close behind the bat was his way of making himself concentrate. He might have looked casual, half standing, hands on his knees, but somehow when the ball came his way, high or low or wide to either side, he could be relied upon to take the catch. With his amazing anticipation, reflexes, great hands and general genius, he was able to do everything wrong and get it right.

When I first started playing with Beefy, I was in awe of him and keen to get his advice on how I could improve my fielding. One day I sidled up and asked him if he had any tips on catching. He swivelled round on his bar stool, looked at me and all he said was, 'Always go for the middle one, Cat.'

I think that was his way of saying, you can either do it or you can't.

Other than Beefy, who I was lucky enough to play alongside a few times at the end of his career, Mark Waugh was probably the stand-out slip fielder during my time. He made the sharpest catch look easy. Both he and his twin Steve were catching balls when they were barely out of nappies. Their parents played tennis tournaments at weekends and used to hit little catches to them off their rackets between games.

When they got older, they also played a bit of indoor cricket, which was booming in Australia in the Eighties, winning a couple of national titles with New South Wales. The indoor game was pretty fast and Mark said that helped him sharpen his reactions in the field.

Then when he was picked for the NSW squad for outdoor cricket, he was lucky enough to be coached by Bob Simpson, considered one of the best slip fielders of all time. Simpson taught him that slip fielders should keep their hands hanging loose, as if they are going to drop off their arms, and wait for the ball to come to them, not go chasing it.

When Allan Border finished as Essex's overseas professional, it was Mark not Steve Waugh he recommended to the club as his replacement, telling them that apart from being a gifted strokeplayer and a decent medium-pace bowler, 'he fields like you wouldn't believe'.

Ian Healy, who fielded hours and hours beside him, remembered his 'ease of movement'. Allan Border talked about his 'soft hands, and ability to not catch the ball flush in the middle, but still hang on to it'. That is a talent – unless I got the ball sweet in the palm, there was every chance of me spilling the catch.

Border also said he'd never seen anybody catch the ball as well one-handed as Waugh. On that score, one of the best must be the one he took off Alec Stewart when Australia hammered England by an innings and then some at Headingley in 1993. When Stewie tried to cut a ball from Paul Reiffel, it travelled so fast that no one in the slips had a chance to move, except Waugh, who snaffled an incredible one-handed catch low down to his right and behind him. Not bad for an Aussie.

My bat-pad hell

While we're talking close fielders, I must salute the bat-pad boys. All of them, really, because that is one dangerous job, as I discovered on the one occasion I fielded there. That was playing for MCC against Worcestershire in a season-opener at Lord's early in my career. It was quite a big deal for me to be selected for the MCC, so I was up for it. Then we went out to field, and the captain plonked me in at forward short leg which, in those days, as all senior players knew, was the ridiculous fielding position where the young rookie should be placed. There or silly mid-off.

Syd Lawrence was bowling and Tim Curtis was facing. It was a freezing cold spring day, I had three jumpers on and a helmet, and I was in position thinking: what the hell am I doing here?

At short leg, you are so close to the bat, you hear the ball *whoosh* down but can't see anything. And big Syd used to bowl the odd wild one, so I was bracing myself for danger. I was crouching down like I've seen proper short-leg fielders do, but I'd have been better off kneeling on a prayer mat.

Sure enough, Syd soon bowled a short one, Tim Curtis hooked it and just as I was starting to take evasive action, I felt the ball thud into my ribs. The padding of three cable-knit woolen jumpers wasn't enough to protect me from a cricket ball hitting me at about 80mph from a distance of two yards. I had to go off with a cracked rib, and that was the end of my day. After that, I vowed never to go back in there again.

So I always felt for my boys who fielded around the bat when I was bowling. They are absolutely crucial to a spinner. I had a couple of batsmen caught off the boot of my close fielders. In a Test for England against New Zealand in Auckland in 1992, Chris Cairns smashed it, Robin Smith jumped in the air, the ball hit him on the foot and the ball looped to Graeme Hick at extra cover. Big bruise for Judge, but a wicket's a wicket.

Joking aside, I was always very concerned for my close catchers, but Judgey had told me before, 'Don't worry, Tuffers, if I get hit, I can go back to the pavilion and have the afternoon off.'

Keith Brown fielded short leg for me for Middlesex and I used to buy him a bottle of scotch at the end of the season in recognition of him taking the blows on my behalf.

Nowhere to hide

Looking at the modern game, it's much harder to pick out the outstanding fielders, because the general standard has improved so much and there are so many potential hall of famers. AB de Villiers is not quite Jonty Rhodes level, but he's up there. Joe Root is a great slipper. Ben Stokes is good everywhere. The list could go on and on.

With the rise of Twenty20, improved equipment and more adventurous strokeplay, dynamic outfielding has become more important than ever. Fielders even work in pairs now to turn a potential six hit into a catch, with one leaping through the air to knock the ball back to his mate inside the boundary rope.

Coaches and teams really work to get an edge, because they know the way a team fields sets the tone – if you're sharp and energetic in the field, it lays down a marker and puts pressure on the opposition.

We always had fielders with good hands, but now they're all athletes as well – and the days of the big fast bowler being hopeless at fielding have gone. Look at someone like Jimmy Anderson, who is a brilliant fielder.

There used to be positions where you could hide, but then the new bats and all these new shots being invented have brought every position into play. Third man and fine leg have become wicket-taking positions.

Batsmen now don't see blokes on the boundary so much as a deterrent but as a mere irritation. I used to place my men on the boundary and say, 'Go on then, if you fancy it' and then I'd play about with the flight of the ball to make them mistime it.

In the old days, only the massive hitters like Viv Richards and Beefy would regularly take on the boundary fielders because the risks were too great. The bowler's field would dictate the shots that the batsmen attempted, but that's not so much the case any-more. Now they calculate that if they have a big swing, even if they don't quite get hold of it, it's going to take some catching.

The amount of times now you see a batsman get to 94 or 95 and go for a six just because they fancy getting to their hundred with a big hit. They feel in good enough nick, have the big old bat to do it and the field placing is almost irrelevant. They just think '**** it' and go for it. And more often than not, they seem to do it.

Talking of boundary fielders, I must give a shout out to my old England team-mate Devon Malcolm. Now, I'd like to think that even I had a safer pair of hands than big Devon, but he did have an unbelievably strong throwing arm on him. You didn't want to be behind the bowler's end when big Dev was winging one in from the boundary, because if he missed and you had to get your hands behind it, it was like trying to stop a missile. *Whoosh!*

If he got it right, he'd run you out from the boundary; he just had to get the ball in his hands first. A prime example was against West Indies in Kingston, Jamaica, 1990. Dev was born in

Kingston and on the first day fielding on the boundary at Sabina Park he was getting plenty of stick from the locals. The Windies openers Gordon Greenidge and Desmond Haynes were scoring runs for fun, and Dev had taken his eye off the ball and let it go through his legs for four, much to the delight of the Jamaican crowd behind him. A couple of overs later, Greenidge flicked another down to fine leg, and under pressure the ball rebounded off Dev's knee a couple of yards in front of him. Seizing the opportunity, Greenidge set off for a second run, but Dev recovered, picked up the ball and fired the ball into Jack Russell behind the stumps. Greenidge was out by a couple of yards – that's how hard he could throw it.

Yes, I'm putting Devon Malcolm's throwing arm into my Hall of Fame for its awesome power, if not the erratic sat-nav.

3

CRICKETING
CREATURES XI

Cricket is a sport to be enjoyed by all, even other species, and there are a few creatures which have made an impression in the game down the years that I want to celebrate in the Tuffers HoF.

For many people, it's the sound of leather on willow that attracts them to cricket, but for some animals, the taste of cricket-ball leather is more appealing. In April 1928, play was suspended in a game in Montagu, South Africa, when one of a number of ostriches loitering near the field of play, ran onto the pitch and fielded the ball. It was a neat bit of fielding, the only problem being that the bird swallowed the ball whole. As no one had a spare, the only course of action was for the (human) fielders to chase down and capture the bird, then massage its neck until it spat the ball out so play could continue.

No such luck in Sydney, Australia, in October 1962, when some boys were having a game and hit the ball towards an elephant from the local circus that was having a walk nearby. The day's play came to a premature end when the elephant picked the ball up with its trunk and swallowed it whole.

The monkey that invaded the pitch during a 1951 tour game between MCC and Maharashtra, in Pune, India, just wanted to play. The little primate dashed onto the pitch and sat down at point ready for the next ball to be bowled, only for groundsmen waving sticks to chase it off the pitch. The next day, the monkey tried again, this time taking up a position at gully – the MCC side were probably grateful for the extra set of hands, but again, the groundsmen denied the monkey its cricketing dream, so it was forced to settle for watching the rest of the day's play from the pavilion roof.

A posthumous award goes to the fish that leapt above the surface of the River Ure one day in 1934 only to be struck a fatal blow by a cricket ball hit out of the ground by a batsman playing in a match between Hawes and Aysgarth. Whether the fish was attempting to take a heroic catch, we shall never know. RIP, fish.

Sadly, quite a few birds have perished in the line of cricket duty. In 1969, a swallow made a fatal intervention during a game Down Under. Western Australia batsman John Inverarity, who was on nought at the time, was bowled by a ball from South Australia's Greg Chappell that deflected off the bird in mid-flight. The umpire called a no-ball, saving Inverarity from a duck, and he took advantage of his extra life to score 89, but, sadly, it proved to be a dead ball for the unfortunate swallow.

There was a much happier ending for a stray dog that joined in an Ashes Test at Trent Bridge in 1993. Stewards tried and failed to catch him, and it was only thanks to Merv Hughes channelling his inner canine and getting down on all fours to calm the dog that team-mate Michael Slater was able to pick him up. The RSPCA were swamped with calls from viewers charmed by the pooch's cameo appearance, and he was found a good home. His new owners named him 'Merv', naturally.

There is a record of a match in Nairobi, Kenya, many years ago where a ball was stopped by a lion that had jumped out of the undergrowth nearby and started playing with it. Now, if a lion rocked up at a cricket match I was playing in, my first instinct would be to run for my life, but these Kenyans were made of sterner stuff. The umpires turned down the fielders' appeal for a lost ball, because it was still in play – albeit in the massive paws and jaws of a lion – so the batsmen kept running while the fielders figured out how the hell they were going to get their ball back. Rather them than me, but they gathered up a few other lunatics and together shooed away the big cat who, luckily, didn't take the ball with him.

The batsmen must have clocked up a few runs in the meantime, but perhaps the combination of lion saliva and scratching on the ball did help the bowlers get some reverse swing afterwards? That is ball-tampering on another level.

The Nairobi lion played a blinder, but perhaps the most dramatic match-saving effort by an animal occurred when a batsman for Nettleton CC struck what looked to be the winning boundary, only for the ball to strike a cow who'd wandered onto the field of play and the Wiltshire club had to settle for a draw.

The creatures mentioned above were uninvited guests to the games, but in the early days of cricket, there was the odd (and I mean odd) match where the animals were selected to play. There was once a money match in Kent between the Gentlemen of the Hill and the Gentlemen of the Dale with stakes of a guinea per man – whether the horses each had to pony up a guinea as well, I don't know. The bats and stumps must have been very long for that game. I'll take the finest horse cricketer from either the Hill or Dale side for my Creatures XI.

In 1813, there was a two-men-a-side match for 50 guineas played in Farnham Surrey. Well, actually, it was two men and a water spaniel called Drake on the side of Lord James Kerr and his servant, against a Mr Cock and Mr Wetherall. Apparently, Drake the dog was an enthusiastic fielder – very quick to the ball – but didn't really contribute with the bat.

At number eleven, to complete my team, a mischievous cat that spent a dozen years of his life meandering around Lord's ... No, not me, this was an actual cat called Peter who roamed the stadium in the Fifties and early Sixties. Feline Pete loved a game of cricket and would often appear on the field of play during big televised matches. He was so well known and loved that when he died, aged 14 on Bonfire Night, 1964, his passing was marked with an obituary in *Wisden*. The MCC secretary paid tribute, saying, 'He was a cat of great character.'

Aahh, I hope that I am remembered so fondly by the club when my time comes. Somehow, I doubt it.

MEN IN
WHITE COATS

_____

Vexed in Visakhapatnam

If you'd asked me to nominate an umpire for entry into a hall of fame early in my playing career, I would have struggled to have given you a single name. No ****ing way. I saw the men in white coats as a foe – and I've always had an intrinsic fear of them actually. And clowns. Not sure why. It took me a while – actually, far too long – to realise that they held the key to getting wickets, because often they're the buggers deciding whether to give it out or not.

My attitude was that they were there to do a job, and they should do it properly whether I'd just called them 'a twat' or not. Of course, that's not human nature. It's like traffic wardens – if you're nice to them and tickle them up a bit, they might give you five minutes on a yellow line to nip into the newsagent's on the high street. If you eff and blind at them, they're more likely to give you a ticket.

That wasn't something I grasped for a while . . . in fact, it was probably a good ten years into my professional career before I stopped seeing umpires as a mortal enemy and realised the value of being a bit more friendly towards them, perhaps starting the day with a cheerful, 'Hello, you're looking well. How's the missus? Is that a new Vauxhall Astra you've got in the car park? Lovely shade of beige . . .'

I was always an aggressive, in-your-face bowler, and when a decision went against me – especially in that first decade – I'd just rant and rave at the umpire, totally justifiably, in my humble opinion. That wouldn't matter if later the batsman got an obvious nick to the ball, but if there was a marginal lbw or caught behind decision for the umpire to make, my earlier antics probably didn't help my cause. If I'd been in their position, I doubt I'd be too inclined to give the benefit of the doubt to a bowler who'd recently questioned my parentage.

My behaviour during a warm-up match in February 1993 on England's tour of India summed up my early attitude towards umpires. We were playing a three-dayer at Visakhapatnam, on the coast of the Bay of Bengal, between the First and Second Tests. I'd not played in the one-dayers before the Test series or the First Test, so I was keen to make an impression. Our opposition was the 'Rest of India', but their line-up did include 'The Little Master' himself, Sachin Tendulkar, so bowling to him would be a good test.

After we made 250-odd for six declared in the first innings, I got my chance to bowl at him on the second day. The weather was typically red-hot, and I'd had the shits the night before so wasn't feeling my best, but I got Sachin out . . . well, I should have.

Early in his innings, he came down the wicket to me. I deceived him in the flight, got the ball to turn and he missed it, leaving our wicket-keeper, Richard 'Dickie' Blakey, with the simple task of completing the stumping. But Dickie dropped the ball, missed the stumping and Sachin made it back to his crease.

Up to that point, I understand that Sachin had never been stumped before in his life, so I had the right hump with Dickie for botching the chance. All I could think was what a feather in my cap it would have been to have got the great Tendulkar out stumped and how much confidence it would have given me for the tour. I've never really forgiven Dickie for missing that one!

After that, normal service was resumed for Sachin as he put on a century partnership with Sanjay Manjrekar and got in some handy batting practice before the Second Test. Meanwhile, my mood deteriorated rapidly thanks to the umpire at my end who kept on calling me for no-balls.

As a spinner, bowling a no-ball really is a cardinal sin, but I know I did sometimes confuse umpires because I had a habit of planting my right foot down to bowl over the popping crease line, then as my arm came over, my foot would sort of screw back, and by the time I released the ball, part of the foot would be on the line which is a legit delivery.

Mind you, *TMS* statto Andrew Samsom told me recently that in my 42 Test matches I bowled 132 no-balls – a ridiculous amount for a spin bowler. I was always pushing the front line; I don't know why. All I had to do was take my bowling mark back half a foot and there wouldn't have been any doubt, but I couldn't do it.

Anyway, so this umpire kept on calling me for no-balls, no matter how much I protested my innocence. 'No, look, I'm screwing back, I'm screwing back,' I told him, like a demented snooker player.

I got more and more annoyed and abusive towards him and, guess what, the no-ball calls kept coming. Eventually, I had a stand-up row with this fella.

'I'm not bowling ****ing no-balls ... right, right, I'll show you ...'

Very unsubtly, I then positioned a fielder – I think it was a very reluctant Michael Atherton – a couple of yards from and directly in line with the popping crease.

'Oh Tuffers, really ...'

'No, Athers. I need to get this sorted. This is a matter of principle.'

'Can't you just move your bowling mark back a foot?'

'No, no, I'm being personally attacked here.'

If he'd been up the other end, Athers would have been at silly point, but here he was just in a silly position. He was sort of 'on the drive', although a couple of steps to my left and I should have been able to stop any balls heading his way, so his main job as far as I was concerned was to check my foot position. So as I was running into bowl, he was crouched there staring at the crease rather than the batsman at the other end, just so I could prove the umpire wrong.

Last ball of the over, the ump calls me again for a no-ball, which sends me over the edge.

'****ing hell!' I bluster and snatch my cap from him.

'Right, you will have to be fined now,' I hear him say as I storm off and proceed to kick my cap all the way down to fine leg. That's quite a long way and I showed some pretty impressive football skills to keep connecting with it.

Think I got fined a grand for that. An expensive tantrum.

Despite my anger – and perhaps because of it in some ways as I sometimes needed something to kick against (not usually my cap) to get myself fired up – I did eventually manage to take four wickets in that innings. No lbws, naturally, and not the prize wicket of Tendulkar, who scored 61 before falling to our leg-spinner, Ian Salisbury. That set me up to play my first Test match in India a few days later in Madras, where Tendulkar scored a majestic 165. I made a decent century myself, conceding 132 runs off 41 wicket-less overs and we lost by an innings.

No, I didn't have the best relationship with umpires, and looking back, I have to give a few of them credit for putting up with me. I didn't know that, like any good marriage, you need to put the work in to get results and appreciate your other half. Mind you, dealing with my outbursts was nothing compared to what the first umpires in the very early days of cricket had to put up with.

Bayonets, bets and brawls

One of the main reasons why umpires were introduced in the first place was to settle arguments before they got out of hand. In the seventeenth and eighteenth centuries when the batsmen were equipped/armed with long curved bats, umpiring was not for the faint-hearted as you could find yourself in the middle of a brawl. Have you ever been hit round the head with a curved bat? It hurts.

In 1715, a player called William Waterfall got done for manslaughter after killing an opponent. My kind of cricketer. Another match, between Kent and Essex at Tilbury Fort in 1776, descended into a murderous pitched battle, after Essex discovered that Kent were fielding a ringer in their team. Two people were shot dead and one was killed with a bayonet in the fight, which, frankly, seems like a bit of an over-reaction for just having a ringer in your side. Always good to carry a bayonet in your kit bag in those days, just in case.

It didn't help the umpires of the day that the rules of cricket were kind of being made up as they went along – it was only in the mid-1700s that the first laws were written down. Different clubs and villages had different rules, so disputes were common. Batsmen who hit the ball up in the air were allowed to charge a fielder who was about to catch them out. Throw into the mix some massive wagers from local aristocrats on the outcome of the match plus an increasingly boozed-up crowd making side bets with the bookies during the day, and the atmosphere could get tense to say the least.

The Artillery Ground, in Finsbury, which opened in 1724, was the big London venue and up to 10,000 people would attend matches there. Spectators would just wander onto the pitch during play to give their opinions or make threats. Fights and even full-scale riots occurred, so security had to be hired to keep the crowd under control and protect the umpires.

The umpires would be under pressure from all angles, because the upper-class chaps who organised the games had big bets riding on their respective teams, too. They appointed the umpires and were likely in their ears trying to influence them.

But before you feel too sorry for the umpires, they often had a bet on the game themselves! I can imagine there were a few dubious 'not-out' calls when the team an umpire had backed were chasing a total. If a 22-year-old Phil Tufnell had been bowling then and getting loads of dodgy calls from an umpire I knew had money on the opposition, I might easily have 'done a Willie Waterfall' myself.

It wasn't until 1835 that umpires were officially banned from betting, but even then no one was really checking up on them so the umps kept on having a cheeky flutter.

It sounds like anarchy, and new rules and developments in the game caused more strife between umpires and players – for instance, when bowlers started to bowl round-arm instead of underarm in the 1800s.

Horseplay and 'Honest Will'

In the early days of bowlers flinging the ball round-arm, there were wides galore. With the bowling arm swinging round the body rather than delivering the ball from above the head, just a slight mistiming of the release and it could fly off line. There's a record of a single-wicket game in 1836 between one Reverend Pycroft and JC Ryle where a total of 149 runs were scored but not a single one came off the bat – with 95 byes, 44 wides and 10 no-balls. Really?

Forget about line and length, the vicar and Mr Ryle clearly had no idea where the ball was going when they bowled, and couldn't get near it when they batted either.

Kent opening bowler John Willes was one of the better exponents of round-arm, but in a match against the MCC, he got no-balled every ball by the old-school umpire Harry Bentley. Bentley had been employed as an umpire by the MCC for 30 years. MCC committee members were very suspicious of the new round-arm trend and it's likely that Bentley was influenced to clamp down on it. Lasith 'Slinga' Malinga would have been in all sorts of trouble.

No-balling Willes every time was a bit extreme, though, and he got so annoyed with Bentley that he chucked the ball down, walked off the pitch, and rode away on his horse saying he'd never play again. I know the feeling . . . although I never usually parked my horse behind the pavilion on a matchday.

When round-arm bowling evolved into overarm bowling, there was a new issue for umps to keep an eye out for, as bowlers started throwing it rather than keeping a straight arm.

An umpire called William Caldecourt — a decent medium-pace underarm bowler himself who was employed by the MCC as a practice bowler — was a traditionalist and no fan of the overarm style. He caused controversy by no-balling all overarm deliveries, whether they were bent-arm or not. It didn't matter how much abuse he got from players and spectators, for years 'Honest Will', as he became known, was the scourge of all bowlers who dared to bowl with their hand above shoulder level.

Bentley and Caldecourt sound like rather stiff and set in their ways for my taste – I think our personalities would have clashed – so I'm afraid they aren't entering my Hall of Fame. However, there was a nineteenth-century umpire called Fuller Pilch who I'm tempted to let in just because of his brilliant name. Pilch had been one of the best all-rounders in England in his day and turned to umpiring in his fifties after retiring. He'd stand in the middle puffing away on his pipe before giving his decisions. Not that any bowler need have bothered appealing for lbws – Pilch did not believe in them and any enquiry would be turned down.

In the days before the Decision Review System (DRS), I encountered plenty of 'not-outers' like Pilch and most of them did my head in, so it's a no to him, too. Instead, my first nomination goes to Frank Chester who has a unique and amazing story.

Wood you believe it?

Frank Chester was a gifted cricketer, who was playing for Worcestershire's county side from the age of 16. In 1913, aged 17, he became the youngest English batsman to score a century in the county championship. But by 19, he was a soldier fighting in the First World War. He served in France and then Salonika, Greece, where he was injured and had to have his right arm just below the elbow amputated.

He was discharged from the army in August 1918. 'Summertime, cricket being played again, and I, a professional with no right arm!' he recalled later of what must have been terrible time for him. '. . . Nothing could restore my ability to follow the only trade I knew and loved.'

He did try to play again, and was so talented that he became adept at pushing ones and twos batting one-handed and taking catches with his left hand, but clearly he could no longer play at the highest level.

Former England captain Sir Pelham 'Plum' Warner encouraged him to take up umpiring instead: 'Take it up seriously, Chester. One day, you'll make a fine umpire.'

Chester took Plum's advice and put everything he had into umpiring. With the help of a wooden arm, he was able to make all the necessary signals. And if you were ever short of a stump, Frank was your man . . . (sorry).

And just as he had as a young player, Frank soon made a big impact on the game.

By 1922, when he was just 26, he qualified to become a first-class umpire. In those days it was uncommon for umpires to give decisions against team captains, because they had a big say in whether you'd stay on the first-class list. Chester had no clue about this and gave both captains out on the first day of one his early county games. His fellow umpire said, 'Boy, you won't last long as an umpire . . . if you give skippers out, you sign your own death warrant.'

I'm not sure that was quite the case in my day, but it was a running joke on the county circuit that being captain and a batsman was worth a couple of hundred runs a season for you.

Umpires also tended to give lots of dodgy decisions against

tailenders in the early twentieth century – a rap on the pads was lbw, and shouts for caught behind even if bat hadn't come close to ball were often given. But rather than follow the traditional masonic code among umpires, Chester decided he'd just give decisions on merit. At first, it didn't go down well with his colleagues, but he gradually earned respect for his honest approach from players, and other umpires followed his lead.

Two years after standing in his first county game, he was umpiring Test matches, and went on to umpire 48 Tests, more than anyone had before him, during the course of 33 years as a first-class umpire.

One advantage of Chester's artificial arm was that it turned him into a human barometer. 'When the stump begins to ache, rain is almost invariably on the way,' he said. 'Often players used to ask me, "Is the arm aching today, Frank?"'

Frank's disability never affected his ability as an umpire, although there was one occasion during a match at Hove between Sussex and Surrey, when he came unstuck . . . or rather his wooden arm did.

A Surrey batsman smashed a half-volley straight at Chester, who took evasive action but couldn't get his wooden arm out of the way in time. The ball hit it solidly and sent it flying one bounce into the sightscreen. Ah, the sound of leather on willow . . . and then on wood again.

Poor old Frank dashed to the boundary to pick it up and go off the field to fix it back into the socket (I don't know whether he signalled four runs first).

'Here – have a brandy, old chap,' said a member as he walked into the pavilion, an offer Frank gladly accepted.

When he returned to the field, Frank positioned himself safely yards back from the stumps, much to the amusement of the crowd.

Frank had a few other funny tales to tell from his long umpiring career. Once at the start of an innings in a charity match, he asked the opening bowler the standard question: 'Over or around the wicket?'

The bowler looked at him quizzically, didn't reply and continued whirring his arms around vigorously to warm up.

'Do you bowl over or around the wicket?' Frank repeated.

'No – at the wicket, of course.'

Frank also told a story from village cricket of a batsman coming out to the crease wearing just one pad – on his right leg. Assuming he was a left-hander the opposing captain changed the field, but, no, he prepared to face the bowling in a right-hander's stance.

In the first over, he got hit painfully three times on his unprotected leg.

'Why don't you change the pad to your left leg?' asked the wicket-keeper.

'That's no use now – I'll be batting at the other end next over,' replied the batsman.

Eh?

Frank never lost his own competitive streak either. On one occasion back at the hotel after a long day in the field at Old Trafford, Frank challenged Gloucestershire opening batsman George Lambert to a game of snooker for half a crown a frame. Frank seemed pretty confident, but Lambert felt a bit guilty about taking on a guy with one arm . . . that was until Frank produced his own special arm rest. Turns out Frank was very handy with a cue and he took George's money for the rest of the evening.

Late in his umpiring career, Frank did get accused of being biased against Australia. During the 1953 Ashes series, he took to turning down their players' appeals by saying 'not out' in an Aussie accent. For a miraculous career topped off by winding up the Aussies, he definitely deserves a place in my Hall of Fame.

In the county game, Chester often teamed up with an umpire called Bill Reeves, who deserves a Tuffers HoF honorable mention. An Essex boy, Reeves was known as a bit of a comedian on the county circuit. During one Roses game, Cecil Parkin made a hopeful appeal for lbw against Yorkshire's England international opener Herbert Sutcliffe. From square leg, Chester could see the ball was going over the top, but Parkin asked Reeves, 'What was the matter with that?'

'Too high,' replied Reeves.

The next over, Parkin made another daft lbw appeal after hitting Sutcliffe's partner Percy Holmes in the stomach.

'Well, what was the matter with that one?' he asked.

'Too low,' deadpanned Reeves.

At another Roses game, Reeves gave a harsh-looking lbw decision against a young Lancashire pro. At lunchtime, Bill saw the lad in the pavilion still looking gutted, so he went up to him to offer some comforting words.

'Don't look like that; you weren't out really.'

'Why did you give me out then?'

'Well, the ground's a bit wet and I was thinking of your rheumatics – what would your poor mother have said to me?'

There were also 'tailender decisions' on the county circuit in my day, and looking back I think the umpires were being as merciful as Bill in some ways. When you were out there facing someone like Malcolm Marshall, avoiding serious injury, not your rheumatics, was at the forefront of your mind. So when you got hit on the pad by a ball slipping slightly down legside, the umpire was almost doing you a favour by raising the finger.

Blind Alec

From the 1930s through to the late 1950s, another well-known character among the men in white coats was Alec Skelding. A good friend of Frank Chester's, but eight years older, Alec had the distinctive red nose of a man who always carried a hip flask of brandy in his pocket to help him keep warm on a cold day in the field. A former racecourse bookie, he also added a bit of flavour to the umpire's normal signals to the scorers by throwing in some tic-tac just to confuse them. God knows what they wrote in the scorebook – the odds on the 4.45 at Chepstow?

Previously, Skelding enjoyed a long playing career with Leicestershire as a pace bowler, and took over 100 wickets in one season (1927) when he was 40 years old, which is some going for a quickie. This is even more remarkable for the fact that he had such bad eyesight, he had to wear glasses with very strong lenses, and on hot days they'd steam up, so when he bowled he couldn't really see what he was doing. 'So I bowl on hearing only and appeal twice an over,' he said.

Bad eyesight? Perfect for an umpire, then, and when Alec took up the job his thick glasses made him an easy target for 'Are you blind?' jibes from disgruntled bowlers and fielders when their appeals were turned down, but Skelding took them in good part. After copping some stick from Aussie star Sid Barnes during a 1948 Ashes tour match, he sent Sid a note before the next Australia game he was umpiring, saying that he had brought his guide dog with him this time.

A dog invaded the pitch when the Aussies were fielding, which Sid picked up and gave to Skelding saying, 'Here's your dog, Alec . . . Now all you want is a white stick.'

Richie Benaud remembered Skelding as the first umpire in England that he'd seen wearing white boots. In Australia that was standard, but in England they used to wear brown brogues or, sometimes, when the weather was dry, brown or navy blue suede shoes. Richie said there was never a dull moment when Skelding was around and he used to love to hear his trademark phrase to call an end to a session's play: 'And that, gentlemen, concludes the entertainment for the morning/afternoon/evening . . .'

Skelding was also a bit of a poet in his spare time. He wrote a poem called 'Duties, Trials and Troubles of County Cricket Umpires' that included these lines:

> *Bowlers who are apt to squeal*
> *At a negative appeal;*
> *Think of umpire Jack, or Jim;*
> *Think kindly, please – and pity him!*

I think I would have been squealing a lot with Alec because he was a dyed-in-the-wool not-outer, who would only raise the finger if he was absolutely sure the batsman was out. Strange then that he was the first umpire ever to give a hat-trick of lbws, to Yorkshire's Horace Fisher in a game against Somerset in 1932. Fisher was a left-arm spinner too, so maybe there would have been hope for me after all. Mind you, even Alec said he shocked himself by giving three in a row, but they were so plumb, he had no other option.

The joy of Smiling Ray

It sounds like the bowlers of yesteryear – particularly the spinners – suffered as I did with the interpretation of the lbw law which was basically unfair right up until DRS was introduced. For almost all umpires, if a batsman was on the front foot, it was not out.

I'd be thinking, 'But the ball's hit him mid-shin so it's not going over the top, and the ball's turned and hit the pad in line, so why isn't it out?'

There was a lot more friction between umpires and spinners (especially temperamental ones like me) because of that. The batsmen would just get their front foot down the wicket and pad the ball away. The way I saw it, the umpires were just getting it wrong. And over a long day in the field, that would drive me mental.

That's why 'Smiling' Ray Julian is an absolute certainty for induction into my Hall of Fame. A wicket-keeper for Leicestershire in his day, he joined the first-class umpires list in 1972 and stayed on it for 30 successive seasons up to his retirement.

Lovely chap, Ray, and his wife was a lovely lady as well. While Ray was umpiring, she would sit in the stands enjoying the game and the sunshine on a summer's day. They both always had amazing tans.

It was only in the last few years of his career that Ray belatedly got some international recognition, standing in six ODIs, but his only involvement in Test matches was acting as third umpire half a dozen times. In my eyes, and those of many other county bowlers, he was a legend, though, because he was that rarest breed of umpire – an out-and-out 'outer'.

'I'm not afraid to give people out, I'm an honest man,' said Ray as he approached retirement in 2001, also acknowledging that his brave decision-making may have cost him the chance to stand in Test matches. 'A lot of umpires go the easy way and keep saying not out. I think at Test level they don't want to be given out so much . . . No doubt when I've retired there'll be a few tears shed by bowlers, but batsmen will be pleased to see the back of me.'

He was voted the Professional Cricketers' Association (PCA) Umpire of the Year in the three years leading up to his retirement, which shows how highly he was rated by all the players – although the joke was that it was just the bowlers voting for him. Indeed, when Ray celebrated his 80th birthday in 2016, all the bowlers turned up for his party.

Ray always looked a very contented man on the cricket field, and never more so than when he was sending batsmen on their way with a big smile on his face. I'm not sure the batters were too happy about that, but it was always a lovely sight as a bowler to turn round to see him raising his finger with a grin.

A bit before my time, there was another renowned outer on the county umpiring circuit, Sam Cook from Gloucestershire, and when he and Ray were working together, championship games moved along rapidly. It certainly wasn't worth buying an advance ticket for the third day.

Ray recalled, 'Sometimes me and Sam would leave the pavilion together at lunchtime and Sam would say: "Only six wickets to go, Ray, I've a good chance of being back in Tetbury by 10 o'clock." And sure enough, he'd shoot out nine, ten and eleven with the consoling words: 'Sorry, son, I've a train at six o'clock.'"

Ray and Sam were like gunslingers in a Western: 'How many have you shot down?'

I have some great personal memories of Ray's umpiring days. During his final season, he was in the middle for a Middlesex–Durham game at Lord's. When I came on to bowl, I turned to him and said, 'I only need one more wicket to reach a thousand in first-class cricket.'

'In that case, you're bowling at the right end,' he replied. 'I only need two myself for 3,000 lbws!'

I should point out that being an honest fella, Ray was only joking and didn't gift me an lbw just to help us reach our milestones despite my appeals – I ended up bowling a chap called Martin Love for my 1,000th wicket.

Ray did have a bit of a Sam Cook moment once when he was umpiring me, though. Again, it was a Middlesex match at Lord's –

I think we were playing Northants. It was just before lunch on a Monday morning, and we only needed one wicket to win the game. It was a beautiful hot sunny day and no one wanted to be kept hanging around by a couple of tailenders into the afternoon session, when we could be grabbing some lunch and getting off home early or to the pub to enjoy a cold one in the beer garden. But these two tailenders were getting stuck in and all of the Middlesex boys are like, 'Oh come on, just **** off. You can't bat and you need about 400 in two sessions; it's not going to happen . . .'

I'm bowling and they're just blocking and blocking, and time is ticking away towards the lunch interval. If they make it to lunch, it's going to add another hour or two of hanging around waiting for the inevitable.

As I'm on my way back to my mark, Ray turns to me and says, 'Tuffers, just hit him on the pads, will you. This bloke's batting me into a traffic jam.'

That creased me up.

A couple of balls later I managed to beat the bat and hit the pad, appealed heartily and Ray's finger went up. In fairness, the ball did look like it sort-of-might-have-been hitting leg stump. Anyway, it was definitely time for all of us to go and for Ray to beat the traffic.

Top man, Ray, and joking aside, he really was a top-class umpire who deserved more international recognition. In the days before DRS, perfectly good lbw shouts were routinely turned down just because batsmen were on the front foot and Ray bucked that trend. In many ways he was ahead of his time – he gave people out because they were out, as DRS technology would have proved.

Sunny days with Dickie

Among the rest of the umpires, the not-outers, I could tolerate the ones who at least communicated with me. If I asked, 'Why wasn't that out?' and they just stood there and shook their head, that would do my nut in.

'Come on, answer me . . . ANSWER MEEEEEE!'

I always wanted an explanation, and some would just say, 'I'm not talking to you', which would wind me up even more.

For me, an umpire has to communicate with the bowler. I don't know if they do this nowadays, but a few would give me a heads-up if I was getting close to no-balling.

'Phil, you're pushing up a bit there . . .'

Or if they'd just turned down an lbw appeal, they'd tell me why.

'Sorry, I thought he hit it, Phil,' or, 'I thought it was going down leg.'

I wanted the ump to give me a reason why the decision had gone against me, otherwise I'd just feel *they* were against me.

That was where Dickie Bird was very good. He was a cast-iron not-outer – unless I was bowling close to the stumps and it was absolutely plumb, I had an almost 100 per cent failure rate with lbw appeals, but I didn't mind so much with him because he was a good communicator, without trying to be your mate.

'C'mon lad, I'm trying me best here,' he'd say. 'It's a lovely sunny day, we're all having a game of cricket – calm it down a bit.'

And he'd also dish out a bit of praise when merited – 'Oh, good over that, Tuffers.' I'm sure he said the same to batsmen who were going well.

Like Alec Skelding with his uncharacteristic lbw hat-trick, it is strange that Dickie, of all people, helped to set a new record for the number of lbw decisions given in a Test match when West Indies played Pakistan in April 1993. On a fast, low-bouncing pitch, the likes of Curtly Ambrose, Courtney Walsh, Waqar Younis and Wasim Akram were lethal and Dickie couldn't deny their appeals. Still, Dickie was quick to point out that of the 17 lbws, he'd only given seven, while his umpiring partner Steve Bucknor gave the rest.

But for someone who was a not-outer as a rule, bowlers got on well with Dickie, which shows his man-management skills. He had the human touch, whereas some didn't seem to have a character, they just stood there and gave the signals.

Even the grizzliest of Aussie fast bowlers had a soft spot for this little Pommie ump. There was a time when Merv Hughes was walking back towards his mark after effing and blinding at batsman Graeme Hick, and Dickie said, 'What unkindness has this man done to you, Mr Hughes?'

That made big Merv smile and reply, 'Dickie Bird – you're a legend.'

Dickie was a great umpire, as his record shows, but it was his unique character that made him famous around the world. All his fidgeting around and tics when standing at the wicket, pulling at his umpire's coat, mopping at his brow with a hankie whatever the weather and hamming it up when nearly getting hit by a ball arrowed past him off the middle of the bat. This chap in a white cap was an instantly recognisable figure on the field. Mind you, he did lose his cap one time in a pitch invasion after the 1975 World Cup quarter-final between West Indies and Australia. A few days later he got on a London bus and noticed the West Indian conductor wearing a cap that looked just like his one.

After asking him where he got it, the conductor said, 'It was from Dickie Bird, the Test umpire.' Presumably, this bloke had no idea what Dickie looked like or someone gave it to him.

Dickie was a good man to play a practical joke on, because players knew he'd take it in the right spirit and they'd get a funny reaction out of him. One time, Ian Botham and Allan Lamb dropped Chinese firecrackers on Dickie's route from square leg to the wicket, and then watched as he trod on them and hopped around amid the bangs.

Dickie used to say that 'rain and bad light have followed me around all my life', and he claimed the credit for breaking droughts in Sharjah and Bulawayo. It hadn't rained for five years in Sharjah before Dickie turned up, and he woke from a deep sleep to find water six inches deep in his hotel room. In 1992, Dickie umpired Zimbabwe's first-ever Test match against New Zealand, in Bulawayo, which was in the midst of a chronic drought. Happily, Dickie took the Yorkshire weather with him, and the spectators cheered wildly as torrential rain stopped play on the second day.

Despite his 'rain man' reputation, Dickie might just be the only umpire who has stood in two Test matches where 'sun stopped play'. The first time, he called stumps 15 minutes early during the 1974 England v Pakistan Test at the Oval when Chris Old, batting for England, found himself blinded by rays of sunshine bouncing off the Shell building a mile or so from the stadium.

Twenty-one years later, a B&Q greenhouse right next to the Old Trafford ground caused a similar problem for Mike Atherton against the Windies, so Dickie called tea early to allow the groundsmen to try and block out the reflection.

In that same game, play was also halted briefly when Dickie dropped the marbles he used to keep track of the balls bowled in an over. 'I've lost me marbles! I've lost me marbles!' he said as he crawled around looking for them.

'Most of us thought he had lost his marbles a long time ago,' noted Athers later.

My old MCC coach, Don Wilson, could vouch for that, as one winter's day he looked out of the window of his office at Lord's and saw the familiar figure of Dickie out in the middle practising his hand signals. Mad, but that shows his devotion to his job.

He was a great worrier, and took the decisions he made very seriously. He was even known to call back a batsman after realising he'd made the wrong decision.

One time at Canterbury, he'd given Graham Cowdrey out caught behind off Northamptonshire's Curtly Ambrose's bowling, only to call a fuming Cowdrey back when he was almost at the boundary. It takes some balls to admit you've made a mistake and put it right there and then, rather than say sorry after the match – especially when you also have to tell big Curtly you've changed your mind.

Dickie carried a lot of useful stuff in his pockets to ensure he was ready for any situation. Like the time when Indian legend Sunil Gavaskar complained about his hair getting in his eyes while batting against England on a breezy day in 1974, Dickie pulled out a razor blade and carefully trimmed Sunny's locks. I just hope he never got stopped and searched on the way to a game carrying a blade.

You can't get much more Yorkshire than Dickie – cut him and he bleeds Yorkshire pudding batter. I know he was very proud to serve as his county's club president from 2014 to 2016, and I understand he still goes to all the games.

Back in 2002, the club installed a 'Dickie Bird Clock' over Headingley's West Stand, which was fitting as I doubt he was ever late in his life. He used to arrive ridiculously early for a day's play – routinely three hours before a Test match – and he never lost that habit. John Major, a massive cricket fan who was prime minister at the time, invited Dickie to Sunday lunch at Chequers soon after his retirement from international cricket in 1996. He was due at midday, but true to form, Dickie rocked up at 9.30am. Luckily, John and his wife Norma were happy to sit and talk cricket with him all morning.

During his time as Yorkshire president, Dickie also kindly paid for a new players' balcony in front of the dressing rooms at the Kirkstall Lane End of their ground. Previously, on sunny days, players were sweating behind glass watching the game, so they were very grateful for Dickie's generosity. I saw an interview with him where he got very emotional about it carrying his name. Mind you, the cost of his balcony spiralled upwards from the initial estimate, and ended up costing him £125k. 'I wasn't sure I liked the players that much!' he said.

They even built a statue of Dickie in Barnsley, where he was born. The statue has him holding up the dreaded finger to point a batsman on his way (a pose I didn't see him in often enough when I was bowling). Apparently they had to raise the statue a few feet higher on a plinth though, because drunks on a night out kept on hanging all sorts of unthinkable things on Dickie's outstretched finger and outraging public decency.

Shep's jigs, Bozo's antics and Eddy's hare pie

I also must squeeze one of Dickie's contemporaries, the late David 'Shep' Shepherd, into the Hall of Fame. Hard to believe that Shep was nicknamed 'Titch' at primary school because he was so small, but he grew up to have a well-upholstered physique – or as Richie Benaud put it, Shep was 'built for comfort not speed'.

He enjoyed a decent 15-year playing career with Gloucester-shire, and although his mid-20s batting average was, well, pretty average, he had a reputation for producing his best when his team was struggling. 'Within my limitations, I always tried my best . . . I played with a big tum and a smile on my face,' he said.

Although he would generally go about his umpiring business with the minimum of fuss, he could always be seen doing a little jig if the score reached the unlucky number of 111 ('Nelson'), 222 ('Double Nelson') and so on to ward off bad luck.

Growing up in Devon and being told all sorts of myths by locals, he was very superstitious, and he started this ritual as a youngster and carried on doing it through his county career. But it was only when Shep became an umpire, and a *TMS* listener wrote to commentator Brian Johnston during an Ashes series to tip him off about his superstitious quirk, that spectators took notice. From then on, whenever the score approached 111, Johnners gave those in the ground listening to their transistor radios the heads-up to keep an eye on him and he'd get a round of applause.

Shep would even refuse to stay in hotel rooms with his unlucky numbers, despite team-mates in his playing days trying to stitch him up by booking him into them. And there was the time when he drove to a hotel in Canterbury for a match, reached the car park and realised he'd driven exactly 111 miles, so he got back in the car and drove round the block until the milometer had moved off the dreaded Nelson. Nutter.

On the way out to the middle, Shep would say to his fellow umpire, 'Good luck, mate, and may your God go with you.' He was well loved by his colleagues and players and it was a sad loss when he passed away in 2009, aged 68.

In recent years, New Zealand's Billy Bowden has been one of the most high-profile umpires, with his 'crooked finger of doom', theatrical 'crumb-sweeping' wave to signal a four and David Brent-style jig to greet a six. He officiated in 84 Tests and 200 ODIs before being dropped from the International Cricket Council (ICC) elite list for a second time in 2016.

Former New Zealand star, the late Martin Crowe, once called him 'Bozo the Clown' and I must say I'm not a huge fan either. I just sometimes think he crosses the line into being a bit too showy.

He umpired a match I was playing in, in New Zealand, when

he'd just arrived on the scene. When I came on to bowl, I said to him, 'If someone hits me for six, you don't want to be jumping around, waving your arms about, mate. I won't be happy. Signal six, put your arms down and get on with it.'

I didn't see it as funny. It might be fun for him and the crowd, but remember the bowler who's just been carted over the boundary. Ray Julian smiling when he gave a batsman out was one thing, because Ray was smiley anyway, but partying like it's 1999 for a sixer is a bit much.

So, sorry, Billy, you're not coming in, but before I step out of the umpires' section of the Hall of Fame, honorable mentions for a couple of lesser-known umpires who've come to my attention.

First off, an umpire in North Yorkshire village cricket who sounded like my kind of umpire. His name was Eddy Cousins and with his frilly teeth had something of the Ken Dodd about him, but batsmen weren't too tickled by his trigger-finger umpiring style. Apparently, Eddy used to keep a count of his 'victims', as he called them, through the season, and the more the better. Any time a bowler rapped the batsman on the pads somewhere vaguely in line with the stumps, he'd appeal in the almost certain knowledge that Eddy would give them out.

The story goes that one season, a very good middle-order batter called Skippy was given out lbw three times in a row by Eddy, and decided he needed to make a gesture to try to prevent it happening a fourth time. So, in good time for the last game of the season, where Eddy would be umpiring him again, Skippy had a hare pie – Eddy's favourite – delivered to him.

When they next saw each other, Skippy asked if Eddy had enjoyed the pie.

'It was champion, lad – one of the best I've ever had,' replied Eddy.

Later, Skippy walked out to the middle, as his team's last recognised batsman in a tight match, but confident that at least he wouldn't be on the wrong end of any dodgy lbw decisions from Eddy. Not that the fielding team knew about that, and when the bowler hit Skippy on the pads, a confident yell of 'Howzat' rang out.

Much to Skippy's shock, Eddy raised his finger.

'Sorry, lad,' he said. 'I needed one more victim to make it a hundred for the season.'

Credit also to John Carr of Hessle, an 84-year-old great-grandfather, who as of 2016 was still umpiring about 30 home games per season for Hessle CC. John was a wicket-keeper for 40 years before becoming an umpire at 58. He once umpired a match in Bradford when a bowler called Bing Crosby delivered the ball and simultaneously something flew down the pitch.

'It's a rat!' shouted the batsman, and John called a dead ball, before realising it was actually Bing's toupée.

Hair-raising action.

Umpire Tufnell?

So what have I learnt from delving into the history of umpiring in search of the finest? Well, one thing's for sure is that I wouldn't be cut out for the job. I couldn't think of anything worse because every day's a bowling day. You're always out there – no chance of a cat-nap in the dressing room.

I'd be good at the chatting to the players part, but the mind might wander. Especially if I was standing at square leg and something interesting was going on in the crowd. The powers of concentration you need are immense, and I could easily imagine me hearing a loud appeal mid-daydream and having no clue whether it was in or out. And my decisions could easily be influenced by which players sent me a nice bottle of scotch at the end of the season.

There wouldn't be too many games going to the wire with me umpiring. I would definitely be an outer, so matches would move forward at a pace, especially if there was a chance of a half-day off.

But no, umpiring wouldn't suit me . . . unless, perhaps, I could be a fourth umpire in Test matches. Travel around the world, go to nice places and not actually have to do much. Bit like the cox in an Olympic boat crew who just sits down, shouts a bit and gets a gold medal while the rowers do all the hard graft.

Bring on the new ball, take drinks on for the umpires in the middle and check the batteries on their light meter, and go out to keep an eye on the pitch during the lunch and tea intervals. I think I could manage that. Then sit back, drink tea, eat cake and wander around looking official and chatting to people in between times. Yes, the fourth umpire's lifestyle sounds like my sort of speed.

I'd just have to hope I never got a promotion.

THE LORD'S WORK

Walking in the footsteps of legends

I was fortunate to play in some fantastic cricket arenas during my career, but there's only one for my Hall of Fame: Lord's, the Home of Cricket.

What a great place that was to go to work every day. Turning up in the morning, walking through the Grace Gates, past the Harris Garden and up to the pavilion, where there was a doorman in an MCC blazer to greet you.

'Morning, Mr Tufnell – lovely day – may I take your bag?'

No one had ever been so polite to me before. The only trouble was that, for home games, they weren't supposed to let you in if you didn't have your Middlesex blazer and tie on. Being a forgetful chap I wasn't always correctly attired, but they lent me a tie if needed.

Then it was up a couple of flights of stairs, past all the beautiful oil paintings in ornate frames, to the home dressing room. It was a nice changing room, not particularly big but very comfortable with chairs and benches to have a cat-nap on (always an important consideration for me in any dressing room). Then there's the little players' balcony, which is a lovely place to sit and watch the game with a couple of your mates.

I think Lord's might be the only major ground I played at that has a thoroughfare for the members going past the dressing room door. The corridor leads to the Allen Stand, and us players had to walk across there to get to the bathroom. Only the occasional person would walk that way, but you could find yourself bumping into a couple of members as you were nipping across for a shower wearing just a towel.

You can feel the history walking through the Lord's pavilion more than at any other ground. Built in 1890, it was designed by Thomas Verity, an architect who'd previously worked on projects like the Royal Albert Hall. Apparently, Verity wanted the pavilion to be made of stone, but stonemasons were on strike at the time so they went for brick and terracotta instead. It still turned out beautifully, and with its huge, elegant windows it makes a wonderful backdrop to a game of cricket.

The club could only afford to build it at all thanks to a low-interest loan from a chap called William Nicholson whose family had made their fortune in the gin trade; hence the pavilion's nickname 'The Gin Palace'. Cheers, Willie.

When it's time to play, whether in a county match or an international, it's a very special feeling to walk down those stairs and into the Long Room. I'd look down at the hundreds of tiny indents in the stairs and floor and think how many great players had clattered through there.

The Long Room is a very unique room. There are not many grounds where you are rubbing shoulders with the members as you head out to play. Going out to bat in a big game, I'd be making my way through a room packed with groups of people having a drink and chatting. Usually, it's more segregated at cricket grounds. Mind you, when you're coming through armoured up with a helmet and pads and waving a big bat, people soon clear out of your way. Nowadays, a route through the Long Room is roped off for the players during Test matches, but when I was playing you just carved your way through the masses, then out and down the steps onto that bright green carpet of an outfield. *Whoosh*.

When there's a big crowd in, there is that unique Lord's hum. It's a different noise from anywhere else; I don't know why, but it is. There's a stillness about the place, and yet you're right in the middle of everything.

A lot of other modern grounds have great facilities, but they are often all concrete and steel. The MCC have managed to modernise Lord's without losing its character. You couldn't have two more different buildings than the futuristic Media Centre building (*aka* 'Cherie Blair's Smile') and the old pavilion, but somehow it works.

It's a bit like when you're buying a house and you're looking for original features. Don't ever rip out the beams or the old fireplace – they are a selling point. Lord's has managed to keep that picket-fence feel, with plenty of trees still poking above the stands. It's like a village cricket ground, only on a massive scale.

In sport, I can only compare Lord's to Highbury stadium, where Arsenal used to play. They talked about the marble halls of Highbury and it was a bit posher than other football stadiums. I felt a bit posh at Lord's.

Playing for Middlesex in my day did give you a superiority complex over other county players, and that was mainly because of Lord's. No doubt, we felt we were better than other teams. One of the main reasons people wanted to play for Middlesex was because the home ground was Lord's. You could turn up at Northampton, Derby or wherever, but no other grounds could compare.

Players from other counties always wanted to be fit to play against Middlesex at Lord's (and not just for the lunches, which were the best – thanks, Nancy). For a county player who might not get to international standard or get to play a one-day final, an ordinary game of county cricket at Lord's is as good as it gets. Even if you were playing in front of 1,000 on a Monday against Glamorgan, you were still playing at the Home of Cricket, running around in this beautiful arena. If you're going to play county cricket, play it at Lord's.

As soon as I walked into the pavilion, I got goosebumps. It could be a bit daunting to play there at first, but playing week in, week out there prepared me for things to come. When I was selected for England to tour Australia for the first time, I wasn't quite so over-awed by the prospect because I was used to the big-game arena, even if I hadn't played that many big games at that point.

Sydney Cricket Ground is probably my favourite ground overseas. Melbourne Cricket Ground might be the biggest, with its 100,000 capacity, but Sydney at 46,000 (18,000 more than Lord's) is plenty big enough and, similar to Lord's, it has a charming, traditional pavilion that stands alone in the middle of a very modern arena.

Incidentally, the scariest place I've played was at Zimbabwe's Harare Sports Club ground. It wasn't the ground itself that was the problem, but Robert Mugabe had a palace nearby and the rumour was that if you went along the road in front of it after about half six at night, you ran the risk of getting shot. Once the day's play was over, everyone was rushing to get showered, changed and out of there. Not even I was late for the team bus at Harare Sports Club.

I never worried about such things happening in St John's Wood.

In England, despite my being a Middlesex boy through and through, my favourite other ground was the Oval. At Lord's, it's all bacon-and-egg ties and 'jolly good shot', which I love, but at the Oval across the Thames it's more of a working man's atmosphere for Test matches. The crowd are more 'oi, oi', a bit more relaxed, and I enjoyed that common touch too.

Nothing can match Lord's, though. It's quite simply 'HQ' – the headquarters of world cricket.

Money games, hopping races and ballooning ... Lord's: the early years

It all began with Thomas Lord, born in Yorkshire in 1755. Thomas' family had once been worth a few quid, but then his dad, William, backed Bonnie Prince Charlie's rebellion in 1745, using his own money to pay for 500 horses to take into battle. When the Bonnie Prince's lot were defeated, William had his property seized and he ended up working as a labourer on the land he had previously owned. To escape the humiliation, he moved the family to make a fresh start in Norfolk, where young Thomas learnt to play cricket.

So, despite his aristocratic surname, Thomas was no rich kid, but he had plenty of ambition. He went to London, became a successful wine merchant and carried on playing cricket. Then a load of members of the White Conduit Club in Islington, led by the Earl of Winchilsea, got together and persuaded Lord to open a cricket ground at Dorset Square, Marylebone, with the promise that they'd cover his losses if it went belly up.

He leased some land in Marylebone from the Portman family (who owned most of Marylebone at the time), built a high wooden fence around it and a hut to store kit and equipment. Lord's Ground was opened and the first match in the history of Middlesex was played on 1 June 1787, a money game against Essex for a 100 guineas stake per side.

Hard to imagine now, but Marylebone then was almost countryside, yet up to 5,000 spectators trekked out there to watch matches, which shows the popularity of cricket and the new venue.

Some epic matches were played there, but also some pretty crap ones. There's a record of a money match played in 1793 where 'Five Gentleman of the Globe challenged Four Gentleman of the MCC'. The Globe club were bowled out for one run with Lord himself taking all five wickets – it was like Botham in the 1981 Ashes, except the bowling was underarm. The MCC then managed three runs between them, with Lord top-scoring with two, before being caught, just 98 runs short of a century.

Lord was an average cricketer, apparently – a good fielder at point and decent underarm bowler, and he had scored a half-century for Middlesex against the MCC in 1790.

To promote the ground, he once offered a prize of £20 to the batsman who hit a ball out of it – a mighty hit with the dodgy old bats they had then. A renowned ball-basher called EH Budd did the business, though, then he kindly said he'd share his winnings with his team-mates. It seems that Lord didn't come through with the prize money, but the club still have the bat that Budd hit that famous sixer with.

Lord wasn't just relying on cricket for his income. He was buying and selling property around London, and he hired out the cricket ground for all sorts of madness, from pigeon-shooting to hopping races.

Not all of his ventures were a success though. Staging the start of a hot-air balloon flight by a French balloonist called Garnerin was a disaster. Ballooning was all the rage since the first cross-Channel flight in 1785, and thousands of people turned up one Saturday for lift-off. Unfortunately, high winds meant the flight had to be postponed, which almost caused a riot. The following Monday, Garnerin tried again. This time one of the stands collapsed, seriously injuring lots of people and killing a child, and when Garnerin did finally take flight people who ran along the road after him were confronted by a bull and one person was gored. The story went that pickpockets had deliberately released the bull so they could grab people's purses amid the panic.

The whole thing was a commercial flop as well, because most of the spectators realised they didn't need to pay to get into the ground to watch a balloon flying in the sky above them. D'oh.

Lord's Ground stayed at the same site for almost a quarter of a century until the landowners stuck the rent up massively. Lord seemed to have seen the rent hike coming, because, a couple of years before, he'd already rented some land on the St John's Wood Estate (where Regent's Park is today) and turned it into a cricket ground. When the time came to leave Dorset Square in 1811, he took the turf with him to the new ground so that the MCC players could 'play on the same footing as before'.

The new ground wasn't too popular with the Marylebone Club members, though – it was in the middle of nowhere, didn't have much atmosphere and they only played a handful of games there over three years.

The players weren't that disappointed when the government decided that the new Regent's Canal would cut right through the ground, but it must have been a pain in the arse for Lord. As usual, he just kept going. Lord got compensation from the family who owned the land, rolled up his sacred turf again and relocated to eight acres in St John's Wood, where the Home of Cricket has remained ever since.

The Dark era

After all his good work, in 1825 Lord blotted his copybook when he proposed to build a load of houses on the edge of the ground. That just wasn't cricket, old chap, but he was in his late sixties by then and looking to retire. Luckily, a London MP from Islington called William Ward immediately got his cheque book out and asked Lord how much he wanted. Ward bought the ground for £5,000, enough for Lord to have a comfortable retirement.

Ward was a serious player himself. A powerful dude who used a bat weighing four pounds, in 1820 he'd scored an innings of 278 for the MCC against Norfolk – the first double-century on record, and the biggest score at Lord's by a mile at the time. (He'd also had the second- and third-best scores of 171 and 162.)

When Ward took over, he didn't try to change the ground's name – Ward's really wouldn't have had the same ring to it as Lord's. However, it wasn't too long before quite a few people were calling it 'Dark's'.

If you wander around the ground today, you can get a beer at Dark's Bar, and there's a wooden sign carved with a tribute to him saying, 'Raise a glass to the man who did more than anyone to make Lord's the Home of Cricket.' The name of the bar harks back to 1835, when an entrepreneur called John Henry Dark (known as 'JH') stepped in to take over from Ward. JH and his brother Ben were both cricketers – JH, who had been a ground boy at the original Lord's at Dorset Fields, was a hard-hitting batsman and a fine fielder, and also did a bit of umpiring. He would stay in charge of Lord's for the next 30 years.

Apparently, JH could be rather short-tempered, but he was a kind-hearted bloke. And he did well to keep things going when the cricket business dipped, offering the venue for other sports and events to keep money coming in, because the 20-odd

MCC cricket matches played there a year weren't enough to pay the bills.

He inherited what was basically a village green, but soon made improvements. He brought in gas lighting in the pavilion, created a billiards room in the tavern, turned an unused rough bit of ground into a bowling green and created an archery ground. Then he had a real tennis court built which attracted lots of new members.

Lord's turned into something of a family business. Ben Dark was a bat merchant and stored his stock in the ground, while another brother, Robert, made balls and leg guards and also worked the gate to collect admission money.

JH himself lived in a house on the corner of the ground, and on his retirement, he wanted to sell the freehold to the MCC, which would have secured its future as a cricket ground, but incredibly the club didn't even bid for it when it came up for auction in 1860.

Fitz makes Lord's the Home

Some of the people on the MCC committee at the time weren't exactly dynamic, and it took an Irishman to shake a bit of life into them. RA Fitzgerald was only 29 when he was voted into the job of club secretary in 1863, the fourth person to take on the role.

'Fitz' had a WG Grace-like beard and had been a member of the club for five years. He was a hit-and-miss batsman himself, but when he connected, he gave the ball a hell of a wallop – he was famous for boshing a ball over the real tennis court into St John's Road, a huge hit with primitive old bats.

Fitz loved Lord's, wanted to establish the ground as the centre of cricket, and he was a fella who got things done. One of his most important achievements was putting right the expensive mistake of not buying the freehold when JH had offered it to the club on a plate. By 1866, he persuaded the committee members to buy the freehold from the new owner, a Mr Moses. In six years, the price had gone up from seven grand to over £18,000, but Fitz understood that it was worth the money to ensure that the club wouldn't have to move again.

With Fitz directing affairs at the club, the pavilion was enlarged, a grandstand and a new tavern were built, and the first turnstile was put in. The first groundsman was also employed, which was a relief for the many fielders who'd twisted their ankles in potholes or batsmen who'd got hit on what was an atrocious playing surface, a far cry from the billiard-table green I would play on years later.

Up until then, sheep were left to graze the outfield between matches to keep the grass down and then put in a pen on match-days. In 1861, a batsman made a century with one shot, because he drove the ball so hard into the slats of the sheep pen, he'd run a hundred before the fielders managed to release it. Baaaaaa-d luck for the fielding side, that . . .

Fitz initially was working unpaid, but he was getting so busy by 1867 that he offered his resignation because he couldn't afford to work gratis any more. Seeing how he was transforming the club for the better, the committee members didn't want to lose him so they approved a £400 salary and he became the club's first permanent paid secretary. Well deserved, too.

Fitz was largely responsible for fellow beardy man WG Grace finally becoming a member of the MCC. Previously, the snobs on the MCC Committee had denied WG entry because he didn't have the right breeding, but Fitz backed his election and they ran out of reasons to stop the biggest crowd-puller joining the club. It proved to be a very good move – with WG wearing his MCC cap wherever he played, it was great branding for the club and helped to increase the club's standing in cricket worldwide.

Sadly, Fitz was forced to retire prematurely due to what the club described publicly at the time as a 'mystery illness'. In fact, Fitz and a few senior members of the MCC had a pretty good idea of the cause.

At first he suffered partial paralysis of the left hand and he got a doctor's note in December 1875 advising complete rest for several months. Instead, the committee voted to pay for a personal assistant for him so he could keep up the good work for the club.

Basically, Fitz's years of womanising – even after he got married – were catching up with him and the paralysis in his hand was an early symptom of syphilis.

By spring 1876 he was unable to work. His physical and mental state went downhill fast, he started having hallucinations that grass was growing out of his skin and all sorts of turns and was taken to a lunatic asylum in Chiswick.

He was only 47 when he died in October 1881 of 'softening of the brain', the polite way Victorians described syphilis. At least he'd been able to leave the asylum and stay with his mum for a couple of years and then spend the last few months of his life back with his wife.

Fitz achieved a lot for Lord's in his short time at the club. Membership had grown massively from 650 to over 2,000. Without him, WG Grace may not have been elected to the club, ground improvements wouldn't have been made ... and some say that the Oval, which was in better shape before he came along, might have become the Home of Cricket instead of Lord's. Never!

Lord Harris' champagne moments

In my retirement, I have spent a few happy hours quaffing inside the champagne tent in the Harris Garden at Lord's. I'd never given much thought to the person the garden was named after, but it turns out Lord Harris was the second-best cricketer behind WG Grace in Victorian times.

By 1875, at the age of just 24, he was president, secretary and captain of Kent and on the MCC Committee. He was the key man in organising the first Test match in England, played at the Oval in 1880 when he captained the England side.

Lord Harris – or Colonel George Robert Canning, the Fourth Baron Harris GCSI, GCIE, CB, TD, ADC to use his full name and various titles he ended up with – was by all accounts a controversial, Marmite sort of character. He went on to become the Governor of Bombay and a lot of people said he didn't do much of job there for the local people.

When it came to cricket, though, the players who turned out for him were very loyal to him. He also loved the MCC and Lord's. His autobiography was dedicated to 'the members of the Marylebone

Cricket Club, the supreme authority on cricket, whom I have had the honour of serving in several capacities for many years, whose unvarying welcome I have enjoyed for half a century; and to their ground Lord's, the home of cricket.'

Lord's book devoted a chapter to his memories of the famous ground. He remembered the days in the Sixties (the 1860s, that is . . .) when people could pay the old groundsman, 'Steevie' (yes, two ee's . . .), two shillings to practise on Lord's not quite so hallowed turf as it was then. Steevie would put them on one of the practice wickets, which were so bumpy batsmen would have to deal with 'shooters' and 'poppers' galore.

He also recalled an incident in the 1866 match between Eton and Harrow that led to proper boundaries being introduced at the ground. A ball was hit to the feet of spectators sitting on the grass. The batsman assumed the umpire had called four and stopped running. One of the spectators threw the ball to a fielder, who chucked the ball in, the wicket was broken with the batter still strolling down the pitch and the umpire gave him out.

A few years later, the MCC committee decided to introduce nets at the boundaries, because some people thought runs should actually be earned by running. So, if the ball hit the net, the batters had to keep running and it was only if the ball bounced over the net or went straight over that a four or six was given. That didn't last long, though, because the season it was introduced was a very hot summer and the players weren't happy about the extra running about . . . and nor were fans who wanted to see a faster game.

'It seems to me that my life has always pivoted to Lord's,' wrote

Lord Harris. 'Even if separated from it for years and thousands of miles, thoughts of it could not grow dim, and the prospect of revisiting it was a beacon to encourage one to live through the years of absence.'

I know what he meant – memories of Lord's often pop into my head and I always look forward to visiting. It's just a very special place.

The Harris Garden was created in 1934, replacing an old lawn tennis court. I shall remember him, Fitz, JH Dark, Willie Ward and Thomas Lord, next time I'm there sipping a glass of fizz.

TERRIFIC TEAMS

The Smokers of 1887

In my playing days, cigarette companies were still allowed to sponsor sporting events. Being the supreme athlete that I was then, I was always keen to play in Benson & Hedges Cup matches – or at least be twelfth man – because a bloke used to come round and drop off a few boxes of Hamlet cigars and a sleeve of 200 Benson & Hedges Gold cigarettes. Even though most of my team-mates were non-smokers, they always seemed to find room in their cricket bag for a box or two to give to their mates, so I got more than my share. If ever I ran out of ciggies, I'd always have a rummage through my team-mates' cricket bags and usually I'd come up trumps with a forgotten, crumpled old packet of Hamlets.

I think I would have fitted in quite nicely to the Smokers v Non-Smokers match that took place in Melbourne at the end of England's tour of Oz in 1887. The Smokers XI was mainly England tourists with a few Aussies to make up the numbers. They lost the toss to the Non-Smokers, which was bad news as they had to bowl on a perfect batting wicket. After walking out to play on the first morning puffing away on cigars, they then wheezed their way through two long days in the field as their clean-living Aussie opponents racked up 803 for nine.

The Smokers scored 356 all out in reply, just about managed to keep their end up and coughed and spluttered their way to a draw in the four-day match.

The contest was sponsored by various cigar companies and there were lots of prizes on offer that seemed rather unfairly weighted towards the Smokers, with 500 cigars each for the Smokers' bowler and batsman with the best figures/highest score. Meanwhile, a Mr Shrewsbury, who scored 236 for the Non-Smokers, received 250 cigars for the highest individual score in the match and Mr Bates, the Non-Smokers' best bowler, received a trophy and 200 cigars for his trouble . . . I guess they sold them to the highest bidders.

Brearley, Top Cat, Captain Pugwash and the Side-step Queen

From overflowing ashtrays to the Ashes and England's boys of '81. The 1981 Ashes series happened slap bang in the middle of my teenage rebellion, when I was more concerned with riding motorbikes, chasing girls and partying than playing or watching cricket, so it was only in later years that I saw footage of the games and really came to appreciate what a great story that was.

Ian Botham had been appointed England captain the previous year after a 3–0 defeat in Australia, replacing Mike Brearley, who had announced he wouldn't be available for tours in future because he wanted to train to become a psychoanalyst.

Beefy did okay as captain in 1980, but after a torrid winter tour of the West Indies, a back injury was affecting his personal form and the worries of captaincy were starting to weigh him down. 'My impression is that Ian found it hard to take advice and even harder to take criticism ... and he became, I think, paranoid about the media,' wrote Brearley later. I know the feeling.

After losing the First Ashes Test of 1981, the pressure on Beefy was growing and growing. England had dropped half a dozen relatively easy catches and a few of the England batsmen looked devoid of confidence after being peppered by the West Indian quicks the previous winter. Beefy himself had scored one and 33 with the bat, and hadn't bowled anything like his best. He'd waited until after fifty overs had passed before he put himself on to bowl in the Aussies' first innings. That wasn't like him at all, a man who naturally led from the front. And he just had that look of stress, weariness and general misery that has come over many England captains down the years.

A draw in the Second Test at Lord's meant England had gone 12 successive Tests without a win. Afterwards, Beefy announced he would only carry on as skipper if he was confirmed as captain for the rest of the series, rather than on a one-match basis, but the selectors had already decided to stand him down. They wanted him to recover his form without the pressures of captaincy.

That evening, chairman of the selectors Alec Bedser rang Brearley . . . well, he actually called him a few times. Bedser was trying to call from a payphone in the pub on the way home from Lord's, but every time Brearley picked the phone up to answer, his coins were rejected. Eventually, Brearley got a call from the operator asking if he'd accept the charges.

'We'd like you to captain the side for the rest of the series,' Bedser told Brearley when he was put through. I suppose if you're going to have to pay for an incoming call, it's one where you are told you're going to be England captain again.

It proved to be the right move. The criticism of Brearley was always that he wasn't a Test-class batsman – his final Test career batting average of a shade under 23 seems to bear that out. In fairness, though, Brearley had actually scored four centuries for Middlesex that summer – more than Geoff Boycott had managed – before he was recalled to the England set-up. He was also a brilliant captain.

What makes a great leader? I think back to one of my first role models as a kid, Top Cat, or 'TC' as he was known to his 'intellectual close friends' Benny the Ball, Choo-Choo, Brain, Fancy-Fancy and Spook. Okay, TC was a TV cartoon character, but bear with me. The leader of a gang of cats living on Hoagy's Alley, he had to manage a lot of different characters. You had Benny, his loyal right-hand cat, a simple soul who might accidentally tell the truth about your latest scam, but also a voice of reason to listen to when TC had his craziest ideas. Then there was Brain, who was generally very stupid, but occasionally came out with a really clever idea which TC would steal and make out he thought of himself. Fancy-Fancy was a suave, good-looking cat who could charm the ladies, while Spook was a fun-loving, streetwise beatnik.

TC had the leadership skills to bring out all their different strengths and get them working together as a team. And even though he took the credit for their ideas and the gang's successes, they all still looked up to him and came running whenever they heard the bin lids crashed together to call them for duty. That takes some kind of talent and charisma.

He also used clever psychology to get under the skin of the NYPD's Officer Dibble, who patrolled the alley. Dibble was forever trying to evict the gang and stop TC using his telephone next to the trash can in which TC lived. On the one hand, TC would keep Dibble off balance by deliberately mis-saying his name as 'Dribble', 'Drabble', 'Dabble' etcetera, but then flatter him to high heaven when he needed something. He'd also nick Dibble's ideas, like in the episode where TC overhears him suggesting ways to improve the police force and presents the ideas as his own to the Chief of Police, who ends up making him an honorary police sergeant and Dibble's boss on the alley.

Yep, as the song goes, he was the boss, the pip, the championship, the most tip-top, Top Cat.

Another favourite cartoon skipper of mine was Captain Pugwash, who spent episodes trying to knock the work-shy crew aboard the *Black Pig* into shape and beat Cut-Throat Jake's mob to the treasure. It was only recently I found out that Pugwash's crew members did not have smutty double-meaning names like

Master Bates, Roger the Cabin Boy and Seaman Staines. It was all a myth that has been passed down the generations. In fact, those first two characters were called Master Mate and Tom the Cabin Boy, and there was no one called 'Seaman' at all. A couple of publications even had to pay damages to the show's creator for repeating these scurrilous lies. So I must stress again here, there was no Master Bates, no Roger the Cabin Boy and absolutely no seamen. It was all fake news. As for Captain Pugwash, he was a two-dimensional cardboard cut-out, so not sure he'd survive in the modern-day game with the demand for 3D cricketers who can bat, bowl and field.

Anyhow, where were we . . .? Oh yes, Mike Brearley. Brearley was a very clever bloke with a Cambridge degree, and those who played under him found he was no snob. As his later career as a psychoanalyst showed, he was interested in what made people tick and seemed to have a knack of getting the best out of cricketers from all walks of life (unlike Top Cat, he didn't try to take credit for their work, though). And England had a real mix of strong characters in the sides that took on the Aussies that summer of 1981, including the likes of Boycs, Bob Willis, David Gower, Mike Gatting and Beefy himself.

Brearley handled Ian Botham as well as anyone. He knew that if he ever criticised Beefy, his first reaction would be to grumble and defy him, but that, while he might never admit to taking the advice, Beefy would usually do what he was told after a while. For instance, on the first day at Headingley, he'd noticed that Beefy was running in more slowly than he did at his best and was losing even more momentum by jinking in towards the stumps in the last strides before releasing the ball. The result was just military medium-pace, gentle swing bowling. Brearley encouraged him to 'come in straight, to *bounce* in, as lively as he could', and ribbed him, calling him 'the Sidestep Queen'. There aren't many who would get away with saying stuff like that to Ian Botham, so Beefy must have respected Brearley.

The next morning when Brearley bought him on to bowl, he riled him up again, telling Beefy he didn't want him 'just floating the ball up like a middle-aged swing bowler'. It did the trick. Beefy bowled beautifully, unchanged, for the rest of the day finishing with a six-fer.

The old Botham, who you couldn't prise the ball away from when he was bowling well, was back. That renewed confidence fed into his batting, as he scored a half-century in the first innings and biffed a match-turning innings of 149 not out with England following on and in massive trouble when he came to the crease to set Australia a target of 130 to win.

Time for Beefy's mate Bob Willis to produce some heroics. Face like a Zombie and big mop of curly hair like a brunette Vera Duckworth, big Bob ripped through the shell-shocked Aussies, taking eight for 43 off 15.1 overs. Everyone was energised by his demonic intensity – even Gatt was leaping around like a salmon taking great catches at short leg and mid-on – as the Aussies collapsed to Nelson, 111 all out. It was only the second time in Test match history that a side following on had won.

Astonishing game, and while Bob and Beefy grabbed the headlines, as with all successful teams the supporting cast had made important contributions. For instance, if it hadn't been for tailenders Graham Dilley and Chris Old scoring runs (56 and 29 respectively) in England's second innings, Beefy would have run out of partners and England would have suffered an innings defeat.

The next Test at Edgbaston was another thriller, and will always be remembered for Botham's decisive spell of bowling of five wickets for one run off 28 balls in the second innings. The former Sidestep Queen charged in and destroyed the Australian batting line-up.

Again, others played their part though, like my future team-mate John Emburey. Recalled to the side, Embers took six wickets in the match and also chipped in with an absolutely crucial 37 not out in the second innings of a low-scoring match. The Aussies were out for 121 and only lost by 29 runs, so without Embers' effort batting at number nine England wouldn't have had any sort of target to bowl at.

England made three changes to the team for the next Test at Old Trafford – Alan Knott coming in as wicket-keeper for Bob Taylor, and Chris Tavaré for Peter Willey, while local lad Paul Allott replaced the injured Chris Old. The changes could have upset the balance, but they all did brilliantly. Taylor had been struggling with the bat, but Knotty's unorthodox strokeplay got the team 72 valuable runs in the match and his keeping was as sound as ever. Lancashire's Allott took four wickets in the match on his debut on home turf. Tavaré, a man nicknamed 'Rowdy' because he was so quiet and a batsman so cautious he made Boycs look carefree, anchored both England innings to score 69 and 78 against very good bowling from Dennis Lillee and Terry Alderman. In the second innings, he held up an end while Beefy, who'd eaten two large steaks before coming out to bat, smashed 118 off 102 balls (and he only scored three off the first 30 balls he faced).

Chasing over 500 in the last innings, the Aussies made a game of it, with Graham Yallop and Allan Border both making centuries, but three wickets for Willis and a couple each for Allott, Embers and Man of the Series Botham clinched a 3–1 series victory (the Sixth Test was drawn).

What an incredible turnaround. A great team effort, directed by a shrewd captain and inspired by a genius all-rounder back to his best. It was such a thrilling Ashes series, no one thought it could ever possibly be topped . . .

The Boys of 2005

After the thrill of 1981, England enjoyed a couple more Ashes victories in 1985 and Down Under with Mike Gatting's team in 1986/87. Then Australia got quite ridiculously good. And they stayed at that level pretty much for the duration of my first-class cricket career, which was really quite annoying.

Going into the 2005 series, the Aussies had won eight on the spin, but under Michael Vaughan's captaincy over the previous couple of years, England had shown the potential to give them a run for their money, and there was plenty of hype going into the First Test at Lord's.

England's performance in the first two sessions laid down a marker for the aggressive brand of cricket they would play all summer to regain the little urn. Our bowlers hit the ground running, with Steve Harmison roughing up Justin Langer and Ricky 'Punter' Ponting early on. The England boys were also under instructions to fire the ball hard into the wicket-keeper's gloves whenever they fielded the ball, and a few throws only just missed the batsmen, which didn't go down well with the Aussies.

I remember a few years before that Gloucestershire had done the same thing because their wicket-keeper, Jack Russell, used to stand up to the fast bowlers. So a batsman would play a forward defensive, no run, turn round to do a bit of gardening, and then the next thing they knew – *whoosh*, the ball's whistled past their nose and thudded into Jack's gloves. Rather than just flicking the ball to Jack, they were zipping it in. It got a bit dangerous because the fielder only had to be a little bit off line with his throw and the ball was hitting people. My old team-mate Mark Ramprakash took matters into his own hands – or head – when Gloucestershire tried it against him, by nutting the ball away and getting some extra runs. Good idea, but he did need a new helmet, and probably a couple of headache tablets too, after doing it.

Ironically, Vaughanie himself had learnt the tactic from an Australian, Darren Lehmann, his coach at Yorkshire, who believed it showed a fielding team had energy and intent. Whatever, they had the Aussies rattled and all out for 190 before tea. Then, of course, it all went wrong and Australia came back to earn a comfortable win.

Vaughanie later admitted he had been 'drained and fairly depressed' after the game, worried about how England's batting would stand up to McGrath and Warne (who had taken 15 wickets between them in the match). Kevin Pietersen, controversially selected ahead of Graham Thorpe, had made two half-centuries on debut, which was encouraging, but he knew that the other batters would have to weigh in with serious runs for England to have any chance.

The Second Test at Edgbaston was absolutely pivotal – England were so close to going 2–0 down and it would have been hard to imagine us coming back from that. It did help (a lot) that Ricky Ponting put us in to bat on an absolute road and that Glenn McGrath did his ankle treading on a cricket ball while playing touch rugby in the warm-up. I always find it a bit strange the way modern cricketers play football or rugby or some other sport before the start of a match. I guess they just want to inject some variety in their preparation to keep things interesting. But if you're going to do something different, why not a nice game of backgammon? Good for getting the fingers loose?

Michael Vaughan and England coach Duncan Fletcher deserve a lot of credit for the way they approached the series. I think I really would have enjoyed playing under Vaughanie. He allowed players to play their own game, and as I've found out working with him in the media, he's also a good laugh.

Him and Fletch had plans in place for every batsman. For instance, they knew they had to stop the Aussie's dangerous wicket-keeper–batsman Adam Gilchrist weighing in with big runs down the order, so Freddie bowled around the wicket and looked to get reverse swing from outside off stump. That had Gilchrist in trouble all series, as his average of 22 shows.

Vaughanie also thought on his feet, like his decision to take out a third slip to Matty Hayden in favour of a shortish mid-off when Matthew Hoggard was bowling to him in the Second Test, because he could see Hayden was hitting it uppishly through there. Almost immediately he was caught in that position, and for the rest of the series Vaughanie loaded the field down the ground to cut off one of Hayden's favoured scoring areas, which worked a treat.

Like Brearley, but in his own way, Vaughanie seemed to have an instinct for how to get the best out of players like Welshman Simon Jones. The Aussies couldn't get to grips with Jones' reverse swing delivered at high pace, and he finished top of the England bowling averages with 18 wickets at 21 runs apiece.

Jones actually asked Vaughanie to be dropped from the team for the Fourth Test after taking a six-fer in the previous game, because he had an injury niggle and he said he never bowled well at Trent Bridge. Michael just told him he was playing, no argument, and Jones went out and took a five-fer in the first innings on the ground where he supposedly couldn't bowl.

The 'King of Spain', Ashley Giles, was another one who benefited from Vaughanie's man-management skills. Ashley got heavily criticised in the press for his performance in the First Test, and he was on a real downer going into the Second. Vaughanie knew that Ashley responded well to a bit of talking therapy, so he sat him down and told him that the whole team had faith in him and supported him. After that pep talk, although Ashley wasn't exactly ripping through the Australian line-up, he bowled tidily and weighed in with some crucial knocks with the bat, not least his steely half-century to keep KP company in the final Test at the Oval and help England secure the series.

Kevin Pietersen of course became a superstar in his first Test series, laying into the Aussie bowlers and averaging over 50. KP was encouraged by Vaughanie to play his natural game and express himself, and that paid dividends, not least in that Oval Test when England needed a draw and the Aussies had us on the ropes in the second innings.

KP went in at number five with England three down, only 70-odd ahead and Ian Bell just out for a duck. He got peppered by Brett Lee, was dropped by Shane Warne on 15 and, while he rode his luck, showed tremendous bravery. At lunchtime, he told his skipper he was in two minds whether or not to take on Lee if he kept on bouncing him.

Vaughanie told to him to follow his instinct and go for it.

KP marched out after lunch ready for battle and absolutely destroyed the Aussies with that wonderful innings of 158. Brilliant stuff.

After a shaky start against that unplayable McGrath spell at Lord's, openers Andrew Strauss and Marcus Trescothick laid the foundations for some substantial England scores – in the Second, Third and Fourth Tests, England posted first innings scores of over 400, which put a lot of pressure on the Aussies. Early on in the series it looked like Shane Warne had Straussy's number, but he came through and was the only player on either side to score two tons in the series. He also took a memorable diving catch to snaffle Adam Gilchrist at Trent Bridge.

Tresco never made a ton, but his positive strokeplay alongside Strauss helped set the tempo for the England innings, which usually rattled along at around four runs per over.

Vaughanie himself had a poor start to the series with the bat, but he showed his class at times, and scored 166 at Old Trafford, the highest innings by any player on either side.

Before the series, Ricky Ponting had said that Andrew 'Freddie' Flintoff was the only English player worthy of wearing the baggy green cap of Australia. A few others proved that statement was wrong, but Freddie lived up to his billing, taking 24 wickets, more than any other English bowler, scoring 402 runs (including a brilliant ton at Trent Bridge and three fifties) at an average of 40, winning two Man of the Match awards (at Edgbaston and Trent Bridge) and Man of the Series for good measure.

Strange to think that even though he'd made his Test debut way back in 1998, it was Fred's first Ashes series. Freddie went in feeling good about his bowling after doing some serious strength and conditioning rehab in recovery from an ankle operation. That work seemed to add bit of extra zip to his bowling, and he was able to get around the 90mph mark consistently in the one-day series leading up to the Ashes Tests.

His batting was another matter: 0 and 3 in his first two Ashes innings at Lord's was not a good sign. It took three four-hour sessions in the nets under the watchful eye of Neil Fairbrother to get his batting in the groove, plus a session with a 'mental coach' to get his mind right after that Lord's defeat. He'd felt a bit too uptight to produce his best and the mental coach asked him what he'd done to relax in the past. The answer was basically music and singing, which led to Freddie blasting out Elton John's 'Rocket Man' and singing along at the top of his voice in the dressing room over and over again until it became the team song.

From the Second Test, Fred was in charge on the pitch and it was thrilling to watch as he played without fear. Adam Gilchrist said Freddie 'was the difference between the two sides' and that summer we did see peak Flintoff, absolutely loving the battle, playing hard but also with great sportsmanship.

England benefited from consistent selection during the series, fielding an unchanged team in all but the final Test – and that change was only enforced by an injury to Simon Jones. In the era I played in, players such as Ian Bell and Geraint Jones could well have been dropped. Bell, then only 23, had a torrid time with the bat, averaging only 17, while wicket-keeper Jones missed a couple of stumpings and dropped a few catches. Bell made an important contribution in the field though, taking eight catches, more than any other England fielder and perhaps that was recognised, alongside his undoubted potential with the bat. Although Belly didn't realise that potential in the 2005 series, the fact that he went on to play a leading role in subsequent Ashes series showed he learnt from a very tough summer personally and being part of a winning team, and the backing he got from his captain and selectors paid off in the long run.

Jones maybe wasn't the safest pair of hands behind the stumps that summer, but again the selectors weighed up the benefits of bringing in another keeper against the possibility of breaking up the team spirit and stuck with him. Jones repaid that faith by taking the match-winning catch down the legside to dismiss

Kasprowicz at Edgbaston, and putting on a crucial batting partnership of 177 with Freddie at Trent Bridge.

Although there were a few run-ins between the two teams on the pitch, as you'd expect in an Ashes series, players from both teams would have a drink together after matches. Win or lose, as the series progressed, they all knew that they were a part of something very special. It must have been a huge buzz to be in the dressing room and part of it all.

Even us ex-cricketers working in the media were carried along with the excitement of it all. Indeed, BBC impartiality may have slipped on the odd occasion in the *TMS* commentary box. Like when Jones took the Kasprowicz catch at Edgbaston and I leapt out of my seat and gave it a 'Get in!' Having played in a few Ashes series defeats, I felt like I was out there on the field myself urging the boys on to achieve what had seemed impossible in my time.

The hype just grew and grew as the series progressed, but the games always exceeded the hype. Cricket had never been so high profile, hitting the front pages for the right reasons, and the players were getting mobbed by the general public and papped by the paparazzi wherever they went. People who'd previously had no interest in the game – such as my wife, Dawn, who I married that summer – were asking how the lbw law works. The atmosphere at the grounds was unlike anything I'd ever seen before, and the England and Aussie fans who attended helped to make it special.

There were some superstar performances along the way, but it was a real team effort, deserving of a place in the Tuffers HoF. The England boys also deserved their MBEs . . . well, maybe not Paul

Collingwood, who only played in the final Test. Although, in fairness, Colly did score a tremendous 10 on the last day at the Oval.

When you consider Shane Warne was at his brilliant best throughout the summer, taking 40 wickets at fewer than 20 runs apiece, dismissing every single England batsman at one time or another, it was some achievement to beat the Aussies. Warne himself admitted, 'I don't think I could have done any better with bat or ball.'

Hate to remind Warney, but he could have done a little better in the field if he'd caught Kevin Pietersen at the Oval. Oops.

Lloyd and his Bouncing Billies

Clive Lloyd captained West Indies for over a decade before retiring in 1985. Between March 1980 and January 1985, the side lost just once under him and set a record of 26 consecutive Test matches without defeat. And in the summer of 1984, they made history by becoming the first touring side to win every Test in a series against England, a feat that has not been repeated since.

The Windies had come to England full of confidence after winning in Australia, but they weren't complacent despite talk in the press of a potential whitewash – or 'Blackwash' as it was labelled at the time.

'This was silly talk,' recalled Viv Richards. 'It had only been achieved four times in Test history and only once by a West Indies team.'

Viv said their players were just focused on winning the series, although he did admit that part of the reason he thought a 5–0 was out of the question was not so much the quality of their opponents as the wonderful English weather: 'If England couldn't beat us in any of the Tests coming up, I was pretty sure that the English weather would.'

Unfortunately for England, it was a lovely warm and sunny summer.

It should be remembered that England didn't lose every match to the Windies that summer, though – in the build-up to the Tests, our boys managed to win a one day international. Warning signs were flashing for England in that three-match ODI series, though, not least when Viv Richards and Michael Holding shared an astonishing tenth-wicket stand at Old Trafford. The score was 166 for nine with 15 overs still left when Holding joined Viv, who was 98 not out.

'Don't worry, just hold on,' Viv told his new partner.

He then proceeded to larrup the England bowling attack of Ian Botham, Bob Willis, Neil Foster, Geoff Miller and Derek Pringle to all corners of the ground and beyond, while Holding mostly stood at the other end and enjoyed the view. Two of Viv's five sixes were absolute monsters that flew out of the ground, one landing on the tracks of the Warwick Road train station nearby.

The Richards–Holding last-wicket stand was worth 106 runs. Holding scored 12. Viv's final score of 189 not out was a new ODI world record. West Indies won that series 2–1 and things went downhill for England after that.

An England team meeting before the Test series didn't exactly inspire confidence. Bob Willis began by offering England's opening batsmen, Graeme Fowler and debutant Andy Lloyd, some advice on how to deal with the West Indies bowling attack.

'Malcolm Marshall and Joel Garner are a good opening pair,' said Bob, in one of the understatements of all time. 'Just try and pick up your singles off them,' he advised.

He then spoke about the problems Eldine Baptiste could cause to the two left-handers as he angled the ball across them, and claimed that spinner Roger Harper was very underrated and would keep it very tight.

Finally, Bob broke the good news: 'So when Michael Holding comes on, he's the weak link. He's the one we've got to get after.'

Bloody hell, when Michael Holding coming on to bowl is the best thing you've got to look forward to, you know you're in trouble.

It is true, though, that the West Indies fast-bowling attack wasn't quite as formidable as it had been a couple of years before. The great Andy Roberts' and Colin Croft's Test careers had come to an end, and the youngster Baptiste was not in their class. Meanwhile Holding, a Rolls-Royce of a fast bowler, was in the autumn of his career and not able to consistently generate 90mph pace like he had in his prime.

The wealth of experience in the side helped to make up for the loss of any firepower. For instance, Holding and Joel 'Big Bird' Garner used to help each other out with their bowling. As well as generating steep bounce, Garner was looking to move the ball both ways, and when he was struggling to make it go one way or the other, Holding would keep a close eye on his action and suggest little adjustments.

Six foot seven tall and very strong, Garner was a remarkably accurate fast bowler with a lethal yorker. He ended up with 259 Test wickets at an impressive average of a touch under 21 runs apiece, but Holding says he could have got 300-plus if it wasn't for his lifestyle. Big Bird was very partial to a big night out and even though he could still pound out 35 economical overs the next day, Holding reckoned that with a good night's sleep Garner would have been able to bowl more wicket-taking balls.

The Test series began at Edgbaston, and the tone was set within the first half-hour when Malcolm Marshall almost decapitated Andy Lloyd. Okay, slight exaggeration, but Marshall's bouncer thwacked Lloyd on the temple guard of his helmet and he was hurt so badly, he had to stay in hospital for a few days, didn't play cricket again that summer and never played another Test match.

Through the series, all of the West Indian players, even the lesser lights, made valuable contributions at key times. The front-line bowlers were all in form. Joel Garner took 29 wickets, Malcolm Marshall took 24 and Michael Holding had 15 victims in the four Tests he played. Off-spinner Roger Harper also chipped in with a match-winning six-fer in England's second innings at Old Trafford in the Fourth Test.

Opening batsman Gordon Greenidge was in imperious form, hitting two double-centuries. The first, in double-quick time on the fifth day at Lord's, turned a likely draw into a stunning victory (see 'The Fabulous Bajan Boys', page 15). The other at Old Trafford showed his ability to dig in when his side were struggling. In partnership with wicket-keeper Jeff Dujon (101) and nightwatch-man Winston Davis (77), he helped his team recover from 70 for 4 to a final score of 500, setting up a win by an innings and 64 runs.

Greenidge's partner Desmond Haynes struggled for runs through most of the series, but weighed in with a century first dig in the final Test at the Oval to hammer one of the last nails in England's coffin.

If Greenidge or Haynes was out early, they had left-hander Larry Gomes coming in at number three to steady the ship. Gomes was a quiet hero of that team – he made a couple of centuries and a 90-odd, plus he averaged 80 in the series and was happy to occupy the crease and allow the flair players around him to attack. As Clive Lloyd said, he was 'a wonderful anchorman on whom we could all depend'.

Gomes was followed by a couple of potential destroyers in Viv Richards and Clive Lloyd strolling in at numbers four and five – Lloyd passed 7,000 runs in Test cricket at Lord's during the series, only the second West Indian to reach that landmark after Garry Sobers.

West Indies used just 13 players in the series and they might have kept the same 11 throughout if it hadn't been for injuries to Holding and Malcolm Marshall which meant they each missed a Test.

Meanwhile, England's selectors used 21 in total, bringing in players on the basis of a couple of good innings or bowling displays in county cricket and then dropping them again straight away if things didn't go right. Playing against the best team in the world with such a muddled selection policy and no longer-term plan was never going to end well. As Desi Haynes said later, 'Some of them were making their debuts against one of the strongest sides they'd ever play in their lives. C'mon! That was just such juicy prey for our fast bowlers.'

Veteran spinner Pat Pocock, recalled to the England side for the first time in eight years for the Fourth Test, got a pair of noughts batting at number ten. Then in the final Test at the Oval, some sadist thought it'd be a good idea to send him out to bat number three as a nightwatchman. Twice.

The first time, poor old Pat stuck around for 42 minutes, a non-scoring knock that Wisden's reporter described as 'one of the most gallant noughts of our time'. Sadly, he only lasted two balls second time, to get his four ducks in a row.

Before going in to bat, he'd told England physio Bernard Thomas, 'I've cleaned my teeth and gargled, just in case you have to give me the kiss of life.'

I'm pleased to say that Pat did finally score Test runs (two of them) that summer at the fifth time of asking, against the slightly gentler Sri Lanka bowling attack when all the big nasty West Indies bowlers had gone home. When Pat got off the mark, the crowd gave him a standing ovation.

Having a settled team helped to create a sense of unity among the West Indies players. A lot of them had played together for years and built up a strong team spirit, and the newer players fitted in seamlessly.

Away from the cricket action, the West Indies boys pulled together too. Some of the players suffered family bereavements, but the news was never made public. '1984 was actually a very difficult year for us,' recalled Joel Garner. 'Things that would normally come out stayed quiet, because we respected each other and trusted each other . . . The enjoyment of that tour is that we pulled each other along at every turn.'

Clive Lloyd's leadership had again been key. 'It was Clive who let us give our best,' said Viv Richards. 'He is the calmest man I know. Never bewildered, always in control. He built us into a great team. We always knew he had the ability to lead us and so we trusted him. It was a complicated thing to bring a West Indies dressing room together. Clive sent a message to the whole region: "Hey, West Indians can be happy together."'

That team spirit was typified by Malcolm Marshall in the Third Test, after his left thumb was broken during fielding in England's first innings. With West Indies just a few runs ahead and nine wickets down in their first dig, and Gomes 96 not out, the England fielders starting to walk off thinking Marshall wouldn't be able to bat. But bat he did, even hitting a one-handed four as he lasted eight balls and allowed Gomes to reach his century. Marshall wasn't done yet though, using his good right hand to rip through the England batting line-up, taking seven for 53. As brilliant as Marshall was when fully fit, knowing he could even beat them one-handed must have been a killer psychological blow for the England team.

Not everyone was happy with all of Clive Lloyd's tactics though. England legend Sir Len Hutton was not impressed when the Windies quicks bowled short-pitched stuff at the tailenders. 'Club cricketers, even village cricketers, know that the best ball with which to dispose of a tailender is the yorker,' said Sir Len. 'I would have thought that Clive Lloyd, with his wealth of experience, might have had a quiet word with his "Bouncing Billies" but, no, it was allowed to continue.'

The game's governing body, the ICC, ended up changing the laws because of the Bouncing Billies, bringing in a limit of two bouncers per over, but Allan Lamb didn't agree with that: 'They were the best side I've ever seen. That [law change] was rubbish. We didn't mind getting bounced. They had the armoury and, if you didn't have the equipment to cope, well, go and suck eggs.' Lamby, shut up!

Allan certainly had the armoury. He was as brave as they come against fast bowling; he loved it. And he can be very proud of his efforts in that series. To make three centuries in consecutive Tests – at Lord's, Headingley and Old Trafford – against that mob was some going.

Joel Garner claimed the West Indies bowling tactics were simply a matter of playing to their strengths, rather than deliberate intimidation, and it was up to opposition batsmen to deal with it. 'If you take away short-pitched bowling, how many fewer runs would Clive Lloyd, Alvin Kallicharran, Viv Richards and Gordon Greenidge have scored?' he said. 'They conquered the bouncer.'

Fair point, but they didn't have to face West Indies' fast bowlers in that series, and tailenders like Pat Pocock were never likely to suddenly conquer the bouncer like Viv and co.

The 5–0 win meant West Indies equalled the world record of eight successive Test match wins and extended their unbeaten run to 23 matches. England had run into a wrecking ball of a team.

'We had the best openers in the world,' said Lloyd. 'The middle order was very solid. We had the best of young and old, the best of pace and superb fielding.'

And that is hard to beat.

Gatt's teams of the Eighties

I have a lot of affection for the Middlesex sides led by my old mentor Mike Gatting in the Eighties. The most successful period in the club's history had begun under the captaincy of Mike Brearley from the early 1970s – his teams had won three county championships in 1976, 1980 and 1982, his final season. So Gatt had a tough act to follow when he took over as skipper, but he managed to do just as well through the 1980s and into the 1990s.

Gatt led the team he inherited to the runners-up position in the county championship in 1983. Earlier in the summer, Middlesex also had the chance to win the Benson & Hedges Cup, something the club had never managed to do before. They faced arch-rivals Essex in the final at Lord's and it proved to be an absolute thriller.

Middlesex batted first and had veteran batsman Clive Radley, who scored 89, to thank for posting a half-decent target of 196 off 55 overs against Essex's bionic bowling attack – I say bionic because it included Neil Foster, who bowled beautifully to take three for 26 and had steel discs in his vertebrae. He also ran out Gatt with a brilliant turn and throw from the boundary. Meanwhile Foster's opening bowling partner, John Lever, had had a lifesaving operation to remove poison from his stomach just a week before and was playing despite a big surgical wound held together by stitches and strapping. Ouch.

Coming in at number three, with his crouching stance and nurdling style, Radley was not pretty to watch but he was effective. He had been a cornerstone of that Middlesex side for many years, and his effort that day won him the £500 Man of the Match Gold Award. Riches, indeed.

Essex looked like they would win easily when Graham Gooch came in and scored 16 off young fast bowler Norman Cowans' first over, they'd racked up 71 after ten overs and, even after Goochy was out for 46 and things slowed down, they were 113 for 1 off 25. Then came the collapse.

Spinner Phil Edmonds and pacers Neil Williams and Wayne Daniel gnawed through the Essex middle order. And after suffering that early shellacking, Cowans showed plenty of grit to come back and take the vital wicket of Gooch's opening partner Brian Hardie, one short of his half-century, before tearing through the Essex tail. Big Norm could generate some revs when he got going, and the last few Essex batsmen couldn't handle the pace as day turned into night. At 8.50pm, with the first ball of the last over, and Essex needing just five runs, he bowled Foster all ends up to clinch a dramatic victory and the club's first silverware under Gatt's leadership.

Gatt then had to oversee the building of the next winning Middlesex team around stalwarts like Radley and Wayne Daniel and younger newcomers like fast-medium seamer Neil Williams. I got taken on by Middlesex in 1984, and while I began my apprenticeship, working on the groundstaff and playing for the Second XI, the first team struggled in the early part of the season. 'It's one thing to lead a successful side, but this year, when things have not always gone well, it's been a much more difficult job,' said Gatt at the time. 'It can be hard to discover exactly what's wrong. Then, when you think you have the answer, you have to decide whom to drop or bring in. And, eventually, if things still don't improve, you begin to doubt your own ability as captain . . .'

He worked out what was going wrong soon enough, though, as the team recovered to a third-place finish in the county champion-ship and qualified for another Lord's final, this time in the NatWest Trophy tournament. The match against Kent proved to be even more nail-biting than the previous season's Benson & Hedges finale.

Kent set a target of 232 off their 60 overs, and it got very twitchy at the end. With six wickets down and the light fading at Lord's, it was up to the spinning duo John Emburey and Phil Edmonds to get the team over the line with the bat. In the second-last over with eight runs required, the legendary Derek Underwood, playing in his record ninth Lord's final, helped by dropping Embers at short mid-on, but Middlesex still needed seven runs off the last over, bowled by Richard Ellison.

It all came down to the last ball. The scores were dead level – both in runs and in wickets lost – and to ramp up the drama even more one of the umpires had to jog over to the scorers' box to check on the situation (no headsets to consult a third umpire in those days). Kent had scored more runs at the 30-over mark, so if the score stayed the same, they would be the winners. With all the Kent fielders in saving one, Embers kept his cool and flicked an overpitched ball from Ellison off his legs for four, to clinch the first NatWest trophy win in the club's history.

Middlesex won the first county championship under Gatt's captaincy in 1985. It was a great achievement because a number of their key players, not least Gatt himself, were called up to play for England in the Ashes series that summer. Embers and Phil Edmonds, Norman Cowans and keeper Paul Downton were all missing for much of the time, but their 'B-side' was still good enough to do the business. In Gatt's absence, Clive Radley was skipper. Fellow veterans Wilf Slack and Graham Barlow opened the innings and were in good nick, featuring in three century-plus opening stands in a row against Leicestershire, Nottinghamshire and Worcestershire. While the old stagers provided a solid platform, youngsters like Jamie Sykes, John Carr (who was brought up in a house right next to Lord's), Keith Brown and Angus Fraser came in and did brilliantly when the stars were away on international duty.

Jamie Sykes was my best mate and we got into plenty of scrapes. Like the time we tried to drink a pint at every one of the pubs along the (very long) Mile End Road in the East End of London and only succeeded in ending up in a police cell. He also initiated something of a revolution at Middlesex.

When I started at the club, the Second XI got changed in a separate dressing room. And the only time the young lads would be allowed in the first-team dressing room was when senior players wanted us to do something for them.

'Oi, twelfer, get my jockstrap and go and put it in the drying room.'

'Okay, Mr so-and-so.'

That was the way. But when an old pro asked Jamie to do that one day, Sykesy replied, 'You what? Hold on, mate – you want me to pick up your skiddy jockstrap and put it in a room a few yards away? Nah. Put it in there yourself.'

'Who do you think you are, son? You do what I say'

'Nah, **** off. I'll get you a drink when you come off after having a bat, but don't ask me to put your sweaty jockstrap in the drying room.'

At first the senior pros were up in arms, saying, 'You don't know the way this club works. Apprentices have to do what they're told.'

The thing was that the old guys were doing it to nause us out, to try and bully us, like we were their fags at a public school. Well, Jamie was from Shoreditch and he wasn't down for any of that.

After a while, people did come round to his way of thinking. Apart from 'jockstrapgate', there was a realisation that the Seconds changing in a different room was not good for developing a squad. The youngsters weren't learning anything over there. Okay, there should be a degree of separation and respect, but you shouldn't have to knock to get in the first-team dressing room door – we're all part of the same club and striving for the same goal. The atmosphere improved after that issue was addressed.

Unfortunately, at Middlesex it would end up being a battle between me and Jamie for the spinner's spot alongside John Embury in the First XI after Phil Edmonds retired, and they went for me over him. (Phil was still a top bowler when he retired, but his business interests were taking over, and the club weren't really up for him taking his big old mobile phone out onto the pitch to answer calls and have meetings over a bottle of claret at lunchtime.)

Jamie was a decent bat as well, but couldn't establish himself in the team. He moved on to play for Durham up north, but he was a London boy, couldn't settle there and his county cricket career petered out.

I must also pay tribute to Wayne 'Diamond' Daniel, our power-house Barbadian fast bowler, who was given a well-deserved benefit year by the club in 1985. A 16-stone all-muscle hulk of a man, Diamond had been a star player in Brearley's Middlesex sides and continued to do the business under Gatt. Wayne had chosen to play World Series cricket as a young lad in the late Seventies, and while he was out of the Test cricket scene West Indies discovered other great fast bowlers who were later selected ahead of him and he didn't win another cap for seven years. For someone of his ability to only play ten Tests in his career when he would have walked into most international teams was ridiculous really, but Middlesex reaped the benefit of having a top-class Test bowler to regularly terrorise our county opponents.

His former Middlesex opening bowling partner Mike Selvey described Wayne's preferred bowling length as 'nasty', although he also bowled a mean yorker which he used to splatter the stumps of many a tailender backing away fearfully to the legside.

The nickname – 'Black Diamond' to use the full version – was given to him by his old Middlesex team-mate the late Mike Smith, who said Wayne was 'our rent and rates, who would pay the way for all of us'. He was that good.

Off the pitch, to say Diamond enjoyed female company would be an understatement. When Brearley was captain, apparently, one of the psychological ploys he used to encourage Wayne to bowl a couple of extra overs was to promise him an introduction to the latest woman to catch Diamond's roving eye in the Lord's Tavern afterwards.

Team-mate Simon 'Yozzer' Hughes ('The Analyst', as he is known now) also recalled an occasion when Diamond was let off fielding practice so he could get some treatment on an injured thumb. When he didn't return to bowl, Simon was dispatched to seek him out. He eventually found Wayne in the physio's apartment. 'The huge, rippling West Indian was face down on the floor, wearing only a jockstrap; the girl in a little white tunic was astride him administering a full massage,' he recalled. I guess she was working her way round to his thumb.

One night before an away match, he was due to share a hotel room with Kevin James. Wayne always used to turn up late, so Kevin had arrived a few hours before him and checked in. By the time Wayne rocked up around midnight, another receptionist was on shift.

'Hello, I think I'm sharing with Mr James,' he said.

The fella looked down his list of rooms, found the surname and gave Wayne the key. Wayne went up to the room, opened the door and walked in. The room was pitch black but he could hear the unmistakable 'noises of love'.

Rather than discreetly edge out of the room, Wayne went up to the end of the bed and started offering encouragement: 'Go on Jamesy, go on Jamesy . . .'

Suddenly, the groans and moans of pleasure stopped, there was a flurry of bed sheets and the bedlight was switched on. 'Jamesy' and the woman looked up to see big Wayne standing there grinning.

'What the . . . !'

It was another Mr James and his partner – Wayne had been given the key to the wrong room.

There was never a shortage of anecdotes with Wayne around. More importantly, on the cricket field, his strike-rate was equally impressive, averaging a wicket every seven overs for Middlesex between 1977 and 1987 and finishing with a total of 685 wickets. He really was a priceless diamond for the club.

In 1986, I was given a full-time contract and made my first-class debut at Worcester that June. I didn't play too often that year myself, but the boys were involved in another Benson & Hedges final thriller. Their NatWest victims of 1984, Kent, were looking for revenge. This time Kent batted second and needed 200 to win on a gloomy July day at Lord's. Embers took an amazing slip catch wide to his right to dismiss Chris Cowdrey as Kent were reduced to 71 for 4 of 35 overs, but Chris's brother Graham biffed a fifty (including a one-handed six off Phil Edmonds) and the Kent tail wagged to get them back in contention.

They needed 19 off the last two overs, and Gatt brought Edmonds back on to bowl the first of them. His bravery in bringing on a slow bowler paid off when Edmonds bowled Richard Ellison who had been motoring along. With 14 still required, Simon Hughes bowled the last over in pouring rain and near-darkness. Somehow the Kent keeper Steve Marsh hit him for six, but they fell agonisingly two runs short of Middlesex's total.

Three out of three epic wins in knife-edge final matches – it can't all have been good luck, could it?

By 1988, Gus Fraser was establishing himself, taking bundles of first-class wickets and playing a starring role in that season's Nat-West final against Worcestershire, capturing the prize wickets of Tim Curtis and Graeme Hick.

Our boys bowled them out for just 161 and should have been able to coast to victory, but at 25 for 4, things didn't look so rosy. It took a man-of-the-match-winning innings of 56 by an 18-year-old prodigy called Mark Ramprakash to win it. Gatt, who played for England himself at 20, said afterwards that Ramps was 'better than me at 18'.

Apart from those cup successes in 1986 and 1988, Middlesex had been struggling a bit in the county championship after the 1985 win. Young talent like Gus and Ramps was filtering through, but the average age of the First XI was over 30. That changed over the next couple of years as the club's youth policy started to bear fruit and the team started to get the right blend of youth and experience.

In 1989, our seam attack of Gus, Ricardo Ellcock, Norman Cowans and Simon Hughes took nearly 244 championship wickets between them at around 20 runs apiece. Ellcock was a surprise package, because he'd been offloaded by Worcestershire who didn't think he was good enough, and he performed so well, he earned himself a place in the England squad for the tour of the West Indies that winter (unfortunately, a back injury meant he had to come home from the Caribbean early).

I'd grabbed my opportunity to team up with Embers in the spin department and we were the only two bowlers to take over 50 wickets each. By this time, I'd begun to get an understanding of the high expectations at Middlesex if you wanted to be a first-team regular. I can't recall the exact game, but I have a very vivid memory after one of my first match-winning bowling efforts for the First XI when I got a six- or seven-fer.

Back in the dressing room, at the end of the game, the players were celebrating and the staff were saying, 'Well done, lads, we won the game.'

But that wasn't enough for me. I was thinking, 'I won this game.'

I chirped up, '****ing hell, is no one going to give me a pat on the back?'

The coach, Don Bennett, looked at me and said, 'You want a pat on the back, boy? What do you want, a ****ing medal? You're meant to do that. Now shut up.'

'Uh-er-oh-uh-er, well ... I thought I was pretty good,' I stuttered.

'Don't ever do that again. There's 11 of you out there.'

I spent the rest of my career trying to get a pat on the back from Don. He gave it to me once (see 'Unique talents . . ., page 272). And I took 1,200 wickets. Hard to please, was Don.

Anyhow, by 1989, I was starting to get the hang of county cricket. Meanwhile, on the batting side, Mike Roseberry was showing the potential to become a key top-order batsman, while Ramps continued to thrive. We had all the senior players, who were lovely, but us young boys were mates. We thought we were the new breed and wanted to prove we were better than the old guard.

Before a game, Ramps and I would gee each other up: 'Ramps, you make sure you destroy their spinners.'

'Tuffers, you make sure you get their batsmen.'

It wasn't idle chat. We used to fight the opposition. I haven't got it in me any more, but I had it then. He had it. Ramps was so intense, he used to scare me. And a couple of times, I scared him, too.

I've never seen someone want to destroy the opposition with such intensity as Ramps. If he got past 50 he didn't give it away. He wanted to grind them into the dirt – with all the shots, but also with immaculate defence.

The downside was that he almost cared *too* much. He'd be physically sick and smash things when he got out. Sometimes I was the only person who could talk Ramps round . . . after giving him a cooling-down period of five to ten minutes, that is . . . and only then approaching him somewhat gingerly. I was, like, 'This ain't good for you, man.' Eventually, he calmed his approach a bit – maybe because he kept destroying his best bats.

I could relate to his explosive temperament, because I had my moments too. Indeed, there was one time I got so revved up that I accidentally knocked myself out. That was when both Ramps and I were on international duty with England against West Indies at the Kensington Oval in Bridgetown, Barbados, in April 1994. West Indies hadn't lost at the ground since 1935 and had won 12 consecutive Tests there since. Going into the match we hardly looked like a team capable of breaking that run, having lost the first three Tests of the series, and been bowled out for 46 to lose the Third Test at Port of Spain. Before the Fourth Test, we also lost by eight wickets to a Board XI with their batsman Stuart Williams hitting me for five fours in a row to clinch victory. Confidence was not high.

Somehow, though, we picked ourselves up and got in a great position to win at the Oval. We'd set West Indies over 400 to win, thanks to two centuries by Alec Stewart and a fantastic eight-fer by Gus Fraser in the Windies first innings.

On the morning of the fifth day, I took one of the best and most important catches of my career (I did catch a few, you know . . .) – a miscued pull by the great Brian Lara off Andy Caddick, running back from mid-on, ball dropping over my shoulder, hung on to it – lovely!

I wasn't bowling well though, and at lunchtime I was fuming with myself. I was desperate to win and we still needed six wickets.

So I took myself away, went downstairs in the pavilion to a little area under the dressing room. I was all on my own, pacing around, ranting and raving to myself, when I saw what looked like a quite flimsy cupboard – wicker or rattan, I think it was.

I headbutted it in frustration. Everything went white.

After I don't know how long – maybe a minute – I came to. I was flat on my back.

My dad had once told me, 'Never take on a man fifty pounds heavier than you . . . or punch a wall.' He hadn't told me about headbutting cupboards, and the door of this one had turned out to be much more solid than it looked.

It wasn't textbook preparation for the afternoon session, but I picked myself up and went out to bowl again. And, oddly, my head-banging seemed to work, because I bowled a lot better and got three of their last six wickets, helping us to clinch a historic victory.

So, yes, although Ramps and I are very different characters in a lot of ways, we both had that side to us.

I was delighted when he was appointed England batting coach in 2014. It was a smart choice, because he not only has incredible technical knowledge but he's been through the mill of international cricket; it chewed him up and stopped him realising his massive potential, so he can warn the youngsters of the pitfalls.

Ramps is a hero of mine. A lovely man. Mind you, if we play a charity match together nowadays, I still give him a wide berth for five minutes when he gets out. Just in case.

We helped Middlesex finish third behind champions Worcester and Essex in 1989 – a few too many draws cost us. We also reached the final of the NatWest (I wasn't selected for that one), this time ending up on the wrong side of a thriller, Neil Smith crashing a slower ball from Simon Hughes (slower ball, Yozzer? Why?) through the darkness for six as Warwickshire got the ten runs they needed off the last over in just four balls.

That was painful, but by the start of the 1990 season, we were ready to do some serious damage. Myself, Ramps, Keith Brown and

Mike Roseberry were all awarded our county caps that year and our first-team squad looked a pretty powerful unit.

John Carr had struggled so much opening the batting the previous year, that he'd decided to change careers and become a banker. (Happily, John did come back to cricket a few years later, and became an assassin at number five for us despite a very strange stance, almost facing the wrong way as the bowler delivered the ball.) In John's absence, Mike Roseberry moved up to partner Desmond Haynes and they just clicked. Desi was in vintage form – he was voted the championship's player of the season – and between them, they scored eight hundreds and 19 half-centuries, so we rarely didn't get off to a good start. Gatt and Ramps batted at three and four and you just don't get better than that in county cricket. Keith Brown at five was our new Clive Radley, and he made a double-century against Notts and an important ton in our last championship game of the season at Hove.

Then there was our always reliable wicket-keeper, Paul 'Nobby' Downton, and his deputy, Paul Farbrace, who came in and did well mid-season when Nobby was sidelined by a very freak eye injury (Embers had bowled someone and the bail flew off and pinged poor old Nobby in the eye – very nasty). Nobby recovered and came back strongly to be named man of the match in our Sunday League final victory over Derbyshire.

We also had bowling options for all conditions with the experience of Norm Cowans and the nagging accuracy of Gus, backed up by Neil Williams or Simon Hughes, and a righty – lefty spin combo in Embers and me.

It did look like Essex would beat us to the county championship title though when they were ahead with four games to play. They had a game in hand, and all their remaining matches were against teams in the bottom half of the table.

Yozzer Hughes, who'd been part of Brearley's championship-winning squad way back in 1980, had struggled a bit during the season, but came in and took 12 crucial wickets in the last two games when Neil Williams was injured and Gus was away on England duty, including the last two, championship-winning, wickets of the season in successive balls against Sussex.

We won by an innings before teatime with more than a day to spare at Hove. I was only twelfth man for that match, but if you check the scorecards you will see that Sussex's third-last second-innings wicket, Tony Piggott, was 'c sub b Gatting' – a rather fine catch on the boundary. Another one for the Phil Tufnell Fielding Academy highlights showreel, that.

There was a great picture of us on the cover of the next issue of *Wisden Cricket Monthly* breaking out the champers in the dressing room afterwards. On a personal level, I had a lot to celebrate, having taken 65 championship wickets in the season, eight more than my mentor, Embers, and I'd been named in England's Ashes touring squad. But it was exciting enough to be a part of the biggest county club, back on top. Brilliant times and there were more to come for us in the Nineties.

My last county championship was 1993 and I would never have dreamt then that it would be another 23 years before Middlesex did it again. After a few lean years, I was thrilled to see the club on top of the pile again in 2016. They won it in dramatic style too, leaving it to the last session of the last day of the season at the Home of Cricket to finally shake off the challenge of Yorkshire (their opponents) and Somerset and clinching it with a hat-trick by Toby Roland-Jones. I was especially pleased for my old mate Gus Fraser, now the club's director of cricket. 'The attitude wasn't great when I started in 2009,' he said afterwards. 'There was a sense from some players that the club was lucky to have them rather than them being lucky to play for this club. We've put the pride back into playing for Middlesex.'

That's how it should be. Looking back, I feel so privileged to have played for Middlesex CCC in a golden period and I'm sure the champions of 2016 are getting that same buzz (and lots of champagne).

Worcester Gents on tour

My next team nomination goes to a side I learnt about in my role as a roving reporter for BBC's *The One Show*. I met Dan Waddell, the author of an award-winning book called *Field of Shadows*, which tells the story of a colourful team of cricketers who went on a tour of Nazi Germany in 1937. If the 'Waddell' name rings a bell, that's because Dan is the son of the legendary darts commentator Sid, and Dan is a witty wordsmith in his own right.

So Adolf Hitler was not a fan of cricket. He had actually organised a game against British POWs during World War One, but came round to thinking it was un-German, decadent and 'insufficiently violent'. Perhaps Adolf would have preferred cricket in the

1700s, before the rules had been properly hammered out and there was a good chance of a ruck on the pitch?

By the Thirties, with cricket-hating Hitler in charge, the chances of an English team travelling to Nazi Germany to have a jolly old game of cricket would have seemed remote. However, cricket had been played and enjoyed by a small minority of Germans since the 1880s, and in the summer of 1937 the Nazi minister for sport, Hans von Tschammer und Osten, came over to England and watched German sportsmen compete in a few sporting events. He went to Wimbledon, the British Athletics Championship at the White City stadium and an England v Germany swimming meet at Wembley. He also paid an unscheduled visit to Lord's for a Middlesex– Worcestershire game.

By all accounts, the sports minister knew bugger all about sport, but he was a big drinker. The details are hazy, but from his research Dan reckons it was while Tschammer und Osten was well-oiled and chatting to the MCC and Worcester bods that the idea of a tour to Berlin came about (he must have been so tiddly he forgot that Hitler hated the game). The next day it was announced that the Gentlemen of Worcestershire would be going to Berlin on their annual tour in ten days' time.

Worcester Gents were a ragtag *Dad's Army*-style squad of ex-county players, oddballs, schoolkids, businessmen and minor noblemen. For example, there was Geoffrey Tomkinson, a 56-year-old big-hitter in the Birmingham League who had once scored a century in 25 minutes and smacked probably the biggest six ever – the ball travelled a distance of approximately 105 miles after he'd hit it out of Kidderminster's ground and onto a passing goods train destined for Cardiff.

The team's fastest bowler was Herbert Oliver Huntington Whiteley ('Peter' or 'HO' to his mates), who was the great-great-uncle of the model Rosie Huntington Whiteley.

Their skipper was a Captain Mainwaring type called Major Maurice Jewell. The Major married into money and gave up work at the age of 26 in 1911 so he could devote all his time to his beloved cricket. He wasn't the most talented, but he was good enough to play first-class county cricket. He had the dubious distinction of captaining the Worcestershire side that went through the 1920 county championship season with a record of one win, 18 losses and one draw . . . and the draw was only due to rain.

He loved the sport though and continued to play the odd game for Worcestershire's full team into his forties, while off the pitch he did loads of fundraising to help keep the club going in the tough years after World War One.

Playing regularly for the Worcester Gents would allow the Major to get his fix of playing cricket into his fifties, but he was under a bit of pressure as captain of the team that went on a tour of Germany. With relations worsening between Britain and Germany, the MCC told him they'd better not lose. Germany beating England at our own game would be humiliating and a great propaganda victory for Hitler and the Nazis.

The Gents paid their own way on the tour, and as most of their players were minted they chose to stay at the Hotel Adlon, one of the grandest hotels in the world. They prepared for the first match against a 'Berlin XI' (Berlin's Second XI) by getting stuck into cock-tails at the hotel bar then hitting the town, so there were a few sore heads when they rocked up at the ground the next day for the first of three matches. Luckily, the Gents' idea of vigorous pre-match warm-up was smoking a couple of cigarettes and a few high catches for the keen young players. That sounds like my kind of set-up.

The English lads had to get used to a few quirks of cricket, German-style, though. They played on bumpy matted wickets. And when the Major and his fellow opener went out to face the first over of the first game, the nearest offside 'fielder' was a pho-tographer at short extra cover. The Major was a bit miffed but was told that in Germany it was normal for a photographer to be on the field close to the action to take photos at the start of game.

Also, all 11 Berlin players cried 'Aus!' – their version of 'Howzat!' – whenever the ball hit the pads, no matter how far off-line it was. The Gents thought that was frightfully unsporting.

Despite the distractions, the Gents ultimately proved too strong for the Berlin XI whose batting was pretty weak (that's being kind). But the first game was really just a friendly before the real busi-ness. The last two games of the tour – two-day matches against Berlin's best players – were being viewed as unofficial Test matches, and the Major's team needed to win them too for national pride.

The Berlin team was led by a cricket fanatic called Felix Menzel who'd toured England with a United Berlin team in 1930. It had been mainly down to Menzel that cricket didn't die in Germany with the rise of the Nazis. He did everything he could to publicise the game and somehow built a good relationship with the sports minister and other senior Nazi figures despite not being a member of the Nazi party himself. Dan couldn't find out exactly how he managed to do that, but suspects that, as Menzel was a jeweller, maybe he sorted them out with cheap jewellery.

As the tour progressed, the Gents got a little more edgy as they saw Nazi flags and SS soldiers all over Berlin, and they even heard machine-gun fire as they were playing. But they kept their nerve on the pitch and dominated the Berlin part-timers over the two 'Tests'. The final match was played at the huge Olympic Stadium, where Mussolini had recently given a speech, and the Gents finished off in style, with the Major top-scoring with 140 and snaffling a five-fer in bowling out Berlin for 19 in the second innings.

The evening after the match, the two teams had an end-of-tour dinner together. Nazi minister for sport Hans von Tschammer und Osten was there and asked Major Jewell for some tips on developing the game in Germany. The Major suggested it might encourage younger players if the senior guys weren't so harsh on them when they made a mistake – he'd been told about an incident when a senior player walked over and chinned a youngster who'd dropped a catch off his bowling.

'Yes, I have heard about the incident,' nodded Tschammer und Osten. 'But I understand it was a very simple catch.'

Aside from the sinister goings-on they'd spotted around Berlin, the Gents had been treated royally during the trip. Official government cars, functions and sightseeing trips had been laid on for them. They couldn't win at the cricket, but the hosts had been desperate to give a better impression of Nazi Germany. The tour reporter for *The Cricketer Annual* wrote: ' . . . it is greatly hoped that other English sides will visit Berlin. Should the Germans ever send a side to England they can be quite certain that they will be most welcome guests, especially with the Gentlemen of Worcestershire.'

Felix Menzel kept banging the drum for cricket in Germany, and the following year he organised a tour to Germany by Somerset Wanderers (with players from four West Country sides). At a lunch to welcome the Wanderers, Menzel made a speech appealing for an international tournament to be staged in England where teams from Germany and across the continent could compete. This got picked up by the British press, but the MCC weren't having any of it as the threat from Hitler grew. A year later Europe was at war and, sadly, Menzel's dream of bringing Europe together through cricket was thwarted.

As for the Gents, most of the squad that toured Berlin contributed to the war effort; even the older fellas like the Major, who took charge of his local Home Guard battalion. At the other end of the age scale was young 'Peter'/'HO' Huntington-Whiteley. He joined the Royal Marines, was given a new nickname, 'Red' (he had red hair), by his soldier mates, and was selected for a special commando unit to steal enemy intelligence. Under the direction of naval intelligence officer Ian Fleming (yes, the Ian Fleming who went on to create James Bond), he was part of a number of dangerous missions inside occupied France. More of a Sergeant Wilson type in manner than the Major, Red was laid back and cool, and also proved to be a brilliant and brave officer, much loved by his troops. Sadly, though, he was killed, aged just 24, in September 1944 in an ambush at Le Havre.

Dan unearthed other stories of service and war heroics by members of that Worcester Gents touring side of 1937, and it was great to learn from him about a team I would never have heard about otherwise. They might not have been the best cricketers ever to represent England abroad, but they are worthy Hall of Famers with a few proper heroes among them.

Waugh? Huh!

I seem to recall there have been a couple of half-decent Australian Test sides over the years who might merit a place in the Tuffers HoF, too. There were the Aussie teams of Bradman and co that won 13 out of 15 Test series between 1930 and 1952. Then there were the teams of the 2000s that played under Steve Waugh and then Ricky Ponting's captaincy – from October 1999 to November 2007 their record was: played 93 Test matches, won 72 with 11 draws. Not a bad record at all. Unfortunately, I've just been told there's no more space in my Hall of Fame's team room. Something to do with overcrowding, health and safety and what have you. Nothing I can do about it. Sorry, fellas.

CRICKETING BROTHERS-IN-ARMS

7

Baths and battles

Winston Churchill is a hero of mine and he had a mantra that I've always followed: 'In times of stress, have a bath.' I'm not sure he said those exact words, but he definitely loved a bath.

There are bath people and shower people. The shower people say you're sitting in dirty water, but I'll have a bath over a shower any day. I want to lie in a bath for an hour and contemplate the world and life. You can't do that in the shower.

Churchill liked to take two long hot baths each day, which were run by his butler and kept at a particular temperature measured with a thermometer. He did some of his best thinking in the tub, and often would have his secretary sitting outside with a portable typewriter so he could dictate to her. He even conducted meetings from the bath. I doubt Churchill would have been able to come up with a winning strategy in World War Two if he'd been taking showers.

As a cricketer, I always used to look forward to playing at grounds with the old-fashioned bathtubs. Nothing better after a day in the field than relaxing in a steaming hot bath. I knew I'd reached the status of a senior player when I could look to the pavilion five minutes before the end of play and give the twelfth man the universally understood tap-turning signal to run a bath. You couldn't do that if you were a junior player. I never asked the twelfer to measure the temperature with a thermometer though.

In an ideal world, I'd do my *TMS* commentary from the bath. Sadly, most of the Test grounds couldn't accommodate that. The nearest I get to it is at the Ageas Bowl in Southampton, where our commentary box is in a suite at the hotel overlooking the ground, so I can spend most of the day padding around in the fluffy white dressing gown and slippers provided. If only the cricket was visible from the bathroom . . .

Apart from a love of bathing, another thing I have in common with Churchill is Blenheim Palace. He was brought up there, and I, well, I once knocked over a suit of armour there. And earlier, an elderly lady had tried to snog me in the library (no, we weren't playing Cluedo).

I'd just come out of the jungle after winning *I'm a Celebrity* . . . and my future wife, Dawn, and I got invited to a dinner at the Palace and there was a charity auction.

'Who's going to bid me 500 quid to kiss the King of the Jungle?'

I didn't even know I was an auction prize.

A bid of £1,000 won the day, and I was summoned to the stage, as was the winning bidder, who must have been in her late eighties.

So I leant forward to give her a peck on the cheek, but the old girl had other ideas and went straight in for a snog. Yikes. Dawn was watching all of this in hysterics.

Then later on my way out, I somehow knocked over a suit of armour in the hallway, which wasn't the best way to make a quiet exit.

Not sure why I am I telling you all of this, but the point is that I'm interested in Churchill and military history and I wanted to find out more about the cricketers who served in the World Wars and pay tribute to them in my Hall of Fame.

When I used to play pre-season games with Middlesex against army teams, we took the piss a bit. There was a bit of sledging and we'd always win the match — as we should have done, what with us being professional cricketers and them being part-timers. Looking back, a silly little game of cricket was just a nice distraction for them. As a young lad worrying about my spin bowling, it didn't click with me that these guys had a real job that might be a matter of life or death.

It's one thing battling for victory for your country on a cricket pitch as a Test cricketer, but fighting on land, at sea and in the air when the future of your country is actually on the line is another. As my dad used to say when I was getting stressed out about my cricket, 'It's only a game of bat and ball, son.' That's why I have so much admiration for anyone who served in the World Wars.

My granddad Bill Tufnell, a silversmith by trade, was a soldier in

World War One, and thankfully he survived, but another Tufnell, one with a cricketing connection, was not so fortunate. His name was Carleton Tufnell and he came from upper-class stock, and to my knowledge was no relation of the Tufnells of Islington, where my granddad was from. Carleton went to Eton and Sandhurst and was apparently a gifted all-round sportsman although he didn't take it too seriously. By all accounts, he played for fun more than anything, but was good enough to play a game for Surrey's Second XI. A lieutenant in the Grenadier Guards, tragically he was killed in action at Ypres within months of the start of the war.

There were many other terrible losses. Take 29-year-old Captain Arthur 'Boy' Collins, who was killed by machine-gun fire at Ypres just a few months into the war. An orphan, he had shown serious cricketing talent as a kid. In June 1899, when he was a 13-year-old pupil at Clifton College, he scored 628 not out (well, 628 give or take 20 runs – the scorers were just kids too and they were struggling to keep track) in a junior school house match. He carried his bat right the way through Clarke's House's innings, finally running out of partners on the fourth afternoon of a match spread over five afternoons. His score set a new world record that wouldn't be beaten until January 2016, when a 15-year-old Indian kid called Pranav Dhanawade scored 1,009 not out off 327 balls (not a bad strike rate . . .) in a schools match in Mumbai.

Not content with his sextuple-century, Boy Collins then took 11 wickets as opponents North Town House were skittled out twice and Clarke's House won by the narrow margin of an innings and 688 runs.

Okay, North Town House may not have been the stiffest opposition, but to score that many runs, boy, Boy must have had some ability. It seems amazing, then, that he never went on to play any first-class cricket. Instead he opted for a career in the military, joining the British Army in 1902, and only playing the odd game when he had time.

Geoffrey Davies was a few years younger than Boy and he was already making an impact in county cricket for Essex as an amateur and being tipped as a future England international when the war began. From Poplar in East London, Davies had been bright enough to study at Cambridge University and was a highly promising spinner and batsman. Not long before volunteering for the military, he took four-fer and scored a century for Essex against Somerset in September 1914. After just couple of months' training, he was sent to the frontline and only a year after that match-winning display in Weston-Super-Mare, he was killed in battle at Calais, aged 22. For various acts of bravery, including putting his own gas mask over the face of a wounded British soldier under threat of poison attack, he was posthumously mentioned in dispatches.

Another young lad making a name for himself when World War One cruelly got in the way was Arthur Jacques. He'd only played county cricket for Hampshire since the start of the 1913 season, but had already taken 168 wickets with his revolutionary method of bowling to an almost totally legside field and looking to swing the ball in and cramp the batsman up. His 'leg theory' tactics laid the blueprint for how Douglas Jardine and Harold Larwood would terrorise the Aussies in the 'Bodyline' series a few years later.

Killed in action aged 27, Jacques never got the chance to fulfil his own potential.

North London boy Harry Lee was more fortunate, and miraculously so. He'd just broken into the Middlesex team when war was declared, so he signed up for the army. Within months the 23-year-old was shipped out to France where he was shot in the leg and left for dead between enemy lines. Instead, German soldiers pulled him from the field and put him on a cattle train for an agonising two-day journey without food. He had a shattered femur, and when he was finally sent home to England after six weeks in Lille, the army doctors told him one of his legs would be permanently shorter than the other and his cricket career was over. Incredibly, he defied medical opinion to play for another 15 seasons and score 20,000 runs, even playing once for England at the grand old age of 40. And, of course, he was a brilliant short leg (sorry).

Another survivor was the Reverend Frank Gillingham, who served as a chaplain to troops on the frontline at Ypres. A wicket-keeper–batsman for Essex, the Rev averaged a decent 30-odd with the bat over a long first-class career before retirement aged 52 in 1927. He continued God's work all the while alongside his cricket, and even worked as chaplain to King George V after the war.

The Rev's other claim to fame was being the BBC's first ball-by-ball commentator, a job he did on a game between New Zealand and Essex at Leyton in May 1927. Apparently, he was a natural, mixing his commentary on the game itself with observations about the goings-on within the ground and passing birds (eat your heart out, Blowers).

The lives of Lionel

The charismatic Lionel Tennyson was a cricketing war hero. The grandson of the famous poet, Alfred, Lord Tennyson, he was from a very privileged background, but on cricket field and battlefield he led from the front.

Born in 1889, he moved to Australia as a nine-year-old when his dad was made governor of South Australia and stayed there for five years. He really got the bug for cricket, going to a 1902 Ashes Test at the Adelaide Oval, where he and his two brothers were presented with a bat signed by all members of the touring team.

It was in Oz that he also got a taste for gambling. He won with his first-ever bet, on the famous Melbourne Cup horse race, starting a habit that would get him in a lot of trouble.

Back in England, he was sent to Eton and Cambridge, but he was no academic. He joined the army in 1909 and soon earned himself a reputation for playing as hard as he worked. Young Lionel would think nothing of going out partying all night in London, then be back to Aldershot in the morning and go straight into training drills with his regiment, the Coldstream Guards, without any sleep.

One Christmas night, Lionel and another soldier were supposed to be guarding the Tower of London, but with senior officers away on their Christmas holidays, Lionel decided to have a party at the Tower, inviting along a load of his army mates and chorus girls. It got very lively, but unfortunately for Lionel and co, the one senior officer who wasn't on leave walked in on the debauchery. They were all summoned to see the colonel the next morning, but,

luckily, he was in festive mood and let them off with the light pun-
ishment of being confined to barracks for a fortnight.

Lionel's dad gave him what was a generous allowance of £500
per year to cover his extravagant lifestyle, but Lionel's gambling
habit saw him burn through a whole lot more than that in a week
of madness.

After a winning streak in 1912, he had five grand in the bank, but
lost a fifth of that in one day's racing at Hurst Park. Then he made
the classic compulsive gambler's mistake of chasing his losses, and
emptied the rest of his bank account and more in a two-day meeting at Newbury. He continued to lump on the bets at the next
meeting at Windsor, until he'd lost a total of £12,000.

Daddy Tennyson was furious, but stepped in to pay his seven
grand's worth of debt to preserve family honour. The shock of mess-
ing up so badly got to Lionel, too, and he reined in his gambling on
the gee-gees (for a while at least) to focus on his army training and
sport, while still enjoying a few sleepless nights on the tiles.

His talent as a big-hitting batsman in army cricket didn't go
unnoticed by the MCC, and he was called up to make his first-class
debut against Oxford University in 1913. As Lionel himself put it,
he had 'some return from Dame Fortune' as he smashed a century
on debut at Lord's (110 off 100 balls). He carried on bashing bowling about for Hampshire that year, averaged over 40 to finish fifth
in the first-class batting averages and was nominated as one of
Wisden's 'Five Cricketers of the Year'.

In 1914, he was able to play less and less, though, as his duties
with the Rifle Brigade increased. He was at his plush flat in

Piccadilly on 4 August 1914 when war was announced. Like many young soldiers at the time, he was keen to go into battle. They'd been led to believe that the conflict would be done and dusted by Christmas. Within weeks he was in the trenches in France, living in horrific conditions, seeing his mates killed, witnessing mass killings, and reality kicked in.

He himself was injured three times during the conflict. The first time, in November 1914, it was reported in newspapers he'd been killed. In fact, he'd 'only' fallen into a deep crater made by an exploded German shell and suffered torn leg muscles and ligaments, but he had to write a letter to his parents to let them know that news of his death had been greatly exaggerated.

One of his brothers, Harold, who Lionel was very close to, was not so fortunate. In January 1916, he was killed when his ship, HMS *Viking*, struck a mine off the Dunkirk coast during a routine patrol.

Tennyson kept a diary during the war and the entries on his experiences at the battles on the Western Front are harrowing. When his brigade were called to the Somme in June 2016, one of his first jobs was to examine the trenches to see if they could be reused, but what he saw was horrifying. 'Never in my life had I been through anything like this,' he wrote. 'Dead faces were looking at one everywhere out of the mud, while the smell was too overpowering and awful for words.'

That September, a newspaper reported that Lionel had been killed again. Again it wasn't true. Stop writing the poor guy off! This time, he'd just sustained a minor wound in hand-to-hand fighting – so he had to send another note to his poor parents.

'Have just read in the papers that I have been killed; please do not believe it; am very well and have just come out of the trenches.'

Just a week after sending that telegram though, he nearly was killed when he was shot in the mouth in fierce fighting in the French countryside. Typical Lionel, after six weeks' rest and recuperation back home in England, he was up and about and willing to serve his country again.

More tragedy struck for the Tennyson family before the end of the year though, when his mother died. She had being doing her own bit for the war effort by setting up a hospital for wounded servicemen. However, the news of the death of her son Harold, and the sickening worry – not helped by false news stories – of having her two other boys, Lionel and Aubrey, fighting on the frontline had worn her down before a bout of pneumonia killed her.

When Lionel returned to France in June 1917, he enjoyed a relatively quiet few weeks including some cricket matches and big dinner parties with plenty of fine champagne, port and whisky to get stuck into. But soon it was back to the frontline, and when he was wounded again in November, it was the end of his war. Tragically, his other brother, Aubrey, was also killed in action before the war was finally over.

It seems pretty outrageous that Lionel Tennyson was never decorated for his bravery at the frontline during the war. While pen-pushing aristocrats who never got anywhere near the trenches were honoured, Tennyson had fought on the frontline in all the major battles on the Western Front, been injured and gone back for more. He was mentioned in dispatches twice, but nothing more.

Considering that he was from such a well-connected family him-self, it seems odd that he was snubbed, but one theory is that either Tennyson's gambling addiction or his scandalous affair with a mar-ried woman (who went on to become his first wife) near the end of the war or both, didn't go down well with the Establishment.

Sod the Establishment, for what he went through this man deserved a medal.

After the war, he continued to live life adventurously. When he wasn't socialising, drinking, smoking his pipe or winning and losing fortunes with the bookies, he was an inspiring captain for Hamp-shire. He was club skipper for 14 years from 1919 and led them to some great wins – one of the craziest against Warwickshire in 1922, when Hampshire only totalled 15 in their first innings, but improved ridiculously to score 521 in the second to win the match by 155 runs.

Funnily enough, Tennyson's butler, Walter Livsey, also played as wicket-keeper for Hampshire during that time. Now that's what you call all-round service.

Tennyson's first-class career batting average was only 23 because of his hit-or-miss attacking style, but when he was on form, he could destroy any attack. He only played nine Tests, but made his mark in the 1921 Ashes series as one of the few batsmen who stood up to the Aussies' dynamite fast-bowling pair, Jack Gregory and Ted McDonald. So much so, he was given the cap-taincy for the final three Tests. After fighting on the frontline, getting a few bruises from fast-moving cricket balls was nothing to Lionel.

The hands of a violinist

The story of Kent and England slow left-armer Colin 'Charlie' Blythe particularly caught my attention. Born in 1879 in Deptford, Charlie left school at 12, and had two choices – either follow his dad into a factory and become an engineer or use his talent to try to become a county cricketer. He went for the second option, joining the Kent nursery system in 1898, playing his first few senior games the following year, and becoming a dominant figure in the great Kent teams that won the county championship four times and finished runners-up once in the years before World War One.

Mike Gatting used to say that I had the 'hands of a pianist' in that they were rather delicate and, in an ideal world, I would have preferred not to have to put them in the way of shots fired at me off the middle of the bat. Charlie literally had the hands of a violinist – he played the instrument in classical orchestras and music hall bands, and his long fingers helped him to give the ball a good rip.

He was renowned for his control of flight and accuracy and being very difficult to get after – the story goes that in August one season, he bowled a full toss and almost before it had reached the batsman, Blythe sighed, 'There goes my first bad ball of the season.'

A very clever bowler, he'd constantly vary his pace and flight during a spell, and adjust his pace and spin levels depending on the pitch. A nice easy action meant he could bowl for hours, too.

He loved bowling against attacking batsmen, and rather than go into defensive mode when they drove him for boundaries, he'd toss it up even more with a bit more spin on it until they fell for the bait. At his peak, he also had a deadly much-quicker-than-it-looked 'arm ball' up his sleeve, which he bowled without any noticeable change in action and could get batsmen out on good wickets. On bad wickets, he was pretty much unplayable.

In the 1909 championship-winning season, he took a ridiculous 215 wickets, including 178 in championship games at 14 runs apiece. In two matches against Leicestershire, he took a total of 27 wickets for 165 runs – he got 14 of those wickets in one day for just 56 runs. Mind you, that wasn't his best day's work. In 1907, he'd taken 17 in a day against Northamptonshire – all ten wickets for 30, including a spell of seven for one run off 36 balls, then slacking off by taking only seven for 18 in the second innings. No one's ever done better than that.

With Kent, he was on a bonus of two guineas for every wicket he took over 80 each season . . . which was a very nice earner in the two seasons before the war, when he took 167 (in 1913) and 159 (in 1914).

He got over 2,500 first-class wickets during his career, including 218 five-wicket hauls. Stellar stats.

Don't be fooled by his lack of Test match appearances – he only got 19 caps. He suffered from epilepsy, which meant he missed a number of games. Also, he played in the so-called 'Golden Era' of cricket, and competed for a place in the team against the likes of Yorkshire spinning all-rounder Wilfred Rhodes.

Opinion was divided among batsmen of the day as to who was the better bowler, but Charlie's Test bowling average of 18.63 was eight runs per wicket, better than that of Rhodes, and he managed a round century of wickets, including incredible figures of 15 for 99 against South Africa in 1907, which no one bettered until Jim Laker's amazing 19-fer in 1956.

When war broke out, Charlie immediately volunteered for service, and passed the medical despite his epilepsy – I guess they looked at a fella who'd played top-level sport for the past 15 years and thought he must be healthy.

He kept his hand in playing a few regimental games, and although he took loads of wickets, he was starting to decline by August 1917 when he played for the Army and Navy against a combined Australia and South Africa Forces XI (really, it was England v Australia though, because there was only one South African in the opposition team). Charlie took one for 54 off 14 overs, and the winning hit for the Aussies was a six off his bowling, which was most unlike him.

He asked to be moved up to the frontline after his younger brother was killed at the Somme. Before he left Britain in late September 1917, his retirement was announced to the press. According to Lord Harris, who'd spoken to Charlie, 'He knew what there was of spin had left his bowling and that without that he would not be good enough.'

He lined up a job as cricket coach at Eton after the war, but having lost his brother, he was well aware he might not come back. In his will, he asked his father to distribute the mementos he'd received for each of his four championship wins – gold cufflinks (1906), a silver inkstand (1909), matching candlesticks (1910) and a silver paper knife (1913).

With the 12th (S) Battalion, he helped to build railway lines to transport ammunition and food to the frontline, relatively safe work, but sadly in November, aged 38, Sergeant Colin Blythe was killed instantly by a German shrapnel shell near Passchendaele in Belgium.

It would be another half a century until Kent had another left-arm spinner, Derek Underwood, in his league, and Charlie will never be forgotten by club or country. There is a war memorial near the St Lawrence Ground in Canterbury to honour him and other Kent cricketers who perished, and at his grave in Flanders a stone cricket ball placed there by Stuart Broad when the England team visited to pay their respects in 2009.

Captain Jack: cool under fire

During World War One, it had been widely felt that people shouldn't be playing cricket and other sports when there was a war on. The War Office even occupied Lord's and kept chicken and geese on the outfield, pecking away at the Nursery End. The Lord's groundsman in my day, Mick Hunt, wouldn't have stood for that.

A quarter of a century later, attitudes had changed. Sport was seen as a 'healthy distraction' and good for public morale. Cricket matches drew excellent crowds and raised funds for good causes like the Red Cross.

Cricket clubs were still expected to do their bit if required, though. For example, the RAF had taken over large parts of the Lord's ground by mid-1941 and that's where many people signed up and got their first experiences as soldiers.

Lord's could easily have become a casualty of the war, too, when in January 1943 a massive 500kg bomb was dropped and punched a hole down to the Bakerloo Line, which used to run under the Nursery Ground. Only the quick work of soldiers and an unusually long fuse – longer than any previously seen on a German bomb – saved the Home of Cricket. It didn't explode and there was time to move it to Hampstead Heath, where it was made safe.

There was another near-miss during a wartime match on 29 July 1944 when a flying bomb passing overhead began to cut out. Players threw themselves to the ground until it cleared the ground and exploded nearby. After the unscheduled break, Captain Jack Robertson got up, brushed himself off and hit the second ball he faced for six. Now that's what you call a calm temperament.

The famous Father Time clock did take a battering though when a cable of a barrage balloon knocked it off onto the balcony seats below – it spent the rest of the war stored in the Committee Room.

It was very fortunate that Lord's didn't sustain worse damage really. The synagogue just across the road suffered a direct hit – the club helped out after that by hosting Sabbath services in the pavilion instead.

Ducat's demise

Approximately 300 county cricketers went to war, and another 150-odd served in other essential war work or civil defence. Cricket writer Jim Swanton estimated that 60 first-class cricketers 'from England and the Dominions' died in active service in World War

Two, and another 200-plus people who played minor counties cricket or were noted schoolboy and club players also perished.

Former players also died during World War Two, notably and, in most unusual circumstances, the former double international cricketer and footballer Andrew Ducat. Born in Brixton, Ducat had been a top batsman for Surrey (making 52 centuries) and played one Test, against Australia at Headingley in 1921. A strange thing happened to him in his first Test innings there, because he was out in two different ways in one ball when a delivery from Ted McDonald broke his bat and the splinter knocked off a bail while the ball carried to slip where he was caught. It went down in the scorebook as caught behind, but he could have been hit wicket too.

Ducat had also played six times for England at football, and captained Aston Villa to FA Cup final glory in 1919/20.

He died from an apparent heart attack while batting in a wartime match for Surrey Home Guard against Sussex Home Guard at Lord's in July 1942. Twenty-nine not out, he patted the ball to mid-on, but by the time the bowler was preparing to bowl the next delivery, Ducat had pitched forward and fallen. He was only 56 years old, but he'd achieved so much in his life and died playing the game he loved (well, one of two games he loved) at the Home of Cricket.

'We must try to win, even if we lose'

Buried in the British War Cemetery in Bayeux, Normandy, is Major Maurice Turnbull, killed during the Allied invasion in 1944 that finally led to the defeat of Nazi Germany. I was amazed to learn of his story and can see why he is considered one of Wales' greatest ever all-round sportsmen.

A Cambridge Blue, Turnbull captained Glamorgan and played Test cricket for England (he became an England selector in the late Thirties, too), and he also represented Wales at rugby, hockey and, later, squash.

Glamorgan had only been accepted into first-class cricket in 1921 and until Mo came along, they struggled to win a match – they only won 26 out of 216 matches through the 1920s. Turnbull was an inspiring skipper and he turned the ramshackle bunch of amateurs and journeyman pros he inherited into a much more competitive force. An optimist even when things were going horribly wrong, Turnbull would urge his players on, saying, 'Get on with it! We must try to win, even if we lose.'

He got the best out of players such as an all-rounder called Emrys Davies. The club wanted to release Davies a few times, but Turnbull believed in his potential and persuaded them not to. His faith was rewarded in 1937 when Davies did the double of 100 wickets and 1,000 runs in a season.

He led by both encouragement and example, because he was an excellent attacking batsman and had the sharp reflexes and bravery to take the catches (and hits) fielding at short leg. He batted with a lot more flair than was usual in those days and wasn't afraid to attempt unorthodox shots. His defence was a bit too loose to be a consistent scorer at Test level, but he was always fun to watch and he managed to score 17,000 runs in first-class cricket. His

CRICKETING BROTHERS-IN-ARMS

greatest innings was in 1932 facing Nottinghamshire's Harold Larwood and Bill Voce, who were experimenting with the 'Bodyline' bowling which would have the Aussies cowering a year later. Turnbull was totally unfazed, smashing a double-century, and forcing the fiery Larwood to give up bowling Bodyline, shift his line away from leg stump and pitch the ball up.

Facing missiles from Larwood was no biggie for Turnbull, who in the winter months was a tough scrum-half for Cardiff and Wales and, according to a team-mate, 'would fall on the ball even if it was in front of a steamroller'. A few months after that double-century, he was part of the Welsh side that won against England at Twickenham for the first time in the country's history.

Turnbull's influence at Glamorgan went far beyond just playing cricket. The club was really struggling financially in the 1930s and Turnbull, who had a sharp business brain, took it upon himself to organise fundraising events all over South Wales to keep it afloat. He even turned down an MCC tour to India and the chance to win more Test caps in 1933 so he could spend the time instead trying to improve Glamorgan's balance sheet.

Soon after World War Two broke out, Turnbull enlisted with the Welsh Guards. Playing a bit of cricket for the Welsh Guards and the army (in 1942, for instance, he captained the army against an RAF team led by Bill Edrich) gave him a little break from his military training which intensified as the war rumbled on.

He was also invited to join the army cricket committee and helped draw up fixture lists for Service teams. In 1943, the MCC also called upon him to sit on a select committee and he contributed to a big report published in spring 1944 on the future of county cricket. Turnbull had hated the negative style of cricket played by some counties before the war, and he must have had a say in one of the committee's recommendations that 'teams should aim for victory from the first ball of a match, and maintain an enterprising attitude towards the game until the last over is bowled'.

Any thoughts of cricket's future had to be put aside though, because there was still a war to be won, and following the D-Day landings on 6 June, Turnbull and the Welsh Guards advanced through the Normandy countryside under heavy German mortar fire, liberating several villages from the Nazis.

He saw many of his colleagues killed and as 'Operation Goodwood' dragged on, his letters home to his wife showed that he was almost resigned to the same fate. Typically, though, he continued to lead fearlessly from the front. On 5 August 1944, he and another officer led a group looking to ambush an advancing column of German Panzer tanks and foot-soldiers, only to be ambushed themselves as they were about to attack the lead tank. Turnbull was killed instantly by machine-gun fire. A tragic loss for his wife and three children, and his many friends and colleagues, as well as a huge loss to the sporting world.

In 1948, Glamorgan won the county championship for the first time in their history. Maurice Turnbull sadly was not alive to witness the achievement, but everyone at the club knew that without his play on the field and work off it to support the club through tough times in the Thirties, it would never have been possible.

The strongman

Turnbull had played his last Test match back in 1936. Of those playing regularly for England when World War Two began, two big names sadly didn't make it through the years of conflict: Ken Farnes and Hedley Verity.

Farnes was a Leytonstone boy and, on leaving school, he became a bank clerk to earn a living, but he dreamt of becoming a top cricketer and after seeing the touring Australian side play live at the County Ground in Leyton in 1930, he was inspired to go for it.

Before that summer was out, Farnes had made his debut for Essex, and went on to help the team become one of the best to watch through the 1930s. Meanwhile, he also earned a degree from Cambridge in history and geography, which led him to a job as a schoolmaster at Worksop College in Nottinghamshire.

Even though he was a part-time cricketer, he was soon regarded as one of the fastest and most dangerous bowlers in the world on his day. People who played against him say he wasn't as rapid as Harold Larwood, but he wasn't far behind, which was all the more remarkable considering that he played relatively little cricket.

His high-arm bowling action and strength meant he could go from the classroom one day to tickling batsmen's ribs the next off a relatively short 11 or 12-pace run-up. Standing six-foot tall, Farnes was a bodybuilding fitness fanatic with a muscular 15-stone physique. According to team-mates, he had a trick whereby he could make a stomach muscle stick out 'like a lamppost' – sounds like a hernia to me, but I'll take their word for it.

His niece remembered how, when she was five years old, Uncle Ken would carry her up the stairs at bedtime. Not by giving her a piggy-back or something like that. No, he would get her to grab his little finger, lift her up and carry her upstairs as she held on. That is one strong pinky he had there.

For all his strength, Farnes was not an aggressive player. Unlike Larwood, he wasn't one for intimidating bowling, preferring to bowl tightly and to a plan. Sometimes, his team-mates needed to gee him up a bit, like the time one went up to Ken and told him, 'Do you know what the batsman said to me just now?'

'No.'

'He said, "I thought Mr Farnes was meant to be a fast bowler, not a twiddly merchant."'

Ken duly upped the revs and sent his next two deliveries whistling past the batsman's chest. The third ball clean bowled him, much to the relief of the batsman, who, of course, had said nothing about Ken's bowling in the first place.

After working in a bank, which he had hated, playing cricket was a dream for Farnes and he never lost that sense of enjoyment and feeling lucky to do what he did. One of the last great gentlemen amateurs, he worked for a living and played cricket for fun whenever he could get the time off. Even though he only played 168 first-class games over ten years – and he would have played a lot fewer but for an understanding headmaster – he had taken getting on for 700 first-class wickets and was in his prime when the war got in the way of his career.

In his first Test against the Aussies in 1934, he had taken ten wickets, and it was only injuries and his teaching job that limited his England appearances to 15. Farnes was England's main strike bowler, seen as the nearest we had to Australia's Ray Lindwall and Keith Miller. He wrote newspaper columns and cricket fans collected cigarette cards with his picture on, and he really was a household name in this country.

Off the pitch, Farnes was a sleepy, laid-back sort of bloke, although he liked a sports car and drove his little MG so fast, few of his team-mates dared to get a lift with him. You were more likely to see a beautiful woman in the passenger seat – modest, quite shy, but good-looking and with a sense of humour, Ken never had to try hard to attract the ladies. It was only when he became a soldier that he fell in love, though. That was when he met Catherine Franklin in the Services canteen in Torquay on 16 December 1940. She was married with a daughter, but her marriage was breaking up by the time they met and it was love at first sight.

Farnes wasn't required to serve in the war because he was in his late twenties by 1939, but he wanted to do his bit and fancied being a fighter pilot. Unfortunately, he couldn't squeeze his big frame into the cockpit, so he went to Canada to train as a night flyer of bombers instead. He wanted to be a flyer, because he said he couldn't be the person who pressed the button that dropped bombs on people thousands feet below.

He earned his qualification and came home a fully fledged pilot officer in the RAF Volunteer Reserve, then volunteered for night-bomber flying training.

Tragically, on his first unsupervised night-training flight, he crash-landed in a village, dying on impact, and his co-pilot died later. Incredibly, none of the villagers were killed in the accident, because he managed to avoid most of the houses. Before the flight, he'd sent a telegram asking Catherine to meet him at the airfield, but sadly he never made it.

An interesting footnote to the story of brave Ken Farnes is that Catherine's daughter ended up marrying Barry Norman, the famous film critic who had his own TV show on the BBC for years. Apparently, Catherine was a great cricket-lover like Barry, so she used to love sitting watching the Tests with him, with the TV commentary turned down and the radio commentary on (just how it should be!).

Hedley the hero

On the morning of Friday, 1 September 1939, two of the three county matches in progress had been called off as it became clear that World War Two was almost certain to begin. However, down at Hove, a game featuring my next Hall of Famer, Hedley Verity, continued after British Prime Minister Neville Chamberlain pledged our support for the Poles against the Nazis.

Yorkshireman Verity was a slow left-armer who learnt his trade from another great Yorkshire and England left-arm spinner, Wilfred Rhodes. He practised by pinning a piece of newspaper to the ground and trying to pitch the ball on it, gradually tearing the paper smaller and smaller to test his accuracy. Verity felt the best length for a spinner was 'the shortest you can bowl and still get the batsman playing forward' and he was capable of plonking the ball on that length time after time.

A lefty like me, unlike me Hedley used to appeal so quietly only the umpire and batsman at the non-striker's end could hear him. And he was generally an everything-in-moderation sort – a pint or glass of wine at the close of play, and the odd cigarette at the tea interval or end of the day. But he didn't have to make a lot of noise, because his bowling did the talking for him.

He took all ten Warwickshire wickets in a single innings for 36 runs in 1931. However, those figures were rather expensive in comparison to what he achieved the following season when he took 10 for 10 off 19.4 overs against Nottinghamshire at Heading-ley, statistically the greatest ever bowling display in the history of first-class cricket.

Verity bowled seven successive maidens before lunch, and as the sun dried the pitch afterwards, he picked up his first wicket in his tenth over having conceded two runs. All his ten wickets came in just 52 balls, including a hat-trick maiden and the last four Notts wickets in six deliveries. Tidy bowling.

He showed he could be equally lethal at Test level in 1934, when he took 15 for 104 (14 of those wickets in one day) to decimate the Aussies at Lord's.

Verity was part of a great Yorkshire team that had already won their seventh county championship of the decade with games to spare when war was declared (he'd topped the English bowling averages for the fifth time in ten seasons). They were playing

Sussex, and had lost the last seven wickets of their first innings cheaply that morning.

The match, which was part of Brighton and Hove Cricket Week, had been played in a very strange atmosphere all the way through. In the car park, people were gathering round wireless radios to try and get the latest news, but also everyone was keen to enjoy themselves, knowing that it might be their last chance for a long time.

On the Friday, the Yorkshire committee wired their skipper, Brian Sellers, suggesting the game should be called off, but as it was also a benefit game for Sussex player Jim Parks, Sellers said his team would like to finish the match. Everyone agreed and that decision gave Verity one last chance to wow cricket fans.

On a blazing hot day and on a wicket that was deteriorating rapidly, Verity took seven wickets for nine runs in 48 balls as Sussex were skittled out for just 33, setting up Yorkshire for a nine-wicket victory. 'I wonder if I shall ever bowl here again,' wondered Verity afterwards. Sadly he never would, but his skills and heroism as a cricketer would be mirrored on the battlefield.

Verity had told his team-mate and close friend Bill Bowes back in 1937 that another World War was coming and predicted that this time it would last six years. He was so sure that, in 1938, he had invited Colonel Arnold Shaw, who he knew from a tour of India a few years before, to the Headingley pavilion to ask his advice. Shaw had given Hedley military textbooks to study and told him to get in touch when war broke out.

'This is no chuffing garden party,' Hedley had told his sister.

'This fellow Hitler means it, if we don't stop him. We have got to stop him.'

And when the time came, he called Shaw and joined the Green Howards at the regimental depot in Richmond, North Yorkshire. Other top Yorkshire cricketers like county captain Norman Yardley, Len Hutton, Herbert Sutcliffe and Maurice Leyland served there too, meaning they could field a more than useful team. 'I reckon we can put out a team from this depot to beat any county side in England,' claimed Verity, before remembering his roots and back-tracking: 'Except Yorkshire, of course!'

That may have been a slight exaggeration, but with Verity bowling, the Green Howards' cricket team were pretty much unbeatable in wartime matches. 'If a side that contained Hedley in it got 60 runs, the match was won,' remembered one fellow soldier.

Hedley impressed with his ability to apply his cricket tactical brain to military manoeuvres. For a top spinner, though, he was surprisingly poor at jobs requiring nimble fingers like stripping down a gun – 'To watch him,' joked Colonel Shaw, 'one would think he had two right hands, mainly consisting of thumbs.'

Verity reached the rank of captain and served in Ireland, India, Persia, Egypt, Syria and, fatefully, in Sicily. He played what would be his last cricket match in Syria – for the Green Howards against the King's Own Yorkshire Light Infantry – and did his usual busi-ness, taking a match-winning six wickets for 37 runs. Shaw had planned to post Hedley at headquarters staff after the Sicily cam-paign. Verity could easily have taken a back seat before then, as he suffered from various ailments like dysentery, which had laid him low in India, but he always insisted on joining the frontline troops.

On 20 July 1943, Captain Verity died after leading his troops in battle against the Hermann Göring Division on the fields of Catania in Sicily. Brave to the end, after being shot in the chest he shouted to his men, 'Keep going – get them out of the farmhouse and get me into it.'

Private Tom Rennoldson, who had often cleaned Hedley's cricket kit ready for wartime games, stayed with him all night while the enemy set alight the cornfields all around.

The next day, they were both picked up by the Germans and taken to a field hospital, where Verity underwent emergency surgery. As the surgeons were preparing to operate, a grenade fell out of his pocket and Rennoldson had to quickly make it safe.

Verity was handed over to the Italians – after an agonising journey by sea and goods train, he was given another operation in Caserta to remove part of a rib pressing on his lung, but he died three days later. He was buried in Caserta with full military honours, his coffin covered in the Union flag.

Tragic to think that if he could have just made it through Sicily, he could have been playing cricket for Yorkshire again after the war, and he was greatly missed by his team-mates. Norman Yardley said, 'We missed him as a bowler, as a tutor to our younger men, but most of all – just as a friend.'

Opponents had just as much respect for him too. Sir Don Bradman, who Hedley had dismissed twice in a day during that incredible day at Lord's in 1934, later wrote, 'Hedley Verity was not only a very great England – Yorkshire cricketer, he was also a gallant soldier and a chivalrous gentleman . . . it is well to record that his opponents no less than his colleagues valued his friendship and manly virtues. Australia mourned his loss and deeply regretted the passing of a great son of the Empire.'

My Hall of Fame isn't good enough for Verity, the other men highlighted here and all the other cricketers who served their country in the two World Wars. Thank God for their bravery.

Gone today, hair tomorrow

A couple of years back, a company got in touch to ask if I fancied having a hair transplant. Last time I'd looked, I wasn't as bald as a cueball; I didn't even have a penalty spot. However, I had noticed I was receding a bit round the edges at the front and I wasn't ready to assume the Ray Reardon/Count Dracula look any time soon, so I decided to find out more.

I went along to their clinic in Marylebone and they talked me through the process. It sounded quite simple – they just grab one in every five follicles from round the back of your head, which you don't miss, then they plonk them in wherever you are bit short of cover. It's like replanting a tree – picking it up, put it somewhere else, then just leave it and it grows. Six months later, once the hair's grown out, you can just go to the barbers and get it cut as normal.

If you don't have enough hair on your head, they have to take it from somewhere else. I met a fella who'd had his taken from his chest, and it looked a bit curly. If you don't have any chest hair, I guess they just have to look further south where the hair only gets more frizzy . . .

Anyhow, I didn't have to worry about that, so I signed up for it.

I went along to my appointment with a few movies loaded up on my iPad to watch while the hair surgeons fiddled with my follicles. First, they give you a load of injections to numb your scalp, which is a bit painful, but once the injections take effect it feels like you are wearing a motorbike helmet. Quite a weird sensation, but five hours later my hair had been successfully repositioned.

Not sure what it is about cricketers and ex-cricketers, but quite a few of us seem to have opted for hair renovation. Here's a very useful Tuffers HoF team of fellow transplantees . . .

Gautam Gambhir and Virender Sehwag

Up top, these two are great mates and formed a terrific opening partnership for India. Sehwag reckoned Gambhir was 'the best India Test opener since Sunil Gavaskar', and Gambhir said that Sehwag was 'the best on-field partner I have ever had'. The savage-hitting Sehwag was the first Indian ever to score a Test triple-century and together the pair averaged over 50 in 87 Test innings together.

The pressure of batting at the top of the order came at a cost for both of them according to Gambhir. 'You lose a lot of hair — especially when you are an opening batsman!' he said once. 'Like Sehwag, I'm losing my hair left, right and centre.'

They've both had a little restoration work done since, so welcome to the team, boys.

Graham Gooch

One of the first ex-cricketers to get a hair upgrade, Goochy was one of the best batsmen I ever played with. Including first-class and List A games, he scored over 65,000 runs in his career, a good 30 times more runs than I scored.

He was a totally dedicated pro and as England captain, he led by example. The problem was that he had blokes like Ian Botham, David Gower and myself in the England team who didn't always want to do it his way. Goochy probably deserves a place in my Hall of Fame just for putting up with us lot.

There's a chapter called 'The Individualist' in his book *Captaincy*, where he talks about the problems involved in dealing with Beefy, Gower and me. Published in 1992, it was written not long after my debut Test series in Australia, so I must have made a big impression on him to earn myself a mention alongside those two legends. A big impression, yes, but not necessarily a good one, and he did suggest that there was room for improvement in my all-round game.

Selected highlights include Goochy's observation that fans 'like seeing someone playing for England who's about as bad as a club cricketer' at fielding and that I appeared to be 'scared of the hard ball'. My attitude in Australia 'wasn't good enough', my general cricket awareness was 'poor', I 'mistook notoriety for celebrity status' and had 'a very short fuse' when decisions didn't go my way. Other than that, I was doing brilliantly!

On the plus side, he did also say that I was 'a high quality spin bowler' with a bright future ahead and that players like me were worth the trouble. Cheers, Graham – I hope I did improve a bit after that.

Michael Vaughan

I owe Vaughanie one actually, because he once selected me in his 'Greatest Touring XI' – I'm not sure that was purely for my cricketing ability, though.

I was in the England squad on his first England tour, in South Africa in 1999, and he claims that he never saw me eat anything other than peanuts and crisps the whole time we were there. Well, that was the easiest food to get at the bar. It was another five years before he saw me eat proper food; a sandwich in the green room before an episode of *A Question of Sport*.

A top-class batsman in his day and one of the best England captains ever, I won't say much more as I've already bigged him up enough for his role in the 2005 Ashes triumph, but I think Vaughanie might be a good man to lead this team.

Jacques Kallis

I played with Jacques for Middlesex for a couple of years back in the late Nineties. I remember the coach, Don Bennett, saying to him then, 'If you put your mind to it, you could be one of the best all-rounders in the world.' Don was a good judge.

Jacques did even better, going on to become the greatest all-rounder South Africa has ever produced, and his statistics put him right up there with Garry Sobers as one of the greatest all-rounders of all time. He scored over 13,000 Test runs, averaging 55, and 11,000-plus ODI runs, and took well over 250 wickets in both Tests and ODIs. To top it all off, he was an amazing slip fielder as well, pouching 200 Test catches.

Jacques wasn't an extravagant, extrovert player like a Garry Sobers or Ian Botham, just quietly brilliant. When I played for England against him early in his career, we actually always fancied we could get him out run out early on in his innings because he seemed to be in a world of his own, but once he got himself in he was very hard to shift.

He never said much; it was like he was in his own bubble, and there was absolutely no point in sledging him. He showed what a cool customer he was when he got his first Test century in front of 100,000 people at the MCG in his seventh Test match in 1997. Aussie bowler Michael Kasprowicz was being rather vocal and Jacques just ignored it. After serving up another bouncer and word of advice without any effect, Kasprowicz turned to his team-mates and said, 'Is this man ****ing deaf?'

Jacques batted through almost all of the final day to grab an unlikely draw for South Africa, and that ability to not be side-tracked has been key to his success. You just can't pop his bubble.

'I've never believed that words get you out,' he said. 'It's the leather ball that gets you out. I've worked at being mentally strong . . . what they say can't take my focus off the next delivery.'

As a bowler, he wasn't pulling up trees early in his international career (he only took 13 wickets in his first 14 Tests, at 40 runs per wicket). Then, in Cape Town during South Africa's 1998/99 home series against West Indies, he became only the eighth player in history to score a century and a half-century and take five wickets in an innings in a Test match. By the end of that series, his bowling average was down to around 27 and it was clear he was a proper all-rounder.

He took a while to get going as a batsman too – after 20 Tests his batting average was a shade under 32. At first he was seen as a steady batsman, but part of that was down to him being a responsible, team player. 'For years I tried to bat through an innings. The side expected to bat around me. Then, when our batting line-up became stronger, I had the opportunity to be more aggressive, especially in Test cricket.'

Even as he became more attacking in his approach, he maintained the correctness of his technique. 'My dad had a philosophy he instilled in me: if you're behind the ball, you can control the ball. So I always try to get behind the ball,' he said.

The great Aussie bowling attacks that played under Steve Waugh could usually come up with a plan to get even the best batsmen out, but Waugh said they examined Kallis and couldn't find a weakness in his armoury.

Bulletproof on the pitch, Jacques has also had a pretty spectacular renovation job done on his barnet, so he can join the team.

Sourav Ganguly

Born into a rich and sports-loving family, to parents who nicknamed him 'Maharaj' because they believed he was born to be a
leader, sure enough, Ganguly grew up to captain his country and
did a very good job. He led India to the 2003 World Cup final, and
helped them improve their Test ranking from eighth to second. His
record of 21 wins from 49 matches made him India's most successful Test skipper to date, and he managed to change the
perception of India as an easy touch away from home and got
them winning matches on tour.

   As a batsman, he averaged 40-plus in Tests and ODIs and Geoff
Boycott said he'd never seen a better timer of the ball than him.

   Sourav could rub people up the wrong way, though. When he
spent a season with Lancashire in 2000, he was known as 'Lord
Snooty' by his team-mates, who thought he was arrogant. Mike
Atherton tells a story about how he was batting with him on a
warm day and Ganguly took off his jumper between overs, handed
it to Athers, and asked him to run it off back to the pavilion for
him. Athers, bear in mind, was a former England captain and actually trying to bat too at the time. Cheeky.

   Then there was that time at Lord's in 2002, when he took his shirt
off and twirled it above his head like a loon on the players' balcony
to celebrate victory over England in the final of an ODI tri-series (Sri
Lanka were the other team). He was getting his own back at his old
Lancashire colleague Freddie Flintoff, who'd done the same on the
pitch earlier that year after clinching a dramatic win in Mumbai to

square a six-match one-day series. Freddie had apologised for his 'ten seconds of madness', but Sourav obviously hadn't forgotten what he did. He got criticism back home in India for his own shirt-waving incident, but it showed his spiky, competitive streak.

Sourav also had a big rivalry with Nasser Hussain, another person who wouldn't back down from a confrontation, when Nass was England skipper. The story goes that at an official India team photoshoot, Sourav was the only player who kept his cap on, and the photographer was desperately trying to get him to take it off.

'Nasser Hussain would never allow himself to be photographed without a hat on,' Ganguly told him.

'That's because he's going bald, but you've got a lovely head of hair,' replied the photographer (or words to that effect).

'Yes, that's true,' agreed Ganguly and, finally, took off his cap, swept back his mane of hair and posed with his head uncovered.

Sourav did have to call the hair surgeons in eventually, so this talented player is eligible for selection. If he wasn't captain himself, it sounds like he might be a handful to man-manage. No worries – I'd leave that to Vaughanie to sort out.

Martin Crowe

The world of cricket suffered a huge loss when Martin Crowe, one of the greatest-ever New Zealand cricketers, passed away, aged just 53, in 2016 after a three-and-a-half-year battle against cancer. He was a wonderful, elegant batsman who set new national records for runs scored in Test matches and ODIs, scored the most

Test centuries (17) and the highest Test score of 299 against Sri Lanka in Wellington in 1991.

Crowe saw the funny side when he was interviewed by a journalist in 2013 and was asked about the effect of chemotherapy on someone who'd had a hair transplant. 'As a fellow desert head, I feel I can ask you this, Martin,' said the interviewer. 'How do you lose your hair from chemo when, well, it wasn't your hair to begin with?'

Crowe smiled and explained that he'd had to shave off the transplanted hair otherwise he'd have had that and nothing else.

An obsessive perfectionist in his cricket career, Crowe said that, ironically, his cancer diagnosis helped him to get perspective on what his life should be about. 'I've probably never been happier,' he said in his last years. Good to hear.

He was a fabulous cricketer and a must for my Hall of Fame.

Greg Matthews

An extroverted hyperactive showman from the Australia teams of the 1980s and early Nineties, Greg would be a lively addition to the team. He bowled right-arm off-spin, batted left-handed and was a fine fielder who absolutely loved playing cricket. He hated running in training, but would chase every ball on the field and sprint for every extra run.

'I love running out there, I don't care if it's 200 degrees,' he said. 'Some of the guys say on hot days, "I wish I was at the beach." I would not be there for quids. No way. I would not swap this for anything . . . Cricket is more than a game for me.'

He never expected to make it to Test level, so he was just grateful for every minute. If he got a wicket, he'd celebrate it properly, not try and play it cool. If he was happy he'd show it, and that enthusiasm rubbed off on his team-mates and fans.

He loved his music and would dance and sing on the field to relax in the heat of the action. One time he was batting for New South Wales against Pakistan at the Sydney Cricket Ground, while, next door at the Sydney Sports Ground, Davie Bowie was doing a sound-check. Greg strummed along to the music on his bat between balls on the way to scoring 80.

He enjoyed himself off the pitch, too. On his first tour of the West Indies he didn't get to play much, but that just meant more time for Greg to interact with the fans and locals. At matches, rather than stay in the pavilion, he'd go and sit in the stand with the locals and have a few drinks – when the Aussies played at Guyana, the spectators around him in the Southern Stand renamed it 'The Greg Matthews Stand' he spent so much time there. Then at night, he'd be seeking out the best clubs and dive bars, and the locals loved him as he was always up for chatting, singing and 'throwing a reggae hip'.

Every team needs a social secretary, and sounds like Greg would be the man. (And he was my first Test victim.)

Doug 'The Rug' Bollinger

Doug might not be quite on the level of some of the other players in this team, but with a nickname like that he has to be included. A left arm fast-medium swing bowler, Doug was playing park cricket in Sydney until his mid-twenties, so he did really well to get to Test level and take 50 wickets in his couple of years (2009–10) playing for Australia.

Back in 2008, balding Doug was preparing to get married and had earned himself a lucrative Cricket Australia contract after taking a load of wickets for New South Wales. He celebrated, as you do, by getting himself some new hair, freshly imported from Russia.

Doug had 'non-surgical skin grafts' (or 'the squirrel' to use the technical term) whereby they stick a false scalp with hair on top of your balding bonce. It's a like a sort of permanent toupée.

'I used to be called the "Bald Eagle"; now they will call me the "Hairy Eagle",' he declared.

Well, no. They called him 'Doug The Rug'.

He had the work done by the same company who'd previously sorted out Goochy, Shane Warne, Martin Crowe and Greg Matthews. Greg Matthews was delighted for his fellow Aussie, saying: 'Doug was broke and bald when he met Tegan [his fiancée]. Now he's got hair and cash and an Australian contract.'

Happy days.

Nothing escapes the all-seeing eye of DRS technology, though, and after taking a wicket for Australia, hotspot not only highlighted the nick from the batsman's bat, but also shone through his rug to reveal Doug's true Willie Thorne-ish hairline to the watching millions.

At the time of writing, I have heard reports that Doug has gone rug-free, opting for a shaven head and a bushy beard instead, so, sadly, that could jeopardise his place in the Hall of Fame.

Darren Gough

A confident, wholehearted performer and a top-class international strike bowler, The Dazzler is the sort of character you'd want in any cricket team. He was also known as 'Rhino' in his playing days. Why? 'Because I'm strong as an ox,' according to Darren. Hmm.

Chest puffed out with pride to wear the England jersey, and charging in to bowl, he was an inspiring presence for both team-mates and fans. Not the tallest for a fast bowler, he bowled skiddy, fuller-length deliveries and developed lots of variations. He was the first English bowler to master reverse swing, and his late inswinging yorker and changes of pace earned him a load of wickets. He ended up with well over 200 wickets in both Test and ODIs, and he would have had more in Tests if injuries hadn't caused him to retire early from playing the longer format.

When Goughie scored 65 on his England Test debut in 1994, he got lumbered with the 'new Botham' tag, but although he could give it a bit of welly, he soon proved he wasn't quite Beefy-class with the bat and could concentrate on his bowling.

Darren actually had the pleasure of rooming with me on his first Ashes tour in 1994/95. That was the tour when I was infamously admitted to a psychiatric hospital before discharging myself. He remembers me coming in one night and kicking and punching the telly. What can I say, Goughie? I'm not a fan of *Prisoner Cell Block H*.

Unlike me, Darren didn't wait until he retired to take part in *Strictly Come Dancing*, having the winter off from international cricket in 2005 and slipping into something more sequinned.

Turned out the Barnsley boy was a dazzler on the dancefloor too and became not just the first cricketer but the first man ever to win *Strictly*.

Shane Warne

Completing the line-up is a good friend of Goughie's – Shane Warne, a legend of the game (and poster boy for hair transplants).

After Warne's first innings of bowling in Test cricket, against India back in January 1992 (he took one for 150 from 45 overs), the ex-Aussie leg-spinner and pundit Kerry O'Keeffe hadn't been impressed. 'Overweight, slightly round-arm, no variation, can't bowl,' he concluded.

Warney must have improved quickly. Just 18 months later, he bowled the Ball of the Century at Old Trafford, a delivery that turned the width of Gatt. To do that with his first ball in Test cricket on English soil and dismiss Mike Gatting, a notorious murderer of spin bowlers, was a statement and a half. That basically ruined my life and the lives of most other Test spinners around the world. How are you supposed to compete with that? And no one (apart from Murali Muralitharan) could for the next decade and a half.

In an age of fast bowlers backed up by the odd off-spinner, leg-spin was a dying art, and he not only revived it but made it the most entertaining type of bowling to watch – when he was bowling it. Every ball had a sense of theatre with Warney. You always felt something might happen at any time, even on pitches that shouldn't help a spinner. Good batsmen could read what he was going to bowl, but he was so good that even if they picked the delivery he still could get them out.

I don't think anyone in the history of the game has spun the ball more than Shane at his peak — he gave the ball a massive rip. Apparently, one of the reasons he built up the strength to do that was because he broke both his legs in a childhood accident and had to heave himself around in a wheelchair for about a year.

As a schoolboy, he mixed up bowling medium pace with leg-breaks, but although he was a good cricketer he wasn't breaking records from day one. He played cricket because his mates did, rather than because he was obsessed with the game. But a Test selector saw him bowling in the nets for district club St Kilda, spotted his ability to spin the ball sideways and invited him to the Australia Institute of Sport in April 1990.

A bit older than the other lads at the institute, and more rebellious, Warney was not exactly living like an athlete. He was on the verge of getting chucked out, and it took a bit of advice from ex-Aussie leggie Terry Jenner to get him on track. Jenner hadn't fulfilled his potential as a player, had just done 18 months in prison for embezzlement, and he didn't want to see Warney wasting his talent. 'You're fat, drink way too much beer and smoke like a chimney and have never had to sacrifice anything,' Jenner told him.

Jenner himself was pulling on a big cigar and holding a beer at the time, but Warney got the message, took it on board and shaped up.

Not that Warney ever became too much of a fitness freak. In later years, he didn't get on with the very successful Australia coach John Buchanan and was not a happy bunny when Buchanan took the squad for a boot camp in 2006. Warney told Buchanan he'd learnt three things from the trip: 'I'm fat, I'm a weak prick, and I want to go home.'

Australia did proceed to smash England up 5–0 Down Under to regain the Ashes, so who is to say Buchanan's approach wasn't right, but I share Shane's lack of enthusiasm for boot camps.

He might not have been an all-round athlete, but he knew what he was doing with a ball in his hand. He was incredibly accurate by any standards, let alone for a leggie, but he reckoned he didn't aim to land the ball on a sixpence. Instead he focused more on trying to guess what shots the batsman might play and then aim to flight and fizz a suitable delivery down to bamboozle them. 'He gives you the impression that he has already bowled the over to you in his head long before the first delivery comes down,' said Andrew Strauss.

Aussie stumper Ian Healy, who said 'Bowled, Warnie' about a million times while keeping to Warne for seven years, admired his ability to quickly change to a new plan if what he was doing wasn't working: 'It took other leg-spinners time to shift their line from leg to off, but he could do it immediately and accurately.'

Bowling over 6,500 Test match overs in his career, and major surgery on his hand and shoulder, meant he had to cut down on some of his variations by the back end of his career, but by then he had the experience to get people out in other ways. He never particularly liked bowling the googly, but he developed the slider that went straight or almost straight and which put less strain on his body than a googly or his flipper. By varying the revs he put on the ball, tweaking the flight, building up pressure on the bastmen with nagging accuracy (and plenty of sledging), he could still take wickets galore. And he could always summon up a match-turning ripper, like the hand grenade to bowl Kevin Pietersen behind his legs at Adelaide in 2006, in his last Test series.

He finished with a career total of 1,001 wickets in Test and ODIs. Not bad for a fat round-armer who couldn't bowl.

So that's my XI. Plenty of superstar quality, even if we are rather heavy on opening batsmen and somewhat light in the pace-bowling department ... oh, and lacking a wicket-keeper. Maybe England Ashes hero Matt Prior will get himself a rug in retirement and help us out?

PUSHING THE BOUNDARIES: INNOVATORS, RULE-BENDERS, GAME-CHANGERS AND LOOPHOLE MERCHANTS

9

The inventive Mr Felix

One of the great cricket innovators in nineteenth-century cricket was a fella called Nicholas Wanostrocht . . . or Nicholas Felix . . . or just 'Felix'. Felix was a kind of stage name that he insisted people used to refer to him in cricket circles. Some say he did so because English people struggled to pronounce his real surname properly (he had Belgian roots). A more likely reason was that he was the headmaster of a school in Camberwell Green, a job he'd taken on at the age of just 19 after his dad, who'd previously run the school, died.

The parents of kids at his school might not have been too pleased to see its headmaster associated with cricket because in the 1820s, when Felix started playing, the game was thought of as quite seedy, with loads of gambling and corruption. So 'N Felix' was the name that always appeared in the scorebook.

Buying and selling of cricket matches was rife at the time, but

Felix was just in it for the love of the game, and never got involved in dodgy gambling shenanigans. As Felix put it, for him cricket was 'a mistress whom he loved, not wisely, but too well' and he became one of the best batsmen and most popular players over the next twenty-odd years.

Apparently, he liked a laugh and played cricket with a smile on his face, and his enthusiasm for the game rubbed off on others. He was very competitive and wholehearted, but also sporting and a good team man – keen to see others do well as much as doing well himself.

As a batsman, he became known for his brutal slashing square cut off the front foot. Whereas others played the cut mostly with the wrists, Felix put his shoulder into it. This was particularly handy against the new round arm style of bowling that was coming in at the time, which meant plenty of short wide-ish balls to tonk around.

Described as 'monkey-built and long-armed' Felix was also a fine fielder at point – in a Kent v England game at Canterbury in 1847, he took seven catches fielding there, which is good going, especially as he was forty-something by then.

I think I would have enjoyed going to Felix's school, because apparently he was often more concerned with getting a game of cricket going for the kids than academic lessons. Felix himself was a specialist left-handed batsman on the pitch, and a multi-skilled all-rounder off it. Schoolmaster, president of the All England XI, French scholar, writer, speaker, ventriloquist, burlesque dancer (wahey, a good bloke to have with you on tour!), amateur artist and inventor . . . he was a busy chap, indeed.

Felix really was a very talented artist. Like an olden-day Jack Russell, he liked to sketch the cricket grounds he played at while touring the country with the All England XI, and there's a fantastic drawing he did of him together with all his England team-mates.

He combined some of his many talents to produce one of the earliest and best cricket training books, *Felix on the Bat* (1845), which he wrote and illustrated himself. The book was packed with interesting tips, such as his advice for hard-hitting batsmen to give their bats a regular rub down with bacon fat to make them last longer. And Felix recommended an Indian-rubber belt to keep your trousers up rather than wearing braces that would be 'exploded in the active exercise of hitting'. Must tell Chris Gayle next time I see him . . .

Also he advised wearing a cotton neckcloth – 'it is much better than a silk one, because silk is a non-conductor of heat, and does not absorb perspiration'. (Personally, I was always a silk neckcloth man, but that's just what my butler packed for me.)

Felix had a lovely way with words – he described a cricket bat as 'a sceptre of delight' – and never knowingly wrote a simple sentence when a very flowery one would do. For example, this is Felix writing about lbw in the book: 'Now come we to touch upon a chord of dissonance, whose shrill note shall vibrate with uneven tension clashing with the silent resignation of those who believe in passive sufferance, with the contention of those who shall dare to move the muddy waters of discontent.'

Okaaaay . . . Translation? The lbw law is quite controversial.

Felix had already made a step towards revolutionising cricket training with his invention of the first-ever mechanical bowling machine, the so-called 'Catapulta'. In the book, he traces the history of the Catapulta back to the Romans, and explains how he adapted it for cricket. Judging by his diagram of the cricket Catapulta, it was a big, clunking bit of kit which certainly looked like it could have inflicted some damage on enemies of the Roman empire. You pulled a latch which released a lever with an Indian-rubber-tipped hammer on the end that struck the ball and sent it whizzing down the wicket.

Felix claimed you could set the pace of the Catapulta so you could imitate all the leading bowlers of the day, and up to a speed so fast it would 'split your bat in two'. In practice, though, the contraption's control of line and length wasn't exactly Glenn McGrath-esque and could just as easily split a batsman's head in two if you were unlucky.

A nineteenth-century Phil Tufnell certainly wouldn't have been volunteering to face up to Felix's contraption, and if he did he'd want to be padded up like the Michelin Man. Felix had thought of that too, though, designing some of the game's first protective batting gear, including socks filled with rubber strips and tubular rubber batting gloves. (He sold the patent for his batting gloves to Robert Dark of Lord's.)

As a tailender who liked to go out to bat wearing a settee, I can only thank old Felix for being a pioneer of protective gear, and he's definitely worth a spot in the Tuffers HoF.

Dodgy cakes and daring declarations

As a crafty sort of player who liked to play on the edge myself, I've always had a sneaking regard for those who push the rules to the limit, so I'd like to highlight a few chancers who did their own thing to try to get ahead.

Some cricketers do go too far in pursuit of victory, though, and they have done since the early days of the game. For instance, the captain of the Cowell's Athletic Association team in a match against Languard Fort in 1891. Languard needed just 58 to win in their second innings and were well on the way when one of their batsmen hit the ball into a tree 'near the pitch'. The captain of Cowell's ordered one of his men to climb up the tree to get the ball and, when he reached it, appeal for a catch. The umpire gave the poor batter out and outraged Languard players refused to play on, so Cowell's were awarded the match. Very unsporting that, really. Worse was a Yorkshire League wicket-keeper called Bill Lilley, who used to stick a hairpin in his boot and subtly flick the base of the stumps to knock the bails off to claim batsmen had been bowled when they hadn't. Nice touch.

More recently, a cricket team in Australia allegedly employed unusual off-pitch tactics to gain an advantage in a match in 2004/05. Inverloch laid on a suspiciously wonderful spread of cupcakes at teatime for the players of visiting club, Nerrena. As one player, who scoffed five of the cakes, commented, 'They usually feed us crap.' Soon after, hysterical giggling broke out among many of the Nerrena players, and their batsmen struggled for up to

20 minutes to put their pads on when they had to go out to bat. After Nerrena had collapsed laughing to defeat, accusations flew around that the cakes had been laced with cannabis. I couldn't possibly condone such (alleged) skullduggery ... or let Inverloch run the Tuffers HoF café.

A Hall of Fame induction is in order for John Shuter, though. Shuter, the Surrey captain during the club's 1887 county championship-winning season, hit upon a clever idea to bend the rules and defeat the previous year's champions, Nottinghamshire. The game looked to be petering out into a draw on the third and final day, as Surrey batsmen built up a comfortable 300-odd lead in their second innings with five wickets remaining. Shuter couldn't declare and set Notts a target, because declarations hadn't been invented yet, so instead the Surrey batsmen sacrificed their wickets in spectacular style. Shuter set the ball rolling by deliberately hitting his own wicket as the ball was delivered. With no regard for their personal batting averages, team-mates followed his example, dollying up catches and wandering out of the crease to allow the wicket-keeper to stump them.

Chuckling spectators wondered what the hell they were watching, but having bought extra time to bowl, the Surrey boys got serious again in the field and rolled through the Notts batting line-up to claim an unlikely win. A couple of years later, declarations were introduced, so Shuter's tactics were game-changing in more ways than one.

Declarations certainly added a new tactical dimension to the game. When I started out as a pro, county championship matches were played over three days rather than the four they are now, so contrived declarations were the norm because we were always up against the clock. If a game was going nowhere, declaration tactics were normally discussed by the captain and senior players over fish and chips and a pint at the end of day two. Then, the next morning the two captains would come together and thrash out a 'deal'.

You need a captain who is a good negotiator/poker player and my Middlesex skipper Mike Gatting was really good. The oppo captain would come in and say, 'Right, we'll give you 55 overs to get 250 . . .'

'No, no, it can't be more than 230 . . .'

Gatt would often shave a few runs off and that could make the difference between winning and losing.

Setting the opposition a gettable-but-hopefully-just-out-reach target in their second innings and gambling on being able to bowl them out took some nerve from a captain, because if you lost, you could look a right plonker. Declaring when your team has scored no runs whatsoever in a local derby, as Middlesex captain Mike Brearley did against Surrey at Lord's in 1977, earns you a place in my Hall of Fame.

Middlesex had gone into that match in a three-way race for the county championship, a couple of points behind Kent and ten ahead of Gloucestershire. Rain washed out the first day. If there hadn't been any play at all on the second day, under the rules the game could have been converted into a one-innings match. Unfortunately for Middlesex, five overs were possible that second day, so going into the third and final day with Surrey 8 for 1, there seemed no chance of a result.

On the third morning, Wayne Daniel steamed in from the Pavilion End taking five for 16 and Mike Selvey took three for 29, and Mike Gatting nicked a couple of wickets as Middlesex bowled out Surrey for 49 in an hour and a quarter. Even then, most spectators expected Middlesex to try and bat through the rest of the day and get bonus batting points. Brearley and his men had other ideas.

John Emburey and Ian Gould were sent out to open the batting. Embers slogged at the first delivery, missed, and he and Gouldy promptly walked back to the pavilion.

Brearley had declared at 0 for 0.

Surrey's batting line-up managed to occupy the crease a bit longer second time around, partly due to Middlesex dropping five catches, but still only mustered 89 leaving Middlesex needing 139 in 27 minutes plus 20 overs to win. Brearley led from the front to score 66 not out and they won with 11 balls to spare.

The extra points from that unlikely win proved crucial come the end of the season, as Middlesex finished dead level with Kent and shared a county championship title that otherwise would have been Kent's alone.

Declarations in two-innings-a-side matches are one thing, but Brian Rose went to another level when he declared in a limited-overs one-day match in 1979. Somerset skipper Rose was captaining a powerful side including the likes of Ian Botham and Viv Richards. After three matches in the group stage they had three wins and nine points, and were three points clear of Worcestershire and

Glamorgan – so in good shape to qualify for the next phase of the competition. Their fourth match was against Worcestershire at New Road, but rain meant no play was possible on the scheduled day of the game.

The game finally got underway the next day and it had hardly started before it was over. Rose had analysed the rules of the competition and worked out that to be one of the two qualifying teams, Somerset just needed to preserve their wicket-taking rate which was better than their rivals going into the game with Worcester.

So Rose and his opening partner, Peter Denning, went out and faced just one over before declaring with a score of 1 for 0 – the run was a no-ball. Rose's original plan was to just face one ball and declare, but he was still weighing up whether to go through with the whole thing when he was out in the middle.

Worcester took ten balls to 'chase' down the target, with New Zealand international Glenn Turner scoring two singles to secure the win, 2 for 1 – it was more like a football score. The entire game had lasted 20 minutes including a ten-minute break between innings.

Rose hadn't broken any rules, and the vast majority of his team-mates had agreed to go along with his plan. He'd even rung the Test and County Cricket Board (TCCB) secretary in advance to explain what he was thinking of doing and he claimed they hadn't told him he couldn't.

Then again, the hardy hundred or so paying spectators who'd waited a day for some cricket action were not best pleased. In the end, Rose's too-clever-by-half tactics were deemed unacceptable by the cricket authorities, who chucked Somerset out of the competition for breaching the spirit of the game and declarations were outlawed.

Nice try, and Rose deserves his place at the top table of loophole merchants. Somerset showed they could actually play a bit too when they returned to B&H action, winning the competition in two of the next three years.

Diff'rent strokes and Mr 360

Nowadays, in limited-overs games, and even at certain stages of Test matches, you see all sorts of shots being played by batsmen to guide the ball between or over the fielders, in front or behind the wicket. Improvised strokeplay and calculated risk-taking are encouraged to put pressure on the bowling team. That wasn't always the way and I'd like to give props to some of the batsmen down the years who've broken the mould and created new strokes.

Back in the 1700s, batsmen would stand still, wait for the ball to come to them and try and give it a whack with no footwork. But when bowlers discovered the benefits of bowling what we call a 'good length' in the 1790s, batsmen had to do something about it. An MCC batsman called 'Silver' Billy Beldham started leaping two-footed to the pitch of the ball like he was competing in a school sports day sack race. Silver Billy's new style delighted the crowds, but needed some refinement, and a lad called 'Young' Tom Fennex from Buckinghamshire came up with the answer, keeping one foot back and stretching his front foot out to the pitch of the ball. And so front-foot driving and – Geoff Boycott's favourite – the forward defensive stroke were born.

A hundred-odd years later, strokeplay was still very limited. Fielders were usually stacked on the offside of the pitch, and it was seen as rather ungentlemanly to hit the ball on the legside. Then a couple of top Aussie batsmen, Victor Trumper and Clem Hill, realised that this was ridiculous and started hooking and pulling the ball, and captains thought they'd better stick a few fielders on the legside to try and stem the flow of runs.

Another legside innovator of that Golden Age of cricket before World War One was the Indian prince and England Test player Ranjitsinhji, whose wristy style of batting was perfectly suited to exploiting the big gaps in the field on the legside.

With the help of Dan Hayward, a local pro who coached him at Cambridge University, Ranji developed the 'leg glance' shot. As a practice drill, Hayward nailed Ranji's right boot to the crease to try to break his habit of backing away to the legside. With his back foot immovable and his front foot forward and across, Ranji found he could use the pace of the bowling to flick the ball for runs behind square.

This type of touch play, getting maximum speed on the ball with good timing and minimum effort, was a revelation to batsmen. And, as Ranji noted, 'the faster the bowler, the easier it is to make hard cuts and glances'.

So Tuffers HoF places for Trumper, Hill, Ranji and coach Hayward for helping to transform batting from an offside focus and paving the way for a more well-rounded game.

It's funny how new shots are often thought of as being rather disrespectful and even illegal. Take the reverse sweep, which Pakistan's Mushtaq Mohammad is credited with inventing. Mushtaq played it for the first time in England against Middlesex in 1964. Chasing a large target, he was struggling to score against the great off-spinner Fred Titmus. The only gap he could see was down at third man, so he attempted the reverse sweep, connected and the ball went for four. According to Mushtaq, Titmus 'went wild and pulled his hair out' and actually appealed for Mushtaq to be given out. 'You've got a ball in your hand, he has a bat. He can do whatever he wants with it,' the umpire told him.

When I started out in professional cricket a couple of decades later, you still didn't see too many people playing reverse sweeps though. If someone did try and play one against you, you saw it as an insult. The cheeky so-and-so.

The first person that I saw play the reverse sweep on a regular basis was Mike Gatting. Gatt was a brilliant all-round player of spin and could play the reverse sweep as well as anyone, but he famously got out playing it to Allan Border's first ball in the 1987 World Cup final. 'I had practised it and at the time I was keeping the momentum going,' he said later. 'Had the ball not hit my shoulder it would have gone for three or four and we would have won the World Cup.'

In Gatt's case, he had practised the shot and was confident it was the right shot at the time . . . so fair enough. But I only tried to play the reverse sweep once in my life, in a game at Derby. I don't know why I did it. Spinner Geoff Miller was bowling. I got down on one knee and had an almighty reverse hack at the ball, missed it, the ball kept low and hit me flush on the box right in front of the sticks.

'Ow, me bollocks,' I cried and keeled over in pain as Geoff appealed.

I was given out and became his last-ever victim in first-class cricket. While the other players walked off, Geoff came over, helped me up and thanked me for being his final wicket.

'Cheers, Geoff. My pleasure.'

In Brisbane in 1994, Mark Waugh got out to me, chopping the ball onto his stumps when playing the reverse sweep. His team-mates watching in the pavilion were surprised because they'd never seen him play the reverse sweep before, and when Waugh got back to the dressing room, Mark Taylor asked him how many times he'd tried the shot before.

'Oh, that's the first time,' Waugh replied casually.

No respect, Mark!

In comparison to Mushtaq's reverse sweep, though, the 'switch hit' popularised by Kevin Pietersen is another level of risk altogether. Even though it's a totally premeditated shot, it requires unbeliev-able quickness and coordination to switch round your stance and grip as the bowler's about to deliver the ball and hit the ball with-out ending up in a tangle.

Jonty Rhodes was actually the first person to switch-hit a six, off Darren Lehmann in a one-dayer between South Africa and Aus-tralia in 2002, but it was KP's two sixes against New Zealand in an ODI in 2008 that everyone remembers best.

It's a controversial shot because bowlers say they have to declare whether they are bowling over or round the wicket and which arm they will be using, so why should the batsmen be able to switch stance? Then again, it's such a risky shot that maybe the bowler should see it as giving them a greater chance to get wickets.

Whatever, it's a spectacular and skilful shot, the game's law-makers have said it's legal, so we should just appreciate when someone like KP is good enough to execute it.

In recent years, the shot-making has only got more inventive. For instance, take the ramp/scoop/flick-over-the-shoulder 'Marillier shot' named after Zimbabwean Dougie Marillier. Marillier show-cased this shot to the world in 2001 when he came in to bat with his side needing 15 off the last over to win a one-dayer against Australia. With Glenn McGrath bowling, the chances were slim, but Marillier, having never faced McGrath in his life before, ramped two consecutive balls – both attempted yorkers which came out as low full tosses – over his shoulder and short fine leg for four. Marillier couldn't quite get his side over the line for victory that time, but he used the shot again a year later coming in at number ten against India to help himself to a 21-ball fifty and his side to claim an unlikely win from needing 65 off 5.2 overs.

The sad thing about Marillier is that he retired in 2003 when he was only 24 years old, because he wasn't getting picked for the international side and needed to earn more money to support his family. If T20 had been as big then as it has since become, he could have made a small fortune. Dougie, you'll just have to settle for a place in my Hall of Fame and I'm afraid there is no prize money attached.

Instead, others have followed his lead and created their own versions of the shot, none more dangerous/deranged than ex-Sri Lanka captain Tillakaratne Dilshan's 'Dilscoop', which he used to flick the ball directly over his own head and the wicket-keeper's for sixes, let alone fours. It takes some balls to play that off straight 85–90mph deliveries, because if you don't get your head down in time it's going to hurt. His team-mates reckoned Dilshan wasn't so much ballsy as missing a screw – they called the shot the 'starfish' because starfish don't have a brain.

New Zealand's Brendon McCullum plays a similar 'McScoop' but he at least gets his body and head inside the line of the ball, even falling over as he plays it to get out of the way. Dilshan just tucked his head down in the millisecond after seeing the ball onto the bat.

Dilshan and Brendon can join Marillier in the Tuffers HoF, but they all have to take their place behind a lesser-known former cricketer called Iqbal Khan who was a good decade ahead of them with his own scoop shot. Khan got the idea for his 'Iqscoop' (I've just made that name up . . .) looking for ways to score more quickly when playing on slow wickets in the English league, and he first played it back in India on his way to a century for Mumbai in a 1991/92 Ranji Trophy match.

Batting really has come a long way since the days when legside play was considered rude, and thanks to daring experiments by the likes of Ranji, KP, Iqbal and co it is now a 360-degree business. And there's no batsman in the modern game more 360 than my next HoF inductee, 'Mr 360' himself, AB de Villiers.

The South African is a ridiculously versatile shot-maker. He doesn't just play every shot in the book, he makes up new chapters as he goes along. Ramps, scoops, flicks, flips, laps, paddles, reverse sweeps, pick-up shots, switch hits . . . they all come alike to AB (or ABD as he's also known). He can pick up the length and line early but even if the bowler surprises him, he has the flexibility, eye-to-hand coordination and strength to adjust mid-stroke and still find the boundary.

Surprisingly, from the huge array of shots he can play, AB reckons his key one is the 'late block' defensive shot. He claims that he didn't master it until 2008, when he was 24 years old and halfway through scoring his first-ever Test double-century in India. Once he had learnt how to get the correct backlift and footwork to prepare to play a simple dead-bat forward defensive shot, he felt he was also in an ideal position to attack different lengths and lines of delivery. Then it was just a matter of letting his instincts take over and his hands flow to play almost all of his shots (bar the really premeditated ones). 'If I have that in place, the rest comes naturally,' he says. 'The minute I'm a bit naughty, I find the other shots much tougher.'

That solid basic technique means that AB always has the option to drop the bat on the ball, and when his team needs that type of innings he has shown he can do it, like in March 2014 when he scored 43 in six hours to try and save a Test match against Australia. More often than not, though, his talent takes over and sends the ball all around the ground, as he did in smashing a 31-ball century against West Indies in January 2015 to set a new world record for the fastest ODI century. Whether he's reverse-sweeping a full toss from a fast bowler over the wicket-keeper for six or dancing down the wicket to cross-bat a bouncer over wide mid-on for a huge six, he is pure box office. Those game-changing shots he's created (and his humble character) are why Indian fans of the IPL worship him almost in the same way they did their own genius, Sachin Tendulkar.

A career batting average of over 50 in Tests and ODIs, a strike rate of around 100 in ODIs and a rate of 130 in T20 internationals show how he has mastered all formats of cricket with his unique brand of batting.

'In my mind, there are no such things as "correct" strokes or "incorrect" strokes,' he says. 'There is an infinite range of available strokes, each carrying a different level of risk and reward. The skill of any batsman lies in selecting the right stroke at the right moment.'

Three-sixty-degree shotmaking? It's as simple as ABD.

The Big Daddy, Den's ComBat and Bob's Run Reaper

Batsmen were using bats that curved upwards at the bottom until the 1760s – handy if you're trying to loft a half-volley over the infield, not so good if you're trying to keep the ball on the deck. Then Hambledon's star batsman and batmaker John Small started making bats with a straight blade.

It was a big change by Small, but not big enough for one cheeky player, Surrey and All England all-rounder Thomas 'Daddy' White. Playing in a high-stakes money match in 1771 for Chertsey against Hambledon, Daddy came to the crease carrying a bat as wide as the wicket, the Big Daddy of all bats. Some reports say he did it to gain an unfair advantage, others say he just did it for a laugh, but with £50-per-side on the game plus plenty of side-bet action, the Hambledon boys were not amused. There was nothing in the laws to say Daddy couldn't use the bat, but apparently the fielders grabbed the bat from him and found a carpenter to plane it down. With Daddy's big bat reduced to a more average girth, Chertsey suffered an agonising defeat by a single run.

Soon after, at a meeting of the Hambledon club, their captain Dick Nyren, bowler Thomas Brett and John Small signed an agreement saying that 'ffour [sic] and quarter inches shall be the breadth forthwith'. That is still the standard bat width nearly two-and-a-half centuries later, so even though Daddy's stunt didn't pay off in the money match, it helped to shape the future of batting. Well played, daddio.

Talking of daft bats, another Hall of Fame gong goes to the 'ComBat' which my hero Dennis Lillee used to (briefly) bring the unusual sound of leather on aluminium into the Test match arena. His infamous aluminium bat came about after Dennis and a mate of his, Western Australia cricketer Graham Monoghan, set up some indoor cricket centres. Inspired by watching baseball players in the States using aluminium bats, Graham made a makeshift bat from a piece of an aluminium staircase. Dennis had a hit in the nets with it and said it felt pretty good. So good, they got an aluminium manufacturer to make some more, did some more tests, added an enamel coating so as not to damage the ball, stuck a picture of a rifle on the back and started selling them as the 'Dennis Lillee ComBat'.

As they could be made for half the price of a wooden bat and didn't need any maintenance, they thought that the aluminium bat could provide a good, cheaper alternative for schools cricket or in developing countries. Although they never intended the bat to be used in professional cricket, Lillee found out that there was nothing in the laws against it, and him playing with it in a Test match could be great publicity.

Before the infamous match in Perth against England in December 1979, he'd already used it in Australia's previous Test, against West Indies. The first sound of leather on aluminium came at Brisbane in the First Test when he defended a ball from Joel Garner and it made a huge 'clanggggg', causing the Windies close-fielders to crease up in hysterics. No one complained about him using the bat then, probably because he was out for a duck shortly afterwards.

But, at Perth, Mike Brearley didn't laugh after Lillee clanged the ball for three runs, claiming the bat was damaging the ball. Lillee, knowing that the bat hadn't damaged the ball in their tests, said the mark had just been caused by normal wear and tear, but the umpires and Brears weren't having it.

Australian captain Greg Chappell sent out Rodney Hogg with a willow bat, but Lillee wanted to double-check the rules situation and walked off the field. An Australian official confirmed there was nothing in the laws, but back in the dressing room Dennis was about to grab a wooden bat when his mate Rod Marsh piped up, 'Are you going to let him tell you that when it's not against the laws?'

So Dennis marched out again still wielding his aluminum blade. With Brearley refusing to let his bowlers bowl at him and the umpires threatening to retire his innings, Aussie captain Greg Chappell came out onto the field carrying a selection of bats.

Furious and knowing he couldn't win, Lillee flung his ComBat away. Chappell admitted later he came out with the bats partly to wind Lillee up before bowling – it worked because an angry Lillee charged in and got both England openers, Derek Randall and Boycs, out for ducks.

When the match ended, everyone started to see the funny side and players from both sides signed Lillee's metal blade – Brears wrote, 'Good luck with the sales.' Unfortunately, soon after, the laws were changed to say that bats had to be made out of wood, which screwed up his business completely. Lillee reckoned he'd plunged about A$50,000 into the venture, and because they had been making the bats to order and they weren't getting any orders any more, they were left with a lot of extruded aluminium which they had to sell for scrap for a cent in the dollar. Ouch.

Lillee might not have been the ideal player to promote an innovative bat in the first place as he wasn't a very good batsman, but worse was to come when lifelong number eleven rabbit Bob Willis tried out an even more ridiculous bat a couple of years later.

The bat was called the 'Run Reaper' – an optimistic name for any bat being used by Bob – but even more so in this case as it had loads of holes drilled through it. The idea was that you'd be able to generate more bat speed as the air whooshed through the holes. 'Dennis Amiss tried it out in the nets at Edgbaston,' recalled Bob. 'He played one shot and it disintegrated in front of all the press men.'

Oh well, Bob's hole-y Run Reaper may have crumpled under pressure, but it's joining the Big Daddy and ComBat in my Hall of Fame.

New balls!

Perhaps the most important change in the history of cricket was the change from underarm to round-arm and then overarm bowling. As I discovered digging into the history of umpires, that change was controversial, and it took years for overarm bowling to gain acceptance before the MCC gave it their official stamp of approval in 1864. Imagine if that had never happened? I could have been trying to bowl underarm spinners to Brian Lara and Sachin Tendulkar. A scary thought. Then again, I might have been harder to hit bowling pea-rollers.

Since overarm became the norm, bowlers have invented all sorts of variations to make batsmen's lives more difficult. Personally, I kept it relatively simple, mixing up conventional left-arm spin with an arm ball and fiddling around with changes of pace and flight, so I do admire the people that have come up with brand-new deliveries.

Probably the two biggest revelations to me during my playing career were reverse swing and the doosra. (Okay, Shane Warne seemed to invent a new delivery before every Test series as well, but I did sometimes suspect he was just making up new names for the same delivery to psyche batsmen out.)

As discussed in an earlier chapter, Wasim Akram and Waqar Younis were the kings of reverse swing in my day having learnt the art from Imran Khan. The invention of reverse swing, however, actually dates back to the late 1960s and is credited to the former Pakistan opening bowler Sarfraz Nawaz. He discovered it by happy accident, practising with an old ball. 'It was rough on both sides but I shone one side and it swung towards the shine – it should not have done this,' he recalled. More trial and error and he realised the trick was to keep the rough side of the ball as dry as possible and weigh down the smooth, polished side with sweat and spit, then point the damper, heavier side towards leg to make the ball drag in that direction.

He shared the secret with his Pakistan new ball partner Saleem Mir, but didn't share it with anyone else until Pakistan's 1976/77 tour of the West Indies, when Imran Khan asked Sarfraz why he was swinging the ball and he wasn't. Sarfraz, the cheeky bugger, was roughing up both sides of the ball on the last ball of his over so it wouldn't swing for Imran! He did show him how to do it in the nets later, though. And so the knowledge was passed on, and Imran reverse-swung a few out in the Eighties before passing it on to the next generation.

As for the 'doosra', some cricket historians claim that Sonny Ramadhin, who played for the Windies in the 1950s, bowled doosras, but most give one of my contemporaries, Saqlain Mushtaq, the credit for inventing it. The doosra, or 'teesra' as Saqlain called it, is bowled with the same finger action as an off-break, but with the back of the hand facing the batsman which means the ball goes the other way. I tried to bowl a left-handed version of it in the nets once and nearly dislocated my shoulder, elbow and wrist, so decided to stick to my deadly(ish) arm ball instead.

I'll never forget the day I first saw Mushy bowl his teesra playing for Surrey against Middlesex at Lord's in 1997. When he first came on to bowl, I was watching from the pavilion balcony and wondering why he'd set such an offside-weighted field. Our batsmen soon found out, as one after the other they played to hit the ball legside with the spin – or what they thought was the spin – only for the ball to fizz the other way. Because none of them had seen it before, they couldn't pick him at all, and a succession of batsmen came back to the dressing room shaking their head in bamboozlement. He took a five-fer in each innings and Surrey beat us by an innings.

May I just mention that Mushy didn't actually get me out in that game. Checking the scorecard, I see I made two not out off one ball in the second innings (strike rate: 200) and I faced 27 balls in the first innings for my seven runs before Adam Hollioake had me caught behind. How many of those 28 balls were bowled by Mushy I can't actually recall – possibly none. But if I did face him, in my case ignorance was bliss.

Packer's game-changing circus

Kerry Packer was a controversial, brash, billionaire tycoon who upset plenty of people, but his bulldozering of the cricket establishment in the Seventies was undoubtedly a game-changer. A huge gambler who won and lost millions – he once lost £15 million simultaneously playing four roulette tables on his own in a London casino – he took a massive punt on cricket that dragged the sport kicking and screaming into the future.

In 1976, Packer had tried to buy the rights to screen Australia's home matches on Channel Nine, and didn't take kindly to the way the old boys at the cricket board had dismissed his offer. 'Cricket is going to get revolutionised whether they like it or not,' he said. 'There is nothing they can do to stop me. Not a goddam thing.'

His vision was to sign up the best cricketers in the world to play in made-for-TV 'World Series Cricket', a sort of travelling cricket circus. When the stars heard the numbers Packer was offering, a lot of them signed up. For example, Gordon Greenidge had been paid £3,000 for the West Indies tour of England, including five Tests and county matches the previous summer, plus his normal county salary at Hampshire of around £4,000. He signed up for three seasons of World Series Cricket at A$25,000 per season – approximately £16,000 – plus expenses.

Financially, it was a no-brainer, and if I'd been a Test player at the time and been offered the chance to play, I think I would have signed up too.

The TCCB were not happy, though, and there was talk of Packer players being banned for life from all other forms of cricket. So the first WSC season, featuring three teams – 'WSC Australian XI', West Indies XI and the World XI – got underway in late 1977 with its players unclear about their future. The cricket establishment wouldn't allow WSC matches to be played on the Test grounds either, so they had to use venues such as Aussie Rules stadiums instead, with 'drop-in' pitches grown in greenhouses and plonked into position by cranes. The pitches were grown in two halves, so they had a big seam down the middle – quite dangerous when you had the world's quickest bowlers flinging down bouncers at you.

The players also had to adjust to another innovation – playing with the white ball in limited-overs night matches for the first time, which took a bit of getting used to. As I discovered when I first played with the white ball in Oz years later, the white ball doesn't shine very well for the bowlers, and it goes green as the match progresses so batsmen and fielders find it difficult to pick up.

On the plus side, television coverage was pushed to a new level, with eight cameras instead of the usual four to give viewers a better close-up of the action than ever before. And while the ICC might have ruled that the matches shouldn't be classified officially as 'first class', the quality of players on show was as good if not better than you'd see in regular Test cricket.

Tony Greig was suspended for a few weeks for his role as Kerry Packer's right-hand man in recruiting players, but the counties weren't willing to lose the services of top-class WSC players in their squads, so the threat to ban them didn't come to anything.

The first season had not been as successful as Packer had hoped, though. Attendances at the Supertests had been largely disappointing, so even though the standard of play was good, there wasn't much atmosphere.

Despite World Series Cricket bleeding cash and legal suits flying around, Packer the gambler doubled down on his investment for the second season with new players signed up and more prize money. The day – night matches had gone down better than the Supertests, so they became more of a focus of the TV coverage. Packer got a big boost when he managed to swing it with the New South Wales government to let his unofficial games be played at Australia's home of cricket, the Sydney Cricket Ground. The New South Wales government even paid for floodlights to be put in at the SCG and a 40,000-plus crowd turned out for the first day – night match there. The new day – night format for Supertest matches, with the last half of each day played under floodlights, also proved popular.

Coloured kits were introduced in January 1979 because the white ball could get lost momentarily against the white of players' clothes. Mind you, some of the Windies players lodged complaints when they first saw the pinkish outfit given to them, which they didn't feel fitted with the macho Caribbean culture.

The Windies boys might have taken a while to get their head round being pretty in pink, but the extra colour and razzmatazz of WSC was attracting more women and children to the games. The old 'official' cricket looked dull in comparison. Without its star players, a third-rate Australian Test team was destroyed 5–1 at home by England in one of the most boring Ashes series ever, and the Aussie public voted with their feet. They preferred to watch Greg Chappell, Dennis Lillee and co and attendances at WSC matches were higher than at the Ashes.

Packer took the teams to the West Indies for five extra

Supertests and a dozen one-dayers and there was also talk of taking World Series Cricket to Pakistan, India, New Zealand and America – Tony Greig, incidentally, recommended shortening the game for a US audience to 25 overs per side, and outlawing maiden overs so batsmen would be out if they didn't score, like the three-strikes baseball rule.

But there was no future for WSC as it turned out. When the ACB caved in and Packer finally got his hands on the TV rights for conventional Tests, the travelling circus shuddered to an immediate halt.

The TCCB and ICC were pretty pissed off with the Aussie board for selling out to Packer after all the money they'd lobbed into supporting it in very expensive legal battles. Looking back now, though, modern cricketers and cricket administrators must be thankful for what Kerry Packer did for the game. For the first time, top-class cricketers got paid decent money. White balls, floodlit matches, coloured kits and fielding restrictions have proved to be visionary innovations and paved the way for new formats and competitions that help to attract new generations and sponsors to the game.

World Series Cricket showed it was alright to shake up the status quo and experiment. Not all of the experiments since have worked, mind – like the first-ever floodlit tournament in England, the Lambert & Butler Cup at the end of the 1981 season. None of our cricket grounds had floodlights then, which is a slight problem when attempting to play cricket at night, so the matches were played in football stadiums on matted wickets instead. And if you think T20 is a thrashabout, it has nothing on the L&B Cup, which was ten overs (yes, ten) per side.

The regional qualifying matches were played at Selhurst Park, the Hawthorns and Old Trafford, with a finals night at Stamford Bridge. Of course, the problem with playing cricket in football stadiums is the pitches are oblong and small, so every other shot was going for four or six even when batsmen miscued horribly. It was a lottery. For the record, Clive Lloyd's Lancashire won the final, biffing 151 off 10 overs, and they are still the reigning champions because the tournament wasn't repeated.

Floodlit cricket has come a long way in England since then and the first day – night Test here is scheduled to be played at Edgbaston against West Indies in August 2017. Day – night cricket in sunny Adelaide is a bit different to day – night cricket in Brrrrr-irmingham and the change in conditions as night falls could favour one team over the other. But, as Kerry Packer showed, you have to be prepared to try new things to shake up the game, and hopefully it'll go well and add another dimension to cricket in England.

From 'Bodyline' to 'headline': Hendren and the helmet pioneers

From my point of view, one of the best things to happen after World Series Cricket was that wearing a batting helmet started to become normal accepted behaviour. Hard to believe that in the Sixties and Seventies, people routinely wandered out to face 90mph missiles with bugger-all extra protection, just a sunhat or cap and a hankie in their pocket. Totally nuts, when you think about it.

The early pioneers of headgear, who braved having the mickey taken out of them for being wusses, are all welcome in my Hall of Fame.

You have to go back a few decades earlier to find the first sensible person who recognised that getting hit on the head by a cricket ball can seriously damage your health. Middlesex and England cricketer Patsy Hendren was first to use a specially designed three-peaked protective cap, in the 1930s. That was in the era of 'Bodyline', so the game was changing and Patsy wanted a bit more protection when he faced up to Harold Larwood and co.

It was made out of rubber and looked more like a Sherlock Holmes deerstalker – very dashing. How much it would have helped if Patsy had actually been hit on the bonce, I'm not sure, but he was way ahead of his time.

After that a few other people experimented with headgear, including Mike Brearley, who had his own version of Patsy's skull cap made with plastic bits to protect the temples, and Indian legend Sunil Gavaskar. Sunny wore a white, padded sort-of skull cap worn round his head with flaps covering the ears and temples. Seen from the boundary, with his hair sticking out the top, it looked like he'd stuck his jockstrap over his head and all he needed was a couple of pencils up the nose for the full Edmund-Blackadder-in-the-trenches pose. Sunny may have resembled someone who had gone loopy in the membrane, but to my mind he was one of the few sane batsmen of his era.

The ante was upped in World Series Cricket, because of the wonky drop-in pitches in Aussie Rules stadiums – even the great Viv Richards, who never wore a helmet in his entire career, took one on the bonce from the medium-pace bowling of Greg Chappell.

I don't think anyone else ever hit Viv on the head. Ex-England quickie Greg Thomas nearly got him and so did a fella called Duncan Spencer who played for Kent – I remember seeing him do that on telly in a one-dayer when Viv was playing for Glamorgan. Google 'Duncan Spencer Viv Richards' to see a clip if you've never seen him bowl. Really rapid, he was; he could bowl at speeds getting up to 100mph. *Whoosh.* Viv said Duncan was the fastest bowler he ever faced. Whatever happened to Duncan Spencer? I think injury problems did for his career, sadly.

In WSC that *mano a mano* battle between quick bowlers and top batsmen was a big selling point, so when Aussie David Hookes had his jaw crunched by an Andy Roberts bouncer and the extra cameras captured the moment in its gory glory from all angles, the marketing people might have secretly smiled at the extra publicity. Hookes wasn't smiling while he was sucking on soup through a straw for five weeks afterwards. Well, it might have looked like he was smiling, what with the wired-up jaw, but it was probably more of a permanent grimace.

Batsmen like Dennis Amiss and World XI skipper Tony Greig had started to wise up to the dangers of, er, an unprotected head a while before the Hookes horror show. On tour in Australia in 1974/75, Amiss had had a torrid time against Dennis Lillee and Jeff

Thomson's bowling, making three consecutive ducks. 'Many a time I walked out to the middle in a Test match knowing it was virtually a waste of time carrying a bat,' he said later. 'I knew it would be used not so much to make strokes as to fend the ball off my body ... There was even talk among some England players of wearing protective headgear.'

'*Even* talk . . .' – it really was seen as a sign of weakness to wear a helmet then.

In New Zealand in 1975, Amiss had also witnessed New Zealander Evan Chatfield hit on the temple and nearly killed by a bouncer from England fast bowler Peter Lever. Only quick work by England physio Bernard Thomas and an ambulance man saved Chatfield's life.

Greig had predicted the introduction of helmets after the West Indies series of 1976. Before going to Oz for the World Series, he'd got a manufacturer who specialised in protective headgear for epileptics to take a mould of his head to create a skull cap like the one he'd seen Brearley wearing in the previous Ashes series.

Amiss had gone further and asked a motorcycle helmet company in Birmingham if they could make him a lightweight version with a plexiglass visor. 'The bowlers were becoming more aggressive – it wasn't "Bodyline", it was "headline" ', reasoned Amiss.

People laughed at him when he first walked out to bat with it in Oz, shouting, 'Hey, Amiss – where's yer skateboard?' but after Hookes' nasty accident, Packer himself ordered some more of the helmets from the Brum manufacturer which Greigy and others gratefully wore.

In the beginning, though, a batsman coming out in a helmet only seemed to encourage the evil fast bowlers. 'The first time I saw Greigy wearing it, I thought, "What a great target,"' recalled Dennis Lillee. 'I bowled a bouncer and hit him on the helmet.' The Aussies took the piss out of Greig for wearing the helmet, and he later admitted that he knew he was past his best when he felt the need to put it on.

Thankfully, by the time I was batting in professional cricket, wearing a cricket helmet was standard (and the designs had got better), so kudos to Hendren, Brearley, Gavaskar, Amiss, Greig and co for dealing with the early sledging and making it socially acceptable.

Lobbying for Howard

In the earliest days of cricket commentary on radio, commentators were under strict instructions to purely focus on the action in a game. So 'X is preparing to bowl from the Nursery End. He's running in now, bowls and Y plays a forward defensive stroke and the ball rolls out to Z at cover point. No run. Z throws the ball back to X as he walks back to his mark . . .' and so on. And on and on. As you can imagine, listening to that hour after hour was unbelievably tedious and nearly killed the game completely as a radio sport. It took a while before people at the BBC realised you couldn't approach commentary on a cricket match in the same breakneck style as a game of football or horse racing, and that they were actually ignoring the advantages of a cricket match stretching over a much longer period of time.

A couple of key men in changing the mentality were a young

up-and-coming commentator in the 1930s called Howard Marshall and the Director of Outside Broadcasts, Seymour de Lotbiniere (*aka* 'Lobby').

Marshall boasted a big vocabulary and wasn't afraid to use it to bring more colour to his commentaries, set the scene for listeners and bring out the characters of the players. He liked to keep things spontaneous and informal, as if he was talking to a mate, and laughed off the times when he made a mistake. He humanised cricket commentary, which was a welcome change from the torturously stiff style listeners had to endure before then.

There wasn't so much ball-by-ball commentary then, so early in his cricket broadcasting career Howard would often watch the match and take notes and deliver reports at the end of sessions. This was made harder because cricket commentary wasn't seen as that important by clubs in those days. For example, the MCC wouldn't let him broadcast at Lord's so he'd have to watch the match from the press box and then head to an apartment nearby to deliver his report for radio listeners. One time, he was about to give his teatime report, when a child in the flat above began her piano practice, and he only just had time to race upstairs to beg her to stop tinkling the ivories for a few minutes while he read out his report.

When he did get to commentate live, his weakness was not keeping up with play. Sometimes the listener would hear applause as the ball zipped towards the boundary rope while Howard was still describing the bowler's run-up!

Lobby supported Marshall's fresh approach and together they laid the groundwork for cricket commentary in the future and the style of commentary you hear on *TMS* today. So Howard and Lobby are definitely two for my Hall of Fame.

The 'vulgar' voice of Arlott

Howard Marshall had what John Arlott later described as a 'deep, warm, unhurried voice' and in many ways he paved the way for Arlott himself as a cricket commentator.

Even though he was a very intellectual sort of chap, Arlott didn't have the chance to go to university, so he became a clerk at a 'mental hospital' (as it was called in those days) and then a policeman for 12 years. He got his break with the BBC after sending in some of his poems, which led to an invitation to read them on the radio and a job as a producer of literary programmes for the BBC Overseas Service.

He'd always loved cricket too, and got a trial as a commentator. Amazing to think now, but his voice was seen as a problem by the BBC bigwigs at the time. The main commentator of the day, who worked with Arlott, was Rex Alston and he was far from impressed: 'At first his delivery was monotonous and his broad Hampshire accent did not make for easy listening.'

Oh, quick story about Rex Alston that made me laugh. One morning in 1985, he picked up the *Daily Telegraph* and saw his obituary, so he thought he'd better ring up the newspaper offices to let them know he hadn't actually died.

Rex told the man he was put through to that the obituary was rather premature.

'Who is speaking?' asked the disbelieving journalist.

'Rex Alston.'

'Are you sure?'

'Absolutely'

There was a long pause and then the man asked tentatively, 'Where are you speaking from . . . ?'

Anyway, back to Arlott – Lobby wasn't that keen on his voice either, but saw Arlott's potential, telling him, 'While I think you have a vulgar voice, you have a compensatingly interesting mind. Would you like to broadcast on next summer's South Africa tour?'

This was in the days when a plummy, King's English accent was mandatory at the Beeb and Arlott even thought about having elocution lessons. Thankfully, he never went through with that idea.

Lobby had another issue with Arlott in his early days as a commentator. For Lobby, one of the golden rules of sports outside broadcasts was to 'begin with the score', so listeners tuning in could quickly discover the state of the game. Arlott was naturally more inclined to give poetic descriptions of the play and atmosphere inside the ground, and he got told off for not saying the score often enough.

A few listeners wrote in to say that they only wanted to hear about the ball being bowled and what happened to it, but Arlott had no time for such dullards. 'We tried that once: the result was seventy-five per cent silence,' he replied. 'There must be other material: atmosphere varies from ground to ground. To describe it is surely part of the essence of cricket-watching.'

Absolutely right, and it was soon clear that Arlott's colourful style was perfect for radio commentary. In that first series of 1947, he came up with a famous line to describe South African spinner 'Tufty' Mann causing batsman George Mann all sorts of trouble. 'A case of Mann's inhumanity to Mann,' he said.

After that, there were so many examples of his verbal dexterity.

Commenting on Clive Lloyd's power-hitting century in the 1975 World Cup final, he described how Lloyd effortlessly swatted a four over midwicket to reach 99 as 'the stroke of a man knocking a thistle top off with a walking stick'.

Or Ian Botham's bowling run-up: 'Botham runs in like a shire horse, cresting the breeze.'

Or this one: 'Butcher drops his head, both hands behind his back, and looks sheepishly down the wicket like a small boy stealing jam.'

Wonderful.

He could even make the covers being taken off after a rain delay sound interesting, as he proved during the 1979 Lord's Test between England and India: 'The mammoth uncovering is going on – you might almost call it an unveiling,' he began, going on to describe the 'team of removers' . . . 'They seem to be in two shifts. Those in red jerkins removing the covers and those in white jerkins admiring them – which is not quite a fair division of toil . . .'

To John, the tractor taking away the covers was 'rather like a First World War aeroplane in its engine note, and it scoots about the place. I should think it's the ambition of every boy on the groundstaff to be the tractor driver.

'There's a strange clamp that joins the two tall covers. The tall ones are quite splendid for the groundstaff because they're a comfortable height for leaning on – and five of them are having a little lean at the moment.'

No wonder so many listeners wrote in and said they preferred *TMS* when it rained.

Arlott was not a fan of limited-overs cricket, finding the 'forty-over bash' of Sunday League cricket boring and predictable. So much so that he did fall asleep during commentary on occasion (hey, we've all done it . . .). One time at Headingley, after a short nap and total silence from the commentary box for BBC2 viewers, John woke and calmly summarised the action he hadn't been watching. 'The last four overs were entirely nondescript and did not deserve comment,' he said.

He didn't like to listen to his fellow commentators between his shifts either. Instead, he'd go for a walk around the ground, returning to the commentary box just in time for his next stint on the mic. The only problem was that meant he might repeat exactly what the previous commentators had said. The listeners didn't seem to mind, though – words sounded better when he said them.

Nowadays, because the lead commentator and summariser are constantly bouncing off each other, there is no break in the chatter. But in Arlott's day, he wouldn't think anything of pausing 15 or 20 seconds before making his next observation and no summariser would dare to jump in. You could call it 'dead airtime', a cardinal sin in radio broadcasting, where silent seconds are like dog years, but it worked because he was such a engaging talker, with his own rhythm, and listeners were hanging on his next word, however long it was before he said it.

His voice was often described as having a 'Hampshire burr', but really it was all his own. And it meant he was in high demand for commercials, and did adverts for everything from St Bruno tobacco and Spanish Rioja wines to Huntley & Palmers biscuits ('I'd almost forgotten a biscuit could taste as good as this . . .') and Qualcast lawnmowers ('A lot less bovver than a hover' – remember that one?)

Before Arlott came on the scene, it wasn't acceptable to drink alcohol in the commentary box, but he used to come to work with a bottle of Beaujolais poking out of his battered old brown leather briefcase. My *TMS* colleague Henry Blofeld recalls how he once carried two briefcases full of bottles of claret up to the commentary box at Lord's for Arlott. 'John's ringing Hampshire tones grew richer and richer over the years as his vocal cords were increasingly marinaded in ever more spectacular bottles of claret,' recalls Blowers.

Arlott loved and was very knowledgeable about wine. His house in Hampshire, where he lived for many years, was a converted pub, so it had a big cellar to keep his wine collection in. But, such was John's appetite for fine wines, it wasn't big enough. Blowers remembers that when he visited it was so packed you had to tiptoe round all the bottles on the stairs down into the cellar.

Arlott used to enjoy a very large glass of red in the commentary box before lunch, but according to his colleagues, he never overdid drinking on the job to the point it affected his work . . . apart, perhaps, from during the Lord's Test of summer 1980, his last as a commentator. He was on duty in the commentary slot before lunch and finished by saying, 'And for his summary of the morning's play, it will be Fred Trueman.' As Fred launched into a familiar rant about England's fast bowlers not being as good as he was, Arlott put his head on the desk in front of him and within seconds fell asleep.

As he talked, Fred was completely oblivious to Arlott's slumbers. 'That's my opinion, anyway,' he concluded, after a couple of minutes, 'I don't know what you think, John'.

He turned to discover his mate face down and away with the fairies. Old Fred was a bit shocked, but recovered the situation very well: 'Well, John is nodding his head vigorously, and with that, back t' studio.'

If there was any criticism of Arlott, it was that he wasn't so good on the technical side of the game because he hadn't played the game at a high level, but that misses the point.

As Mike Brearley said, 'He knew cricket more in the way of a lover than of the critic and, as such, tended to romanticise the performers.'

In 1986, Arlott was interviewed by Mike Brearley for Channel 4 and he reminisced about his life and career. 'I have been lucky, desperately lucky, in many ways to think that the cemetery keeper's boy was going to be a commentator, a poet, an author,' Arlott said. 'Sometimes you tell yourself you have done it yourself, but you know really that there is a vast element of luck in it, being in the right place at the right time . . . I am sure there are fifty better commentators than me about the place, who are not doing commentary, but I was there when the chance happened.'

Fifty better commentators than John Arlott? I don't think so.

Jolly japes with Johnners

Arlott's long-time colleague in the *TMS* commentary box, and my next Hall of Fame inductee, Brian 'Johnners' Johnston took a very different approach. Blowers compared Johnners to 'a bottle of champagne which has just been opened, and the bubbly is spraying out of the top'. On the other hand, 'Everything about John was more measured,' he reckoned, adding,' . . . well, except perhaps the amount of wine in his glass.'

Johnners and Arlott were very different types of people, and they weren't close friends, but they shared a passion for the game (Johnners once said, 'I understand there are some men who do not like cricket, but I would not like my daughter to marry one') and their different personalities helped *TMS* to become a special institution. While Arlott was the grammar school kid, more serious, and with a dry wit, Johnners, the public schoolboy with the posh voice and love of music hall comedy, had a silly, childish sense of humour. Johnners came out with accidental (or were they?) double-entendres like 'Ray Illingworth has just relieved himself at the pavilion end' or 'Welcome to Worcester, where you've just missed seeing Barry Richards hitting one of Basil D'Oliveira's balls clean out of the ground.' My old *TMS* friend the late Christopher

Martin-Jenkins put it well, saying, 'Arlott treasured words like the poet he was and mulled them over as if he were testing the nose of a vintage Château Lafite. Johnston used them with gay abandon, without art or pretension.'

Sometimes the same things did tickle the pair of them, though. On one occasion they were commentating together when news came through of the death of a regional reporter/commentator called Emrys Walters. Neither John nor Johnners knew Walters personally, but neither had rated him highly as a commentator.

'Good Lord, he must have been listening to one of his own commentaries!' they both joked simultaneously before feeling rather guilty.

'Who are we going to attribute that remark to?' said Brian.

'Oh, put it down to me,' replied John. 'You're supposed to be the nice one.'

Johnners loved a practical joke, like the one he pulled on Tony Cozier. Tony was another fabulous commentator, by the way – on radio and television. He was so knowledgeable and had that wonderful Caribbean lilt to his voice. I had the pleasure of working with him on a few occasions and found him to be a lovely, warm and witty bloke. Away from cricket, he loved a rum punch and a good time, too.

Anyhow, Johnners' joke on Tony occurred during a rain delay at Queen's Park Oval in Port of Spain. Tony had been doing some press work on the other side of the ground and headed straight across the outfield to get back to the commentary box. Brian saw him coming and by the time Tony arrived, out of breath after climbing the steps to the box, Brian was talking into the micro-phone and the red light indicating a live broadcast was on.

'Ah, here's Tony Cozier, so I'll hand over to him as I know he has all the latest averages for the series, which he'll pass on to you.'

Poor old Tony had no stats to hand so started to waffle on about anything else that would come to his mind about the state of the match and the weather prospects.

'No,' interrupted Johnners. 'We've promised the listeners the averages and we know you can provide them . . .'

With Tony in an utter state of panic and scrabbling around for scoresheets, Johnners finally cracked up and revealed they weren't on air at all.

Cruel.

Johnners didn't mind being the butt of the joke either. David 'Bumble' Lloyd, who had a spell with *TMS* before he became England coach and then joined the Sky commentary team, played a good one on him. Johnners was due to interview a conductor (music not bus) called James Judd in the 'View from the Boundary' lunchtime slot, but didn't know much about Judd and wanted to get some background information. Bumble got hold of some BBC headed paper, wrote down some random and totally made-up notes about Judd and then put them through the photocopier so they looked like a fax coming in from BBC researchers.

Johnners was always wary of practical jokes by his *TMS* col-leagues, but this time he didn't twig when the 'fax' was handed to him. So when he got to meet the composer, Johnners was asking him about his supposed Weetabix sponsorship deal, love of

Aldershot FC and his nickname of 'Ratty', which, according to Bumble's notes, was given to him because he had pet ferrets.

James Judd found the interview as hilarious as Bumble and co, and he later sent the *TMS* team a load of his CDs signed 'Ratty Judd'.

Alternative voices

Talking of 'View from the Boundary', Peter 'Backers' Baxter, the producer of *TMS* from 1973 to 2007, deserves an honourable mention for bringing in alternative voices on cricket. He was inspired by a radio interview with 90-plus-year-old playwright Ben Travers during a car journey back in winter 1979/80. Travers had been much more interested in talking about cricket, and his memories of watching WG Grace play, than his theatre productions, and so the idea of 'View from the Boundary' took shape.

Apart from being reasonably well-known among the general public, Baxter decided that the only requirements to be invited into the commentary box for a chat was a lack of any professional involvement in cricket and a love of the game.

Initially his idea was the commentators would share interviewing duties, but Johnners made the spot his own because he was so good at it, and in recent years Jonathan 'Aggers' Agnew has taken up the mantle.

There have been hundreds of great guests over the years. Actually, you could select a colourful team of 'Bounders' from them. Together, this lot might not be world-beaters, but they would've certainly drawn a crowd . . .

Bounders XI

John Cleese

Or 'Cleesers' as Brian Johnston called him, naturally. Cleesers told Johnners that he was six feet tall at 12 years old, very thin and weak. 'I used to run up quite a long way and then bowl slow – which was quite a good trick first ball.' Don't know what Cleesers' batting was like, but I'd like to think he gave the ball a 'damn good thrashing'.

Christopher Lee

Famous for playing Count Dracula, the late actor was also a natural sportsman. He stood six foot four, and on *TMS* described himself as a 'fairly rapid' bowler in his youth with a 'whirling windmill action like Mike Procter'. He also relived his greatest performance, for his RAF squadron on a matting pitch in the desert, where he took nine wickets. Would have been useful in day–night cricket . . .

Michael Parkinson

A cricket fanatic, the legendary chat show host did nets with Yorkshire at the same time as the likes of Brian Close and Ray Illingworth, but wasn't quite good enough to make it at county level. Opening the batting for Barnsley, though, with Dickie Bird, they once had a double-century partnership against Harrogate – Parky scored a century and ran out Dickie for 98. Very Geoff Boycott.

Parky at his best would have been a handy player to have on your side . . . and he could have interviewed himself after the game.

John Major

The former Prime Minister's cricket dreams were dashed as a young man by a car accident in Nigeria. In his words, the cricket world was robbed of 'an extremely mediocre medium-paced bowler'. Never mind, John could go behind the stumps instead.

Hugh Cornwell

When the Stranglers singer was a guest on 'View from the Boundary', Aggers was keen to find out what it took to be a punk back in the day. 'Did you have to be angry as a 20- or 18-year-old to be into punk?' Aggers asked. 'I actually was quite happy at the time, which is perhaps where I fell down.'

Gary Lineker

Lineker was still a superstar player for Barcelona when he was interviewed by Johnners in 1988. One of those people who seemed to be good at every sport he turned his hand to, he played for the MCC in a few matches when he was still a footballer, and by all accounts, he was an excellent batsman, fielder and wicket-keeper. He could probably sort the team out with an unlimited supply of free crisps, too.

Piers Morgan

KP's mate would be the official sledger in the team. During the 2013/14 Ashes in Australia, he said that England's batsmen had 'gone soft' and should 'grow a pair', something he may have regretted when he was then challenged to face an over from Brett Lee in the nets at the MCG. Brett steamed in and Morgan, who was hopping away to legside quicker than me in my batting prime, suffered a broken rib for his troubles. That experience hasn't shut him up though.

Peter O'Toole

Proud to say I got a name-check from the late and legendary actor/hell-raiser when he was interviewed during my spell of six for 25 against West Indies at the Oval in August 1991. 'I'm often asked why cricket means so much to me,' he said. 'And it's high drama. Tufnell comes on – takes a wicket. Botham returns – takes a wicket.' With Peter around, high drama – and a long night out after the game – would be guaranteed.

O'Toole was a qualified cricket coach. In breaks between filming scenes for *The Lion in Winter* on location in France in 1968, in which O'Toole played King Henry II, he even tried to teach his American co-star, Katharine Hepburn, how to play, but she struggled, admitting baseball was a lot easier.

Stephen Fry

A keen cricket-watcher, but never a player, Stephen told Aggers that at school, he preferred to 'lie in the long grass, make a daisy chain and be camp and foolish'. Never mind – with his amazing vocabulary and storytelling ability, he'd be a good laugh in the dressing room when the Bounders were batting, and he can pick daisies down at fine leg when it's time to field.

Russell Crowe

When I heard Russell Crowe was coming to be interviewed by Aggers, I made sure I was back in the commentary box a few minutes before the end of the morning session so I could listen in. Russell, cousin of former Kiwi international batting legend the late Martin Crowe, and Martin's brother Jeff, also an ex-New Zealand international, was already there when I walked in. The cricket was still going on, so at first I just stood there at the back of the box, trying not to say out loud what I was thinking: 'Bloody hell, it's Gladiator!'

Gladiator is one of my favourite films, so I was a bit starstruck.

Eventually, I said, 'Ah, Mr Crowe,' and he replied in that familiar gravelly drawl of his, 'Alright, Tuffers.'

He was very nice, but he certainly lived up to that Gladiator aura and struck me as someone you'd want leading your side into a battle.

Sir Terry Wogan

Ah, Sir Terry. RIP. Charm personified. I don't know about his cricketing ability, but I'm sure he would have been a horizontally laid back, calming influence on the pitch. Terry had a wonderful voice for radio, but *TMS* listeners didn't hear it at lunchtime when he was a guest in 1984. He was running so late, they had to draft in an actor called Robin Bailey to take his place. Terry finally rocked up for a chat at teatime. So Bailey became the first person ever to be on 'View from the Boundary' twice. Two 'Views.' in one day – that was also a first.

My dear old Blowers

My commentators Hall of Fame wouldn't be complete without 'my dear old thing' Henry Blofeld. He came up with that phrase after a heavy night drinking illicit champers at a hotel in Iran (typical Blowers). Checking out early the next morning, Blowers was nursing a massive hangover, to the extent that when he started writing a note to leave at reception for his friend, he realised that he couldn't remember what his name was. So instead of 'My dear Michael', the note began, 'My dear old thing . . .'

When Blowers calls me that during commentary now, I'm not sure whether he's forgotten my name as well.

Blowers started out as a commentator in 1968 after a journalist friend of his, John Thicknesse, who thought he might be good at it, suggested that he write to the BBC Head of Outside Broadcasts and ask for a trial. He had to do a couple of 20-minute spells of commentary on a county game at the Oval, and then was summoned to Broadcasting House for a meeting with Henry Riddell, Assistant Head of OBs, and to listen back to his efforts. It was the first time Blowers had heard a recording of his own voice and he didn't like it, but Riddell and his colleagues thought he had potential – 'You try and paint the picture,' Riddell told him – and Blowers was duly added to the BBC commentators list.

Riddell gave him some great pointers that day about radio commentary, about the importance of telling the listener exactly where you are sitting in the ground, what you can see and where – to your left, right, near or far away. That way, the listener can imagine he or she is there with you and picture the scene, and it can help to liven up the periods when nothing much is happening in the game. Obviously, Blowers took that to heart, with his keen eye for pigeons and other wildlife invading the pitch, plus passing aeroplanes and buses.

Blowers was actually a very talented cricketer himself – a fine wicket-keeper and batsman for Eton in his youth – but his playing ambitions were scuppered by injury after he got run over by a bus while out riding his bicycle. He was unconscious for a month and lucky to survive. No wonder he always keeps an eye out for buses when he's commentating . . .

In 1974, Blowers got his *TMS* debut at Old Trafford, commentating on the First Test between England and India. The weather forecast was terrible, and he was terrified that he wouldn't be able to fill airtime when there were stoppages in play. On the plus side, he thought, old hands John Arlott, Johnners plus Freddie Trueman and Trevor Bailey would be on hand to help him through.

The weather held the first day, but after lunch on the second day, the rain, in Blowers' words, was coming down 'like stair rods'. When Johnners handed over to him, a nervous Blowers started off with great gusto, talking away for a few minutes and forgetting to bring his colleagues into the conversation. But as he was starting to run out of steam, he looked around the commentary box to discover all of his colleagues who should have been there to help fill in the chat void had disappeared.

All he could see was a piece of paper with a message in Brian Johnston's handwriting: 'Keep going until 6.30, and don't forget to hand back to the studio.'

In a state of some panic and with his mind now going blank, Blowers started stumbling over his words. Johnners and co, who were waiting outside the back of the commentary box, let poor old Blowers blather on for a minute or two before coming back in to relieve the rookie.

Cruel, but funny, and Blowers says that he got Johnners' message, which was to remember *TMS* is a team game.

People may forget that Blowers actually left the Beeb for Sky for a while in the early 1990s. 'They made me an offer my bank manager couldn't refuse,' he explained. 'But they wanted me to scream and shout and do all this frightful nonsense, so back I came.'

I'm glad he did, because I've had so much fun working with Blowers – and wondering what amazing Technicolor outfit will greet me each day.

I've learnt a lot from him over the years, too. Blowers' advice is that 'commentators must tell the story in the way that suits them best'. He is always trying to identify incidents and battles going on within the game that are important to certain players. He believes that even in a seemingly dull passage of play, there is a little sub-plot he can focus his commentary on to get him enthused and listeners engaged ... And if all else fails, seek out the nearest pigeon.

The rise of the summariser

Up until the 1980s on BBC radio, the lead commentator would be the only voice heard while an over was being bowled, and the 'expert summariser' would be called upon to give his opinions at the end of each over. That has changed; now it's more of an ongoing conversation between the two people at the microphones, so the job for me and others in the role nowadays is to be more of a 'co-commentator'.

You need to break down the technicalities of what's going on, give your reading of the game, offering the listener an idea of what the batsman is trying to do and how the fielding side is looking to counter that, or vice versa.

The lead commentators have their hands full simply describing what's going on ball-to-ball, so you can chip in and help to add a bit of context. You work around them, and don't interrupt unless you've seen something that they may not have spotted. Usually, there's a natural break where you can make your point. And at the end of the over, they might hand over to you to go into a bit more detail about what's happened and what to expect next.

We're getting employed to speak from our experience as players and from watching cricket for many years. Some people have a joke on Twitter when I talk about batting – 'What does Tuffers know about getting behind the line, etc . . .' – but I have no problem giving an opinion on it. Just because batting wasn't my forte, that doesn't mean I don't know about it, because I spent quite a few years bowling at the best in the world. I'd be a very good batting coach – because I couldn't bat myself, I can spot a batsman's weakness a mile off.

Everyone has their own style as a summariser. For instance, Geoff Boycott is known for being very opinionated and blunt. I tend to frame my criticisms a little bit more sympathetically than Boycs – 'He'll be disappointed with that . . .' is one of my favoured phrases when someone's made a hash of it.

As an ex-player, especially when you first start out as a summariser, it is hard to be too critical because you know how players can make horrendous mistakes in the heat of battle. Wide long hop – yes, it's crap bowling, but we've all bowled the odd crap ball in our time. None of us in the commentary box like to see a player having a nightmare, because we've been there and done that ourselves.

There comes a point where you have to say it's not good enough, though. In India in winter 2016, five or six England batters were out hooking in an innings. Well, then the commentators were entitled to criticise them for continuing to play the hook shot. As long as you're not slagging people off without reason, most Test players will take it on the chin. And if they don't like it, they can always use it as fuel to motivate themselves to stuff your words down your throat in future.

Once you've covered the action on the pitch, you can drift off at tangents, especially when there is an uneventful passage of play. Then just see where the conversation takes you, whether it is about serious issues of the day such as which of the array of cakes sent in by listeners to eat first, or where Aggers went flying last weekend (for those who don't know, he's a qualified pilot). I really enjoy that part. And sometimes, like the listeners in Arlott's heyday, I like it when it rains and we can just have a chinwag.

You have to be careful not to lose the plot when the game's in progress, though. When I first started out in radio, I was co-commentating with Christopher Martin-Jenkins in Sri Lanka and got rather over-excited by the brightly coloured kites being flown in the blue sky close to the ground.

'Ooh, look CMJ, there's another kite! CMJ . . . look, there's a purple one! Look at that . . .' I was going on about them a bit too much and CMJ very politely had to give me a hint to pipe down and instead focus on Muttiah Muralitharan who was in the process of decimating England's batting line-up.

'Yes, yes, Tuffers – well, they do like to fly kites here,' he said, pointing his forefinger towards the pitch. 'Anyway, back to the cricket . . .'

Johnners had started involving the summarisers more during the Seventies. He wanted the atmosphere in the commentary box to be more like a group of friends having a chat about cricket (among other things). By the time John Arlott retired, some people felt the fun and games had gone a bit too far, to the point where the cricket commentary suffered, and they criticised Johnners for being the ringleader of the silliness. Jonathan Agnew has since done a great job in getting the balance right, knowing when to get serious and when to loosen the leash.

Aggers joined *TMS* at a tricky time. Don Mosey had written an autobiography where he'd been very critical of some of his colleagues, and it had poisoned the atmosphere in the commentary box. Mosey retired from commentary soon after the release of his controversial book and, being an affable sort of chap, new boy Aggers was just the right person to help get the team spirit going again among the *TMS* crew.

Before his first Test for *TMS* at Headingley in 1991, working as summariser alongside Fred Trueman and Trevor 'The Boil' Bailey, Aggers asked Blowers what sort of approach he should take – whether he should follow Johnners' jovial style or take Christopher Martin-Jenkins' more serious approach and focus just on the cricket. Blowers told him, 'My dear old thing, you can't possibly try to copy anyone. Your style will simply come out naturally, so for goodness' sake, don't force anything.'

It was the best advice, and it turned out that Aggers naturally had that balance.

Aggers also credits Johnners with giving him the confidence to be himself and not worry about the occasional cock-ups, which are inevitable when you are broadcasting live for hours on end. And the cock-ups are, of course, part of the joy of *TMS*, as with their comical 'Botham leg over' meltdown at the Oval in Aggers' first summer, er, on the job.

Aggers knew what he was doing when he said the line, because it was fed to him by journalist John Etheridge, who he'd bumped into a few minutes before. Etheridge had told him, 'I know what our headline will be tomorrow – Botham cocks it up by not getting his leg over', which made Aggers smile, but he couldn't have predicted the hysteria caused by his own 'Botham failed to get his leg over' comment on air.

All these years later, replaying the audio of the incident still has audiences in stitches at Aggers' theatre stage shows. When you listen back to it, you can hear the sound of scorer Bill Frindall's china teacup hit the saucer. Then as Aggers and Johnners try and fail to speak for laughing, you can just about hear producer Peter Baxter, at the back of the commentary box, pleading, 'Will somebody say something.'

Aggers recalls that Johnners was actually rather upset at their lack of professionalism at first, but that changed when the letters started pouring in from listeners who'd loved it and Aggers persuaded him to listen to a recording of the best minute or so of 'dead airtime' in cricket radio broadcasting history.

Before 1991 was over, Aggers was appointed BBC Cricket Correspondent, succeeding CMJ, who I also later had the pleasure of working alongside. Aside from his sharp, knowledgeable commentary, there are lots of funny stories about CMJ's mishaps. He was a technophobe like me, and there was the time in Jamaica in 2000 when he was trying repeatedly and unsuccessfully to ring his office back home on his mobile phone and getting more and more frustrated. It was only when a friend pointed out that he was trying to make the call on a TV remote control he'd picked up from the hotel instead that the problem became clear.

A notoriously bad timekeeper who'd usually arrive in time for his shift by the skin of his teeth, he had a particularly good excuse for running late for a one-day international at the Oval in 2006. He called in to explain, saying, 'I may be a little late. I went to Lord's.'

A well-spoken man, CMJ didn't like to swear, so created his own alternatives. If he was annoyed, you might hear him exclaim, 'Ffffotheringay Thomas!', 'Ffffishcakes and buttercup pie!' and all sorts of filth like that.

CMJ passed away on 1 January 2013 and is much missed by all of us in the *TMS* team to this day.

A letter from Baghdad

Nowadays, we have a constant stream of tweets and emails coming in for listeners giving their instant feedback on the cricket (or some random stuff we've been talking about), but Johnners was the one who first got listeners involved by reading out letters on air. That helped to build *TMS*'s following in the UK and abroad.

Aggers tells a story about the time he was on air when Johnners read out a letter from a 'Mr Richter in Baghdad', who had written in to say how much he enjoyed listening to the show as it reminded him of home. Johnners thanked him for the letter and started rambling on about how lovely the weather must be in Baghdad at this time of year and what a wonderful city it is. Aggers, who was sitting next to Johnners at the time, vaguely recognised the name of the listener. The next day, another letter arrived from 'Friends of Ian Richter' explaining that Ian was listening to the programme on a radio from a prison cell in Baghdad, where he'd been held the past four-and-a-half years on trumped-up bribery charges.

Johnners apologised profusely on air, and there was a happy ending to the story when Richter was released a year later and invited to be interviewed by Brian on 'View from the Boundary' where he confirmed that he'd heard his letter read out and the apology when he was in his cell.

Another time, at a tea interval, Aggers launched into reading one of a pile of letters handed to him by the producer. But he had only got a sentence into the note before he spotted the name at the bottom of the letter and burst out laughing.

Johnners picked up the letter and only managed to splutter, 'This isn't from the prime minister, William Pitt, but from William H Titt . . .' before he was gone too.

While the two of them were holding their sides, crying with laughter, Trevor Bailey had to step in to announce the umpires coming out for the evening session and hold the fort until they could speak again.

'Morning, everyone . . .'

So those are the greats of radio in my eyes. But when it comes to television broadcasting, Richie Benaud was the absolute don.

An abiding memory of my childhood was sitting down on the sofa with a cup of tea and a digestive biscuit, turning on the telly and there was Richie Benaud: 'Morning, everyone . . .'

For me, Richie was synonymous with a day watching the cricket on the telly. It always felt like he was addressing me personally. When he was being interviewed by the presenter, he even did that thing where he slowly turned to look down the camera and gave his answer to the viewer rather than the guy asking the questions. Richie seemed very aware at all times that his job was to connect with the millions of people watching at home. Many have tried to do that same answer-to-camera thing since and it can look a bit odd and forced, but with Richie it seemed natural somehow.

Richie explained the difference between the job of the TV and radio commentators well. The radio commentator, he said, is 'being there, capturing the moment and being able to describe the picture for those not so fortunate', whereas a TV commentator needs the 'expertise to add to whatever is on screen – television commentators would only last one day if they tried to paint a picture because the picture is already there'.

Richie had a reputation for speaking less than other TV commentators because he only wanted to say something beyond what viewers could see with their own eyes. 'There is nothing worse than a pompous cricketer, a pompous sporting official or an overbearing cricket commentator,' he said (I can't think who he could have been talking about . . .).

He realised that it was not easy to get the balance right, though, because there are so many different types of people watching, from cricket novices who want everything explained to them and club cricketers with decent knowledge of the nuances of the game to know-it-alls who would rather you'd just shut up. It's a very tricky job.

Dennis Lillee made his debut in the commentary box alongside Richie. When it was his turn to speak, he started gabbling on until Richie turned to him and put his finger on his lips to tell him to stop talking.

At the end of their stint together, Richie told him, 'There are pictures and people can see what's going on . . . you really shouldn't say much at all . . . it's not like radio where you have to paint the pictures in your own words.'

Richie himself had picked up a few good tips from David Hill, his executive producer at Channel 9 in Oz in the 1970s, who wrote ten commandments for his team of commentators. These included the following little gems:

2. *Never talk over your fellow commentator – just as your fellow commentator shall never talk over you.*

4. *Listen to your director with an ear as keen as a ferret's – just as your director will listen avidly to the commentary, thus ensuring your magic phrases are pertinent to the viewer's picture.*

7. *Remember this is a game of many and varied hues. As a commentator you will keep foremost in your mind that cricket contains venom and courage, drama and humour, and you will not be backward in bringing out in your commentary those aspects of the noble and ancient pastime.*

9. *Remember at all times that, having practised the ancient art at the highest possible level, you may occasionally dwell on the sacred mysteries to the utter confusion of the uninformed. Therefore, you will keep it simple, never talking down to the viewer by using those bastard phrases: 'of course', 'as you can see', or 'as my fellow commentator said'.*

All good advice that Richie said he always had in mind when behind the mic.

With Richie around, TV producers and viewers knew they were in safe hands. He was meticulous in every detail and was always willing to help out his fellow commentators. For example, he worked out that the best way to hold the lip-mic was to gently rest it against the end of your nose, so that whether you are looking down at a monitor or out of the commentary box window at the action, the mic goes with your mouth and the volume stays even. And before the Australia–Sri Lanka Test series in 1995/96, he spent an hour teaching other Channel 9 commentators how to correctly pronounce the names of Sri Lanka's players.

On the rare occasions when things went wrong, Richie would handle the situation as coolly as you like. Once in Brisbane when he was doing a piece to camera, the alarm on his watch went off – he had the alarm on because as well as his TV duties he had deadlines to meet for various newspapers. Unflustered, he leant forward to turn it off, but in doing so dislodged the backdrop behind him, which slowly fell forward onto his head. At which point he calmly suggested going to a commercial break.

Early in his commentary career, he was being interviewed by Peter West on top of the Edgbaston pavilion in a storm with only an umbrella held by Peter to protect them from the driving rain. They didn't have an indoor studio at the time. Richie gave his usual forensic summary of the previous session's play. It was only when the interview had ended and the cameras were off them that Richie thanked Peter for holding the brolly in such a way that water had been pouring off it and down the back of his neck.

Like a world-class ODI bowler, Richie had a fantastic economy rate. He could sum up moments in a couple of words, and was already ready with a dry quip.

He was commentating with Richard Hadlee once, watching Mike Atherton batting, and poor Athers got hit right in the crown jewels.

'That ball did bounce,' said Hadlee.

'Which one, Richard?' deadpanned Richie.

Another time, summing up a morning watching Geoff Boycott bat, he said, '"Slow" is one word for it. "Torturous" is another.'

When Rod Marsh, who'd not been having his best day, grabbed a streaker during an ODI at Edgbaston in 1981: 'That's the first thing Rodney Marsh has caught today.'

I also liked this one: 'Glenn McGrath dismissed for two, just 98 runs short of his century'. As a tailender myself, I had many such near-misses.

Richie's words carried real weight because he'd had a distinguished playing career. A cunning leg-spinner who took 248 Test wickets at 27 runs apiece, he was also a charismatic leader who never lost a Test series as captain, including three successful Ashes campaigns. I used to love the way he brought all that experience into his commentary.

'Great delivery, edged ... but dropped at third slip by Peter Willey ...'

Then there would be a pause.

'Reminds me of 1959 at the Gabba ...' and he'd go on to relive a similar incident from his encyclopedic memory.

Richie was already planning for his future as a TV broadcaster when he was only four years into his Test career. He spent the spare three weeks between the end of Australia's 1956 Ashes tour of England and flying out to Pakistan for their next match doing a crash course in TV broadcasting at the BBC. Every day for 21 days, from 11am to midnight, he was going to Outside Broadcasts or on set at dramas trying to learn as much as he could. People had only just started watching TV in Australia, so it tells you how forward-thinking he was.

He made his debut as a BBC commentator covering the West Indies tour of England in 1963 alongside the likes of Brian Johnston and Peter West, a year before playing his final Test match. When he started at the Beeb, people were a bit wary of this Australian interloper, but he was so unbiased in his commentary that he soon won people over.

I've occasionally been guilty of getting a bit 'us and them' in commentary on an England match – particularly when we're playing the Aussies – but I don't think Richie ever did that in his many decades as a commentator (and a writer). He had that ability to remain totally clear-headed in his analysis of the game. 'I believe one of the worst words a commentator can use is "we",' he said, 'because there is no such thing in a contest where you are adding to the picture for the viewing public.'

That's probably why he became so loved by Australian and England supporters and cricket lovers all around the world. At the Sydney Ashes Test in 2014, there was a sea of fake Richie Benauds in the crowd as Aussie fans dressed up with silver wigs, beige blazers, ties and big fake channel 9 microphones in tribute to the great man. But there was only one Richie. Back in the Eighties, *Spitting Image* made a puppet of Richie which was a sure sign you'd made an impression here – and with Richie, that impression was all good.

Aggers had it right in his tribute to Richie when he died, aged 84, in 2015: 'He was cricket on TV in England. He was our Richie – and that is the ultimate compliment for an Australian.'

Yes, Richie was a big hero of mine. If you look at his contribution as a player, commentator and general ambassador for the game, he has to be one of the most important people in the game's history. And what a unique voice.

UNIQUE TALENTS, TALISMANS AND GENIUSES

Messing with Viv

Looking back on my list inductees so far, there are a select few among them that I'd place in the category of cricketing geniuses. Ian Botham, Shane Warne and Murali Muralitharan, for definite. Then there are others who, if not geniuses, were certainly very special talents and talismans for their teams: the great Wasim Akram; Hedley Verity and Jacques Kallis in their own quiet ways; Jonty Rhodes as a fielder. In modern times, I think AB de Villiers has a touch of genius about him, too. All of the above could qualify for this next Tuffers HoF section, but they can't be inducted twice, so they'll just have to stay where they are.

Instead I'm going to start by inviting in the 'Master Blaster' Viv Richards. To my mind, Viv was a genius. And he was cool with it. Viv was so cool, when he was awarded the MBE in 1994, he forgot to turn up at Buckingham Palace to collect it.

Eight-and-a-half thousand runs in Test cricket with an average of 50 place him in the top bracket, but it was the manner in which he scored the runs that made him so special. He could absolutely destroy any bowler because he had the skill and power to hit perfectly good balls for fours and sixes, and he did so with more swagger than the Hofmeister Bear. It wasn't arrogance, just absolute self-confidence, because the fact was he was better than anyone else.

I loved watching Viv play, but he was a very intimidating player to bowl to. Looking back, I don't know how I had the bottle to do it. I must have been quite strong-minded, then. Gradually, that erodes over time. Steve Parrish, the former TT motorbike racer, once said, 'When I was 20, I didn't see the bends; when I was 25, I started seeing the curves; when I was 28, I started to see the spectators; when I was 30, I started to see the potholes; when I was 32, I gave up.' I can relate to that, but as a young lad, I was daft enough to take Viv Richards on . . . on a cricket pitch, at least.

In the 1991 Oval Test against the Windies, I had the thrill of getting him out for just two. Before I bowled to him, he looked at me and I looked back at him. We were like a couple of gunslingers ready for a duel. The first ball, he put his front foot down the wicket and played a textbook forward defensive stroke, except he didn't look at the ball as he played the shot, he just continued looking at me. That put me on edge.

The next ball, he ran down the wicket, tried to hit the ball out of the ground . . . and nicked it to Alec Stewart behind the stumps.

That was great, but I nearly got myself in more bother than I could handle with Viv when I bowled to him during an incredible game between Middlesex and Glamorgan in 1993. By then, Viv was getting on a bit, in his early forties, but he could still play as he proved in the first innings, when he made a double-century as Glamorgan racked up 562 for three declared.

We didn't get to bat until the afternoon of day two, but Desi Haynes and Mike Roseberry got stuck in, with Desi making a nice 70-odd before being trapped lbw by Steve Watkin right at the end of the day.

It shows you what a good batting track it was, though, because John Emburey, who came in as nightwatchman, went on to score a century the next day, as did Mike Gatting, who weighed in with 173.

By the end of play, we were still 90-odd behind with just one day to go, so the chances of a win looked slim. We went for it, though, and the next morning our stumper, Keith Brown, made some quick runs to edge us past their score to 584 before the last wicket fell (mine — I had contributed a stylish five runs).

I then went out and produced the best bowling display of my life to date, taking eight for 29 off 23 overs as we skittled them out for 109.

The key wicket was Viv's. I'd knocked over their first three batsmen, so when he strolled in, I was on a roll. Viv didn't look remotely worried though. As usual, he sniffed the air deeply — almost a snort, like a bull ready to charge.

Then as I came into bowl my first ball to him, he stepped away from the crease and waved his arm casually to indicate he wasn't ready.

Unimpressed, I stood there, hands on hips and said, 'What?

We've all got to ****ing wait for you. Are we all here to play your game?'

He gave me an icy stare. I stared back then turned and walked back to my mark.

As I turned, he was still standing up having a look round the field, so I waited a second or two while he took his guard, then ran up. As I reached the wicket, I stopped.

'Frase, can you just move a little bit that way,' I said

Viv glared at me daggers. I looked back at him.

I was still on the wind-up, though.

'Right, are we all ready now?' I announced loudly. 'Okay, good . . .'

By this time, Viv's old Windies team-mate Desi Haynes, who was fielding nearby, was hopping about, looking at me as if I had lost my mind.

'He'll punch you, Tuffers. He'll punch you, man!'

Eventually, a game of cricket broke out again.

I ran up, bowled, Viv got his front foot forward, the ball gripped and bounced a bit higher than he expected, hit him on the glove and John Carr took the catch at short leg.

Got him first ball.

As I walked into the dressing room, Don Bennett came up to me and said, 'Well bowled.'

'Thanks, Don.'

Don set a high bar. I'd been striving to get that 'well bowled' for a long time. And it really was well bowled – up the other end, Embers had taken one-fer off the same number of overs.

There was still work to be done, but everyone was buzzing now and Desi and Mickey Roseberry went out and knocked off the 90-odd runs required before time ran out. It was the most amazing game.

Back in the dressing room all the boys were slapping me on the back, then Desi comes over.

'You might have ****ed up there,' he said.

'What do you mean?'

'Viv's going to come and have a word with you.'

'Wh-wh-wh-wh-what do you mean? He's coming to have a fight with me?'

'I don't know, but he told me he's coming to see you.'

Shit!

Sure enough, a couple of minutes later, Viv sauntered in and all the boys melted away from my corner of the dressing room.

Viv came and sat down beside me.

'Well bowled, man' he said. 'But be careful.'

'Er, thanks. I will, Viv.'

Then he got up, said, 'Very well played, everyone' and walked out.

Viv's actually a lovely man and we get on really well when we bump into each other. Every time he sees me, he says 'Alright, Tuffy' — always Tuffy, not Tuffers. The great man can call me what he likes.

The Little Master

In 2011 an Australian university researcher called Dr Nicholas Rohde came up with a formula for working out who is the best batsman of all time, by comparing their career total runs to the total number of runs an average player of their own era would score over the same number of innings. By the Doc's calculations, Sachin Tendulkar was number one, ahead of Sir Don Bradman at two, Jacques Kallis at three, then Rahul Dravid, Brian Lara, Garry Sobers, Allan Border, Sunil Gavaskar, Steve Waugh and Javed Miandad from four to ten.

Better than The Don? That's debatable, but Bradman himself likened Tendulkar's batting to his own, and I can say from personal experience that he was very useful. At five foot five inches tall, Tendulkar was even shorter than Bradman, but he had a huge aura about him at the batting crease too. I bowled against him in two Test matches in 1993. In Chennai, he scored 165 and India beat us by an innings. Then in Mumbai they beat us by an innings again, but Sachin 'only' got 78 and I got him lbw to keep his average over the two games down to a respectable 121.5.

To get Sachin out in India, with an Indian umpire, it must have been plumb. And I always remember the umpire raising his finger, because it looked like the top half of it had been run over with a steamroller. It was like a lollipop or a table tennis bat.

Sachin's ability was obvious from a young age, but he actually fluffed his lines when his brother Ajit first took him along to nets with a well-known cricket coach in Mumbai called Ramakant Achrekar. Sachin was so nervous he couldn't do a thing right, and at first Achrekar sent him away, telling him to come back in six months' time. Luckily, Ajit persuaded the coach to give his brother another chance that day, and it was the beginning of a beautiful coach–player partnership (Sachin always visited Achrekar before every Test series for many years to come).

Achrekar believed match practice was the best way to learn, and there was never any lack of that available to Tendulkar as a kid. On the famous Shivaji Park, where loads of matches are played side by side every Sunday, he'd play as many as a dozen matches per day, moving from one game to another to bat if he got out.

He was practising like a pro (well, actually a lot more professionally than many pros) long before he became one. By the age of 12, 13, he was practising from seven to nine in the morning, then playing a match (or matches) from half nine to 4.30, and practising again from 5.30 until 7pm.

Sourav Ganguly recalled meeting Tendulkar for the first time at a training camp for the best juniors in India, and how he batted in the nets for hours until the coach had to tell him to stop and give the others a chance. 'Sachin stopped immediately, because he is a fair guy – but until you told him, he wouldn't,' said Ganguly. 'He had a massive hunger to bat . . . His way of working was to bat. No running, no gym, just batting.'

Tendulkar also fancied himself as a fast bowler and even went to trials at the MRF Pace Foundation in Chennai, where Dennis Lillee coached. Five-foot-five fast bowler? Hmm, no. He was told to stick to batting.

In 1988, aged 14, he was one half of a world-record-breaking unbroken partnership of 664 in a school match, with him and his mate Vinod Kambli both scoring triple-centuries. They might have got more, but they made one of the opposition bowlers cry and his team-mates refused to play any more.

I don't think I ever made anyone cry with my batting, although there may have been tears in the eyes of the Aussie close fielders laughing hysterically at my attempts to keep out Shane Warne at Brisbane in 1994.

That schoolboy innings by Tendulkar led the then Indian captain, Dilip Vengsarkar, to invite him to net practice with the national team. 'Tendulkar appeared a genius to me at first sight,' Vengsarkar said later. 'It was simply impossible for me to ignore him.'

He made his Test debut when he was just 16, and although he was only a little fella, he already had man-strength. He had such strong arms – probably from using a bat that was far too big for him when he was a young kid – that he could beat all bar one of the players at arm-wrestling. That arm strength allowed him to use a big heavy bat throughout his career, which, as Brett Lee once put it, 'he just waves around like it's a toothpick'.

On Tendulkar's first tour of Oz in 1991/92, as an 18-year-old, he was already bashing the Aussie bowlers around. In Melbourne, fast bowler Craig McDermott was getting the right hump, and after seeing another bouncer effortlessly hooked to the boundary, he followed through down the pitch and told Tendulkar, 'Bastard, come to Perth – I'll see you there.'

The next Test in Perth, McDermott and Merv Hughes targeted him again with some chin music, but even with the extra zip off the notoriously fast pitch, their bouncers just pinged off the middle of Tendulkar's bat to (or over) the boundary rope even faster.

Big Merv told his captain, the Test record run scorer, Allan Border, 'AB, this little prick's going to get more runs than you.'

He was right – Tendulkar ended up scoring 15,921 Test runs, a good four-and-a-half thousand more than Border managed in his career, to set a new world record, including 51 centuries, also a world record.

Of batsmen who scored over 2,000 Test runs in the 1990s decade, only Tendulkar (58) and Lara (51) averaged over 50 (in the Noughties, 19 batsmen averaged 50-plus). There were bowlers of the class of Allan Donald, Shane Warne and Glenn McGrath, the Walsh–Ambrose and Younis–Akram combos around and in their primes, so to record those kind of figures, you had to be very special. Allan Donald reckoned what set Sachin apart was his ability to adjust to different surfaces. 'You didn't work out Tendulkar in days. You had to plan for him weeks in advance,' he said.

Tendulkar and Rahul Dravid scored nearly 7,000 Test runs in partnership with each other, and Dravid remembers how Sachin made little tweaks to his technique while he was out there in the heat of a Test match, things that mere mortals would need weeks of net practice to perfect.

Tendulkar could flay any attack in the world, but he could also dig in if his team needed that kind of innings. He was also smart enough to adjust his game as he got older, cutting down on shots that were getting him into trouble. For someone capable of playing all the shots, his discipline was incredible. In Australia in 2004, for instance, he was getting out early in his innings playing the cover drive, so he decided to completely cut it out in the next Test in Sydney. Even when Australia brought on their part-time bowlers, he never deviated from his strategy and made a double-hundred.

Most players if they cut out scoring shots get bogged down, eventually lose patience and get out playing a rash shot, but

Tendulkar absolutely backed himself to play as he wanted to play, even if it meant blocking for hours on end. A classic example was the New Year's Test between India and South Africa in Cape Town in 2011, where he faced lightning-fast swing and seam bowling by Dale Steyn on an uneven pitch. He played out maiden after maiden, leaving as many balls as he could and when he did play, just dead-batting it. He did not want to risk playing away from his body at all, as that was what had got him out twice in the previous game. Mid-innings, he decided to stand outside his crease to Steyn to cut down the movement and bounce. Brave, and doing that also cut down his time to react, but no problem for Sachin.

'I am a batsman who goes by feel,' he once said. 'If I feel like doing certain things, I just do them.'

Apparently, he hated it if someone said 'good luck' to him when he went out to bat – luck didn't really come into it when he was at the crease and he didn't believe in it. If I'd known, every time he came out to bat against me I would have got all of my fielders to wish him 'good luck' on the way to the wicket. Then again, it might not have been a good idea to upset him.

Tendulkar was always more than a cricketer in India. People worshipped him like a God. Even his team-mates. VVS Laxman recalled how he stayed around the house of one of Sachin's Mumbai team-mates and found that this guy had a big poster of Sachin on his bedroom wall. That would be like me having a poster of Graham Gooch on my bedroom wall when he was my England team-mate – as great a player as Goochy was, I didn't, but in India, with Sachin, different rules applied.

Despite his God-like status and the riches he made from being a superstar, as an opponent Sachin always came across to me as a humble, respectful sort of chap. He might destroy your bowling, but he did it without lording it over you.

'I've always respected Sachin the person more than Sachin the cricketer,' said Laxman. 'He never thinks he is bigger than the game. He respects his fellow cricketers, junior and senior. Whether in India or abroad, everybody wants a piece of Sachin ... Never have I seen him irritated.'

He must be some guy, if he is a better person than he is a cricketer.

A Lara Lara runs

If having to bowl at sodding Sachin Tendulkar wasn't hard enough, I had another batting genius to contend with during my career: bloody Brian Lara. Lara once said, 'Sachin is a genius; I'm a mere mortal', but I'm not so sure about that and nor was Sachin who called Lara 'God's gift to cricket'.

Another little fella, standing just five foot seven tall, Lara had more moving parts in his batting technique compared to Tendulkar but was just as brilliant.

Lara had an uncanny ability to score runs quickly without hitting the ball in the air. He generated great power with that lovely generous backlift, a flourish of the blade and the absolute purity of his ball-striking, flicking the wrists and angling the bat to thread the ball through gaps in the field. His light footwork and

exceptional hand-to-eye coordination meant good balls were routinely dispatched to the boundary, and that makes life almost
impossible for bowlers. How do you set a field to that?

He hardly seemed to break sweat, because in his prime he was
getting around two-thirds of his runs in first-class cricket in boundaries. He would just casually bully bowlers into submission.

Lara set the bar high for himself from a young age. Aged eight,
he told his sister of his ambition 'to become the greatest cricketer
there has ever been'. It wasn't long before other West Indians – and
especially people from his home island of Trinidad – saw that he
was a special talent, too. At 14, he played in an under-16 national
tournament and scored 745 runs at an average of 126.

Unlike Tendulkar, Lara was in and out of the West Indies team
early on in his Test career. While others wanted to fast-track Lara,
captain Viv Richards felt that it was best to bring him on gradually,
include him in the squad but not play him all the time so he had a
chance to see what Test cricket was all about without too much
pressure. Viv got plenty of criticism for that, and Lara was frustrated, but Viv said he'd rather take that criticism than throw Lara
in at the deep end too early.

When Viv retired from Test cricket in 1991, Richie Richardson
took over as skipper and soon Lara took a leading role in a new era
for West Indies cricket.

The Aussies got a taste of Lara's genius during the West Indies'
1992/93 tour of Oz, hitting a magnificent 277 in the drawn Third
Test to help his team past Australia's big first innings total of 503.
Lara himself was a bit disappointed as, after reaching 265, he said

he was counting down towards reaching Garry Sobers' world record of 365.

After that innings, which tilted the momentum of the series in West Indies' favour, it was impossible to hold back Lara any more as Viv had tried to, because all the world now could see how good he was.

When he made his new Test world record score of 375 against us in Antigua in April 1994, he was unplayable. He didn't give up a single chance in more than two days of batting. From early on, it looked almost inevitable that he'd beat Sobers' record. My captain, Mike Atherton, said as much when he brought me on to bowl on the first day. Brian had only scored 60-odd at the time and at the end of my first over, Athers came over to me.

'Brian's playing well today, he might break the record.'

This was not really what I wanted to hear at the time, but Athers was right.

The outfield was very slow at the Antigua Recreation Ground, which meant some of his shots that would normally have gone for fours only got him two, but that just prolonged the torture for us. With hindsight, it was a beautiful kind of pain though, because it was a privilege to watch one of the greatest innings ever close up.

Brian dedicated that innings to his father, who had died when he was 20, before he had made his Test breakthrough. He credited his dad with instilling in him the three Ds – dedication, discipline and determination – which allowed him to make the most of his talent, and we saw all of those qualities in that innings.

After smashing us, he then came over to play county cricket for

Warwickshire and left a trail of destruction in his wake in his first season. His county statistics in 1994 were ridiculous, and never more so than when, a few weeks after his 375, he hit 501 not out against Durham, beating the previous world-record first-class score of 499 by Pakistan's Hanif Mohammad. He scored 390 of those runs in one day, hitting 62 fours and ten sixes, and rattled along at a rapid rate throughout the innings – his first fifty was the slowest, scored off 60 balls, the following nine took 58, 55, 27, 25, 33, 33, 39, 48 and 28 balls.

It was unfortunate for Lara that a lot of his career coincided with the decline of West Indies cricket. There was a lot more pressure on his shoulders than there would have been if he'd been part of their great sides of the Eighties. He also had the responsibility of three spells as captain to deal with, but there were times when his brilliance allowed West Indies to compete at a level that they could not have done without him.

Take the fantastic 1999 series in the Caribbean against Australia. West Indies were coming off a 5–0 defeat by South Africa and ex-Windies star Michael Holding called the decision to keep Lara as captain 'shocking'. Backed into a corner, Lara showed his battling qualities against an Australian side that looked stronger in almost all departments. After a humiliating First Test thrashing, when West Indies were bowled out for 51 chasing 364 to win, Lara's stunning double-century (213) at Sabina Park in the Second Test, which turned another possible defeat into a ten-wicket victory, was hailed as one of the greatest ever played. But then many people thought his 153 not out in the fourth innings of the Third

Test in Barbados, to guide his team from 105 for five to reach the 308 victory target, was even better.

After watching that, Michael Holding's opinion had turned 180 degrees: 'Brian is a changed man and a better captain these days,' he said.

Lara's third successive century – off 84 balls – in the Fourth and final Test, couldn't prevent an Australia win to square the series 2–2, but without Lara's God-like displays, West Indies wouldn't have had a prayer.

In some relatively thin times for their team, Lara was always a ray of hope for West Indies fans and joy to watch for any cricket lover. I was there in Antigua as an England fan ten years after the 375, watching live as he became the first person to score a quadruple-century in Test cricket. England had already won the series 3–0 going into that final Test, but Lara's 400 not out stole the show with its historic achievement. Wonderful player.

The Don

Lara's 400 also saw him become only the second player after Don Bradman to score two triple-centuries in Test matches. Whereas I had first-hand experience of bowling to Tendulkar and Lara, I've only seen the odd video snippets of Sir Don Bradman in action. But going on his mind-blowing stats and the many people who've said he's the greatest batsmen who ever lived, 'The Don' is a cert for any sporting hall of fame, let alone just cricket.

A *Wisden* poll in 2000 asked 100 eminent cricketing people

around the world to nominate the five greatest players of the twentieth century. All 100 voted for Bradman. That's a better result than a dictator could hope for in a rigged presidential election.

Bradman's Test average of 99.94 was ridiculous. Even if you subtracted all of the centuries he scored in first-class cricket – and he scored 117 of them in 338 innings – the average of all his other scores under 100 was 58.20, higher than the lifetime averages of players of the calibre of Geoff Boycott, Denis Compton, Garry Sobers, Viv Richards and Wally Hammond. 'Bradman: a genius and twice as good as any other batsman,' was Boycs's verdict.

I guess the nearest equivalent in team sport today where players' records stand out way above the rest is in football, with Lionel Messi and Cristiano Ronaldo. The difference is that in cricket back then, there was no Ronaldo to Bradman's Messi (or vice versa, depending on who you reckon is the better of those two football legends). There was only one Don Bradman and everyone else was streets behind him. As Bradman's team-mate Bill Woodfull put it: 'He's a freak.'

Bradman scored centuries (including three doubles) in eight consecutive Tests against England either side of World War Two. His lowest batting average in a Test series was in the notorious 'Bodyline' series of 1932/33, but his average of 56.57 was still the best on either side of any batsman who played at least eight innings in the series.

So how did he score his runs?

Bradman was only five foot seven inches tall and always used a lightish bat weighing somewhere between 2lb 2oz and 2lb 5oz because he found it easier to place the ball with a lighter blade. Also, a lighter bat was less tiring for him to carry around when he was batting all day – not a consideration I ever had to worry about when I was choosing a bat.

Technically, he wasn't textbook. He had a strong 'bottom-handed' grip, so when he lifted the bat up, the face was closed and it went towards the slips rather than straight back. He picked up that style as a kid practising on his own, bouncing the ball off a water tank and hitting the ball with a cricket stump. There was a wall right next to him on the offside, so he naturally developed a grip to whip the ball legside.

On trial at the SCG in 1926, Bradman was advised to change it, but he couldn't get on with a more neutral grip, and he felt that while his grip restricted his offside play a little, it helped him roll the wrists over onside shots and keep the ball down.

During Bradman's first Test series, in 1928/29, England bowler Maurice Tate told him, 'You'll have to learn to play with a straighter bat before you come to England.'

He didn't need to because of his freakishly quick reflexes, foot-work and hand-to-eye coordination. And although his bat may not have come straight up and down, when it met the ball with a defensive shot, it was as straight as could be.

Denis Compton said Bradman 'had a marvellous gift of getting into position quicker than any batsman I have ever seen, playing the ball very late, and was never off-balance, or stretching out of control'.

Don hit the first six of his first-class career against Oxford University in 1930 off a no-ball by a slow bowler called Ian Peebles. Peebles later described the experience of a Bradman innings like this: 'Think of all the best strokes one has ever seen, all played in the course of an afternoon.'

Gubby Allen reckoned that Bradman 'had two shots for every ball when he was going well'. He was particularly destructive on the back foot, hitting fours with everything from powerful pulls to delicate late cuts.

It is believed that two-thirds of Bradman's first-class centuries were scored without him offering up a single chance to the opposition fielders, because he rarely hit the ball in the air until his team was fully in control of the match. Indeed, he only hit six sixes in his entire Test career, and most of those came after he'd reached a century or even double-century.

Plenty of players nowadays can score very quickly, but Bradman's genius – like Lara after him – was being able to do so without taking a risk. He turned batting into an exact science, exploiting gaps in any field setting. 'He must have memorised the exact position of every fielder to the inch,' reckoned Sir Len Hutton. 'He could pull the ball exactly where he wanted it to go and that's no exaggeration.' The dashing Keith Miller (who was my dad's cricketing hero, despite being an Aussie) agreed with Sir Len, saying, 'When Bradman hooked the ball, he could almost choose the picket it was going to hit along the boundary fence.'

On top of pinpoint ball-striking ability, he had the insatiable appetite for scoring runs, to build big innings after big innings. Alec

Bedser, who actually had more success than most bowling to Brad-man, said of The Don, 'He had all the strokes – and the will and nerve to crush a bowler's heart.'

'Once he goes to the crease, Don Bradman forgets everything else but the scoring of runs,' remarked Denis Compton.

As you'd expect, Bradman was also super-competitive, and that competitiveness applied to all sports he played. For example, when he was 26, he was invited to play a game of billiards with Walter Lindrum, one of the great billiards players of all time. Bradman was pretty good at the three-ball game and scored a 56 break first go, before Lindrum stepped up and reeled off his usual effortless cen-tury break. Getting beaten by a top professional in their sport is no disgrace, but Bradman was so annoyed he had a billiards room built at his new home and practised for a year until he could make a century too.

He was cricket's first superstar, long before people had TVs let alone social media to spread the word of his brilliance. His legend grew by word of mouth and he got so much fan mail, his mum once complained, 'If Don breaks any more records, I don't know how I will manage to get through the clerical work involved in answering congratulations.'

He was the greatest crowd puller Australia had ever known. Some-one once looked at the daily attendances over seventy-odd days of Australian Shield matches, comparing when The Don was batting to when he wasn't, and the crowd was almost double the size if it was a Bradman batting day. But it didn't matter if you weren't Australian, everyone wanted see him play. Wherever he was playing, as soon as the first wicket fell, there was a buzz of anticipation as the great Don Bradman was about to walk out at number three.

Some opposing clubs that faced Australia on tour even put Australia into bat on good batting pitches so the spectators could watch him bat (and to swell the club's coffers as well, no doubt). When he came over to England, English fans almost willed him to do well against our bowlers, because they just wanted to see genius at work. Dickie Bird said that his dad walked the 17 miles between Barnsley and Leeds, there and back, every day of the 1934 Headingley Test to see Bradman play live. It was worth Mr Bird's effort as The Don scored 304, his second triple-century at Headingley (he'd scored a world-record-breaking 334 in 1930). In a total of four Tests and six Test innings at Headingley, he averaged 192.60.

I was amazed to discover that he nearly played for Accrington in the Lancashire League. In 1931, they offered him £600 to come over from Australia and play. Don was considering it, because at the time he was earning much less working for a sports retailer in Australia. It caused a hullabaloo in Australia and England for weeks, but eventually three companies in Australia clubbed together to offer him a A$1,500 two-year contract, which he accepted even though he could have made more in England with media work and endorsements. So Lancashire League spectators were denied the honour of watching Bradman week in, week out – and bowlers the chance to have their bowling averages destroyed by him.

Were there any chinks in his armour? Some said he wasn't so good batting on a 'sticky dog', but Hedley Verity wasn't having that criticism after bowling to him on such a pitch. 'Don't ever tell me Don is just ordinary on sticky ones,' said Verity. 'It was a pig of a pitch and he played me in the middle of the bat right through.'

In the field, Bradman was renowned for being very quick and had a very strong, accurate throw from the boundary, but his catching was somewhat less assured, and he dropped a few along the way. His occasional leg-breaks were nothing special either, getting him two wickets in 52 Tests. Another thing he wasn't good at was winning the toss. In nine Tests as captain in England, he called 'heads' every time and was wrong eight times out of nine. What's wrong with 'tails', Don?

But I'm picking holes here. The Don really was the don. As Denis Compton put it, 'He was unique; a batsman appearing not just once in a lifetime, but once in the life of a game.'

Pleasantly weary with Richard Hadlee

On to the all-rounders and an era when Ian Botham, Imran Khan, Kapil Dev and Richard Hadlee were all vying to be considered the best all-rounders in the world. Of the Big Four, Hadlee was the one who perhaps had to carry the biggest burden, because he was often playing for a relatively weak New Zealand side and so much responsibility rested on his shoulders. He was the talisman who set the example for team-mates with his skill and professionalism and helped them reach new heights.

A brilliant bowling all-rounder, he was the first bowler ever to take 400 Test wickets. He had a textbook bowling action, was able to swing and seam the ball with tight control at speed, and was right up there with the best specialist fast bowlers of his time. His batting wasn't as consistent as his bowling at Test level (as his average of 27 shows), but he was capable of some destructive innings; for instance, when he smashed 99 to set up an innings victory against England in just three days in Christchurch in 1984 (he also took eight wickets in the game).

Amazingly, only a year before that wonderful all-round performance, Richard had suffered a mental breakdown. It happened soon after playing in New Zealand's first-ever Test match victory on English soil, at Headingley. By then he was a national hero, travelling around the world for months on end, in demand by the media, getting loads of commercial work. He was also writing books, doing guest-speaking, working as a PR officer, not to mention running his own promotions company. So he was mad busy and one day, during a festival match in New Zealand, it all got on top of him.

'I started the game, but couldn't go on,' he recalled. 'I came off the pitch in a daze, wondering what the hell was happening to me. I couldn't see properly and my head was splitting. Somehow I got home and went to bed.'

He started getting severe chest pains and went to bed each night convinced he was going to die. He was convinced he had heart trouble, but when his family finally persuaded him to see a doctor, the doc told him he just needed to slow down.

He lost his mojo for a while, and didn't want to do much of anything let alone play cricket. Then, in Auckland he bumped into a cricket-loving motivation expert called Grahame Felton, who helped him out of the trough. Felton had never applied his techniques to cricket before, but within a couple of weeks, Hadlee was on the road to recovery.

After that, Hadlee always carried a 'motivation card' in his cricket bag with trigger phrases he had worked out with Felton. For instance, 'Never get tired – just pleasantly weary', the idea being that if you walk off the pitch saying you are shattered, you will feel shattered. I wish I told myself something similar when I pulled an all-nighter and had to go straight to training. 'I'm not knackered and still pissed, I'm pleasantly weary and unsober...' It's all about positive thinking.

Another line on his card read, 'Goals, aims, targets – be better than opposition – beat opponent', and the opponent Hadlee was obsessed with beating was Ian Botham to prove he was the best all-rounder. 'I had a fixation about him,' admitted Hadlee. 'He was the one I had to beat, whether with wickets or runs.' And in his next series against England, in 1984, he turned it into a personal duel with Beefy (Hadlee took more wickets, but Botham edged him on the runs, so we'll call it a draw). He also encouraged the other New Zealand players to pick their opposite number in the England side and try and beat them too. Nowadays, sports psychologists are part of the setup of all top teams, but Hadlee was some way ahead of his time with the methods he picked up from Felton, and it all came about by chance after his breakdown.

Once he recovered, his big target with his county club, Nottinghamshire, in 1984 was to become the first cricketer in modern times to score 1,000 runs and take 100 wickets in an English season (the last person to do it had been Middlesex and England's Fred Titmus in 1967, but that was before the number of county games was reduced from 28 to 24).

Hadlee was a military planner, and he plotted exactly how he would hit his target. Allowing for a decent British summer and days lost to rain, he reckoned he had the equivalent of 20 full games to hit his target, so he'd need to average 50 runs and five wickets per game. Then he broke down in detail how he would achieve his goal – yup, time for another list for his cricket bag. The list of targets included: 'Ten bags of five wickets'; '60 wickets at Trent Bridge, 40 away' (he even worked out which grounds he had his best chance of getting his wickets); 'three centuries and six fifties'; 'better career-best batting/bowling' and so on. He even went as far as to budget how many overs he expected to bowl, how many maidens, how many runs he'd concede, how many innings he'd bat, and his expected averages with bat and ball.

He beat some mini-targets, fell short on others, but ultimately reached his goal taking 117 wickets (74 at Trent Bridge, 43 away, averaging 14 runs apiece) and scoring 1,179 runs (averaging 51, way over the his 'budget score' of 34).

Maybe I should have made more lists, but it makes me pleasantly weary just thinking about it.

Pleasure in Proctershire

A great all-round cricketer who perhaps maybe doesn't get the recognition he deserves is Mike Procter. Procter was unfortunate that most of his career was at a time when South Africa were excluded from international cricket due to apartheid. One of his great admirers was Sir Garry Sobers, who said it was 'tragic' that Procter never had the chance to play more Test cricket. International cricket's loss was English county cricket's – and, more precisely, Gloucestershire's – gain, but he might not have come over to England if it hadn't been for a rule change.

The game was in the doldrums over here in the mid-Sixties. With attendances down, the authorities needed to do something to bring the crowds back, so they made it easier for clubs to import talent. There was a regulation that said players had to have lived in a county for a year before they would qualify to play for that county's team. Procter said later that he wouldn't have been prepared to spend a year twiddling his thumbs in Gloucestershire, as it would have meant missing the South African cricket season and perhaps, with South Africa still in Test cricket at the time, his chance to attract the attention of international selectors. The removal of the 'gap year' demand meant Procter did come over, and English cricket fans got a chance to see a lot of him in action in years to come when South Africa were isolated from the international game.

He did get to play some Test cricket and when the Aussies toured South Africa in 1966/67, they got a taste of young Procter's bowling ability. Twelfth man in the first two Tests, Procter took match figures of seven for 98 on debut in the Third Test. Sadly, he didn't get much chance to build on that, playing only seven Tests in total – all against Australia, including a 4–0 massacre of the

Aussies in 1969/70 – taking 41 wickets at a cost of 15 apiece, before South Africa were completely excluded from Test cricket.

He never made a Test match fifty in those early days, but he was already developing into a tremendously destructive batsman. Playing for Western Province against the Aussies during that 1969/70 tour, he thrashed 155 in 130 minutes, hammering five of his nine sixes off successive balls from Ashley Mallett, which helped him zip from 100 to 150 in 12 minutes.

When Procter joined Gloucestershire in 1965, it was a fairly lowly team, but his talismanic presence and ability lifted them to heights they hadn't experienced for many years. So influential was he that Gloucestershire's supporters rechristened their club 'Proctershire'. Playing against Procter in his prime could be as enjoyable as a proctoscopy, but with Mike on their side Gloucester fans enjoyed a lot of success. His century of wickets in 1969 helped the team to the runners-up spot in the county championship, and victories in the 1973 Gillette Trophy and 1977 Benson & Hedges Cup followed.

He was a muscular fast bowler, who thundered in off a long run-up, released the ball chest-on – and off the wrong foot – with a great whirl of the arms. He was so strong he could generate the same sort of pace off his short run. It might have looked an awkward action, but it was the way Procter had naturally bowled from a young age, and luckily neither his dad (a decent cricketer whose career was cut short by a wartime injury) nor his junior coaches tried to change him. Instead, they let him deliver the ball in his own way, and focused on drilling him on line and length, changes of pace and using the crease to change the angle of attack.

Procter's the sort of bowler I would have dreaded facing. His bouncer was one of the most feared in world cricket, because his open-chested action meant the ball speared in at the batsman and kept chasing him – I'd have been nearer the square-leg umpire than leg stump if he'd bowled to me. He knew how to get the ball to straighten up, too, setting a record as the first bowler to take two hat-tricks of lbw decisions.

He wasn't afraid to mix things up either, as he did on the way to B&H success in 1977, taking six for 13 – including four wickets in five balls – bowling round the wicket against Hampshire, knocking out Gordon Greenidge's middle stump and getting Barry Richards lbw along the way. Two good scalps there.

A powerful middle-order destroyer, Procter could have got into any Test side on his batting alone. Unlike his bowling, his batting technique was textbook and he was a fantastic straight driver of the ball. Playing for Rhodesia in 1970, he equalled the world record held by Sir Don Bradman and CB Fry, of six first-class centuries in a row. Back in England, he hit seven tons for Gloucestershire in 1971, and was leading century-maker in the county championship in 1973 with six hundreds.

If all that wasn't enough, he had a safe pair of hands too. In 1969, he took the most catches (33) of any fielder in the county championship, winning a hundred-quid prize from the sponsors, Ceylon Tea Centre. Riches indeed.

Former team-mate David Graveney summed him up: 'Procter was a champion. "Give me the ball, the bat and I'll make it happen." That's what he was like. He could do anything.'

Sobers: the six-in-one-cricketer

An all-rounder worthy of an honorable mention is Bermudan Alma 'Champ' Hunt for one very special all-round performance. Alma moved to Scotland in the 1930s to play as a pro for Aberdeenshire and in 1939 he produced an incredible display against West Lothian. First he took seven for 11 as Aberdeenshire bowled out their opponents for 48. Then he knocked off all the runs required himself in 25 minutes, hitting eight fours and two sixes. As the match finished early, Alma then kindly gave the West Lothian players a coaching session.

That's impressive multi-tasking, but old Alma has nothing on the big daddy of all-rounders, Sir Garfield Sobers. Sir Don Bradman called Sobers a 'five-in-one cricketer', because Sobers could bat, bowl three different styles and field brilliantly too. Make that a six-in-one cricketer, because he was a good captain, as well.

Let's look at his batting first. He made his West Indies debut at 17 and batted down the order at number nine. It was almost four years before Sobers made his first Test century, in his fourth full series. When he broke the three-figure barrier for the first time, at Sabina Park in Jamaica against Pakistan in February 1958, he just kept going until he'd racked up a Test world record score of 365 not out. Only two other cricketers in history – Aussie Bob Simpson (1964) and Karun Nair of India against England in the winter of 2016 – have managed to turn their first Test hundred into a triple. A very special achievement.

Sobers had an excellent defensive technique, but he preferred to attack. He knew how demoralising it can be for a bowler to have good-length balls dispatched to the boundary and he was also a crowd-pleaser. 'We have to give the spectators entertainment when we are batting,' he said.

Sobers was confident of dominating any kind of bowling: pace, swing, seam and spin. He was fearless, too. He was so confident in his ability against fast bowlers, he didn't even bother wearing a thigh pad against the likes of Dennis Lillee and Wes Hall – that is just mental.

On the rare occasions that a bowler got the upper hand on him, he'd get them back soon enough. For instance, on his first tour of Oz in 1960/61 he scored two and a duck against New South Wales when Richie Benaud bamboozled him with his googly. After the match, Australia's team manager came in to the Windies' dressing room and said to Sobers, 'Don't you worry, son. You'll get to pick him sometime . . .'

Soon after, at the First Test at the Gabba (which ended in a tie), the Aussies were picking the ball up from the boundary as Sobers smacked 132 in better than even time, with Benaud suffering brutal treatment.

'It's a good thing that you could not pick Richie or you would have murdered him!' Bradman joked to Sobers afterwards.

He learnt how to keep the ball on the deck playing lots of 'pick-up' games with a tennis ball as a young kid, where everyone would join in and there could be 20 or 30 fielders at any time. With so many pairs of hands to catch you out, Sobers taught himself how to strike straight balls on the rise and roll the wrists over cross-bat strokes to keep the ball down.

Tall with strong arms, wrists and shoulders, he had a big backlift, a high and straight follow-through on drives, and perfect timing, which together gave him the power to take the aerial route too. With unforgiving old-fashioned bats, Sobers knew that he could beat fielders on the boundary even with a mishit. On the golf course, he could carry the ball over 300 yards, further than most professionals at that time. He was just a natural ball-striker.

Famously, Sobers was the first person to hit six sixes in an over in first-class cricket, and there is nice little story behind that which I hadn't heard before.

He'd joined Nottinghamshire in 1968 even though they had been scrapping around at the bottom of the county championship for a few years. It was a case of going to the highest bidder, but when his agent told him that he'd be going to Notts, Garry was happy enough because he liked the Trent Bridge pitch. So much so that when the move was confirmed during England's tour of the West Indies, Sobers struck a bet with Bunty Ames, the wife of England manager Les Ames. He bet her six bottles of champagne that he could get Notts into the top six in his first season.

He went into the last game at Glamorgan in August with his bet almost won. He'd scored well over 1,000 runs, taken 80-odd wickets and they just needed a few points from the final match for Sobers to get his champers. But Glamorgan were a good side and chasing the title, so it was not a foregone conclusion.

A big crowd were in for the first day on Saturday, and Notts got off to a flyer and had racked up 300 before captain Sobers came in at number seven. When he'd got 40, he decided to just bat one or two more overs before declaring.

The bowler of the next over, Malcolm Nash, had opened the bowling at medium pace but had changed to Derek Underwood-ish-speed spin by this point. Unfortunately for Nash, Garry had his eye on the short legside boundary and planned to thrash every ball he could as hard as possible in that direction.

He middled the first four balls for sixes, and the Welsh crowd, sensing history in the making, were urging him on. The next ball pitched outside his off stump though and he didn't quite get hold of it, skying the ball to the long-off fielder, who caught it but toppled over at the boundary markers. Sobers thought he was out and was ready to walk off, but even the Glamorgan fans were yelling 'Six!' and after the umpires went to check a six was signalled.

A shellshocked Nash obligingly dropped the last ball too short on middle and leg and Sobers smashed it out of the ground and down the street, his biggest hit yet. Fortunately, the TV cameras were there that day to record the moment – 'My goodness, it's gone way down to Swansea!' said commentator Wilf Wooller.

Peter Walker, fielding at slip, said later, 'It wasn't a six, it was 12!' and the ball was a still rolling when a local kid picked it up – he brought it back to the ground the next day, which was very honest of him.

Glamorgan captain Tony Lewis described Sobers' blitz as 'not sheer slogging, but scientific hitting with every movement moving in harmony'. Watch the video of the over on YouTube and you see that Tony was right. Amazing batting.

As a member of the slow left-armer's union, I've got to feel sorry for Malcolm Nash, who was a decent bowler and had a good career. Nash himself saw the bright side almost straight away, though. When Sobers bumped into him at the end of the day, he was surprised just how chipper Nash was and told him so.

'And why not?' replied Nash. 'You're not the only one who goes into the record books, you know. I do, too!'

Good attitude that, Nashy. And for that he's entering my Hall of Fame as well. Especially as he added to his legend by getting boshed for five sixes and a four by Lancashire's Frank Hayes in 1977 to become the bowler who conceded the highest and second highest number of runs ever scored in a first-class cricket over.

As for Nottinghamshire, they got their top-six finish and Garry got his bottles of bubbly from Bunty.

What about his bowling? I can only compare Sobers to the best chefs on *Professional Masterchef*, who always seem to be cooking ingredients three ways in a bid to impress the judges – roasted cauliflower, cauliflower puree and a cauliflower foam . . . that sort of thing. Well, Sobers wowed the crowds by bowling batsmen out with either seam bowling, wrist spin or orthodox finger spin.

There's never been another Test bowler like him – in his prime, he would swap effortlessly between the different methods and take wickets. Apart from the skill required, it takes some nerve to bowl in three different styles at Test level. Incredible.

He started out in the Test team as a slow left-armer. As a wrist-spinner, he could bowl a mean googly until 1966, after which shoulder trouble stopped him doing so any more and he had to rely on his leg-break and top-spinner, which limited his effectiveness.

He developed his seam bowling playing league cricket in

England where the conditions were more suited to it. He had such a smooth, rhythmical bowling action, he found that he could generate plenty of pace running in off a dozen paces, which made his bouncer a lethal surprise weapon.

He was capable of bowling the odd ball as fast as Wes Hall when he wanted to, but it was his ability to swing and dip the ball into the right-hander and get the odd one to move away off the pitch that got him most wickets.

Whatever method he was bowling, he used to hustle through his overs. His logic was that the quicker he got through his overs, the quicker he could get wickets, and he wasn't one for deliberately slowing down over rates.

One of the few bowlers of his time to get 200 Test wickets, his average of 34 isn't the best, but there were some reasons for that. He bowled to get batsmen out, not just contain them – especially when bowling wrist-spin or fast. Also, he played most of his international cricket in the Caribbean at a time when the pitches over there favoured the batsmen. West Indies had the great fast bowlers Wes Hall and Charlie Griffith and spinner Lance Gibbs around, too, so Sobers often got second choice of which end to bowl. And he also did a lot of batting, so there were a few factors which made it harder for him.

Opponent and admirer Trevor Bailey still reckoned Sobers was the most complete bowler at international level he ever saw: 'If he had not used a certain amount of effort in scoring more runs than anybody else, he must surely have broken the record for the number of wickets taken.'

Sobers was also a brilliant fielder anywhere on the park. And as captain, he won his first three series after being given the West Indies job in 1965, including their first-ever victory over Australia. His record suffered over the next few years as the overall standard of the Windies team dropped.

He was always an attacking captain, and occasionally that went against him. He got loads of stick for losing the Fourth Test during England's 1967/68 tour of the Windies, after declaring and setting them 215 to win, in two-and-three-quarter hours. The Windies even rattled through 21 overs per hour, when even bowling 18 an hour (which is loads more than you'd see nowadays) would have meant England couldn't have reached the target.

'That never entered my mind – I was trying to win,' said Sobers, even though that defeat ultimately cost his team the series. 'I made that declaration for cricket. If I had not done so, the game would have died.'

That sums up his principles, his desire to play entertaining cricket for the paying punters, and that's what made such an exciting cricketer who was loved worldwide.

Sir Garry, welcome to the Tuffers HoF.

Deadly duos, top teams, game-changers, war heroes, legendary spinners, speed merchants, batting geniuses, awesome all-rounders, magic fielders, the best umps, classic commentators, hair transplantees, the Lord's cat, and even a few Australians . . . I reckon that I've covered most bases. But before I pull the rope across and roll up the red carpet, there are just a few others I want to squeeze into my Hall of Fame.

Iggy nose best

My mate Alan Igglesden, the former Kent and England cricketer, is a hero to me for the way he's dealt with having a brain tumour that was discovered just after he retired in 1999. At the time, it was thought that he might not live five years, but, happily, he's still with us, living a full life, and does a lot of work to raise awareness and money for Brain Tumour UK to help fund more research into the disease. I always look forward to the annual Iggy Golf Day, which raises a few quid for the cause.

I first got to know Iggy when we toured the West Indies together with England in 1994 and I'll always remember a night out we had at Millers beach bar in Antigua. About four in the morning, there were me, Matthew Maynard, Robin Smith, Devon Malcolm and Iggy still standing (just about), when a load of yachtsmen who were doing a race around Antigua parked up nearby and came in. They thought they were Joe Bananas and picked a fight with us. I remember getting pushed about and looking around for help.

Devon and Judgey weren't looking fit to do anything, but Iggy ran up behind this bloke who was having a go at me. Now, Iggy is six foot six tall, a big unit, and I'd have fancied him to knock him over with a solid rugby tackle. Instead, for reasons best known to himself, he reached over the top of the guy's head and stuck two fingers up his nostrils.

'I've got him! I've got him!' he cried.

Strangest way I've ever seen anyone break up a fight. It worked though and it was hilarious.

The odd couple

Gladstone Small and Andy Caddick were two very good bowlers and a very lively opening pair for England, but I'm voting them into the Tuffers HoF for their comedy value when we were warming up.

Stoney is a stocky figure who famously has no neck — his head just sits on his shoulders – whereas Caddy is a tall, wiry string bean of a man with, shall we say, prominent ears.

The physio would go, 'Arms forward . . . arms back . . . now put your right ear to your right shoulder . . .'. Stoney's head didn't move independently of his shoulders so his right ear didn't get any closer, while Caddy hardly had to move to get his ear to his shoulder. Always made me laugh that.

Stoney was also a favourite of mine because he was fond of a having a nap in the dressing room. We'd have to wake him up when it was nearly time for him to bat. He was a senior pro and I thought, 'Thank God, there's someone else like me here.'

The unlikeliest SPOTY ever

Only four cricketers have ever won the BBC Sports Personality of the Year award. There were Jim Laker in 1956, after his amazing ten-fer against the Aussies at Old Trafford, and all-rounders Ian Botham (1981) and Freddie Flintoff (2005) for their Ashes heroics, and the other was a grey-haired batsman who had played just three Tests, hadn't scored a century and was part of a losing Ashes team.

In summer 1975, David Steele, a journeyman Northamptonshire player, had been called up to play for an England team that was in dire straits. They'd been murdered 4–1 by the Aussies Down Under the previous winter, had lost the First Test by an innings, their captain, Mike Denness, had been sacked, and new skipper Tony Greig was desperate to find a top-order batsman who could defend against the firepower of Dennis Lillee and Jeff Thomson. Geoff

Boycott had made himself unavailable for selection since Denness was made captain instead of him, so Greigy asked county umpires who was the most Boycs-like alternative and Steele was the name he kept hearing.

When Steele turned up at Lord's for his Test debut, the other England boys laughed at his tatty old gloves and boots that looked like they could fall apart at the seams at any moment. England selector Len Hutton called him 'Derek'. In net practice on the morning of his first Test innings, Steele was bowled so many times that he stopped batting because his confidence was being destroyed. New team-mate Dennis Amiss said, 'I could not imagine anyone who looked less like an England batsman.' Then when it was Steele's turn to go out and face the chin music from 'Lillian Thomson', he went down one flight of stairs too many inside the Lord's Pavilion and found himself by the gents toilet rather than striding through the Long Room.

Out on the pitch, though, he played Lillian Thomson better than any of England's other batters. Wearing just a cap on his head, he defended fearlessly on the front foot, hooked bouncers from in front of his face, and continued to do so throughout the series. His valuable innings of 50, 45, 73, 92, 39 and 66 helped England steady the ship to get three draws. England were denied the chance to square the series when the final Test was called off due to the Headingley pitch being vandalised, but cricket fans – and people in general – warmed to Steele's Churchillian spirit and voted for him in their droves to be their SPOTY.

It's just a lovely story of a really good cricketer taking his chance at the top level after years of hard graft. And winning Sports Personality of the Year without winning a match is some achievement. That's why I'm inducting you in my Hall of Fame, Der– I mean, David.

WG the lifesaver

WG Grace played first-class cricket for 44 seasons from 1865 to 1908, scored 54,211 runs, took 2,809 wickets and was the first superstar all-rounder of the game. He was also, by all accounts, a mercenary and a bit of a cheat. I'm going to give him the benefit of the doubt and have him in the Tuffers HoF, though, because he did once save a team-mate's life.

That happened in June 1887, playing in a match for his team, Gloucestershire, against Lancashire at Old Trafford. Gloucester were fielding when Alexander Croome dashed to prevent a boundary at Old Trafford. Running at top speed he missed the ball, then tried to hurdle the railings at the Stretford End. Croome had been a competitive hurdler for Oxford University, but he misjudged his leap and succeeded only in impaling himself through the throat on one of the spikes. Ouch. Luckily, WG, a qualified doctor, was there and held the wound together with his bare hands for half an hour while medical assistance was summoned. Well played, Doc.

Best teeth

The first time I came across David Ward was playing a Second XI match for Middlesex against Surrey, so it was a big grudge match.

He walked out to bat, number four, and he had his helmet on to face the faster bowlers, then me and my mate Jamie Sykes, an off-spinner, came on to bowl in tandem. As Sykesy was about to begin his spell, David took his helmet off.

'Whoa, ****ing hold on!' said Sykesy loudly. 'Have you had a look at this geezer? Everyone? Have you seen this bloke?'

Jamie, in his own subtle, sensitive way was drawing our attention to Wardy's front teeth. And they were pretty eye-catching – big tombstones, and so frilly he could eat an apple through a tennis racket.

'Yeah? And? What's the matter?' Wardy replied, not in an aggressive way, just standing up for himself. Straight away, I admired him for that, not letting Sykesy psyche him out with his school playground sledging.

I played against 'Gnasher' (as he was inevitably nicknamed) a few times after that. He seemed like a top bloke and I would have liked to have got to know him better, but he was a Surrey boy, so I couldn't get too close. He was a bloody good attacking batsman, too. And he remains, to this day, the cricketer with the most spectacular set of Hampstead Heaths I've ever seen.

Fielding farce

As the founder member of the Phil Tufnell Fielding Academy, I do enjoy a good fielding cock-up, and I found out about an all-time great Pythonesque fielding farce that occurred on a hill in Sussex many years ago. Rottingdean Cricket Club is one of the oldest clubs in England and in the 1800s their home ground was on top of Beacon Hill, and in the days before boundaries were introduced, that meant some long chases for the fielders.

In one game, a batsman hit a lofted drive that ran down the hill into the village. The fielding side dispatched a man to get the ball, and the others formed a chain gang so they could throw it to each other back to the pitch. When the ball finally reached the wicket-keeper, the batsmen had already run 30-odd, but the keeper sensed the chance of a run-out and launched the ball at the stumps. Not the brightest idea, as all his team-mates were still behind him chugging up the hill at the time. He missed and the ball rolled off down the other side of the hill and down the main road towards Brighton, so the fielders had to do it all again while the batters ran 67. Buzzers!

Kohli and Rooty

Looking at the current crop of cricketers around the world, the two that stand out for me most as future legends are India's Virat Kohli and England's own Joe Root.

Kohli is in his late twenties, a couple of years older than Joe, and actually might already have reached that status. By the end of 2016, he was averaging 50-plus in Test, ODI and T20 internationals, which is a phenomenal record, especially as he has had the added responsibility of captaining India's Test team since the end of 2014. He also took on the captaincy of India's limited-overs sides in January 2017, and judging by the century he scored in his first

ODI as skipper to successfully chase down the target of 350 set by England (our highest-ever score against India), that is not going to be a problem for him either. That was his seventeenth second-innings century in one-day internationals, putting him level with Sachin Tendulkar as king of the ODI run chase, and he's scored them in just 96 matches, 136 fewer than Sachin. Michael Vaughan tweeted after the match 'Best Test player . . . KOHLI. Best ODI player . . . KOHLI. Best T20 player . . . KOHLI' and I couldn't disagree with that.

Rooty has played much less international limited-overs cricket than Kohli, and his averages are not quite as sensational, but still very good. In Tests, though, by the start of 2017, they had both played 53 matches, and Rooty actually had the better average – 53 compared to Kohli's 50. As England's newly appointed Test captain, it will be interesting to see if he copes with that role as well as Kohli has with India and keeps piling up the runs. I'm confident Rooty will and I don't think it's too much of a leap of faith to add him and Kohli to the Tuffers HoF roster.

Dedication's what you need

When I was younger I was always more attracted to flair players in sport, the ones who seemed to play off the cuff. For instance, in snooker, Alex 'Hurricane' Higgins and Jimmy 'Whirlwind' White were the players I was drawn to – indisciplined off the table, inconsistent on it, but exciting to watch and, at their best, capable of blowing any opponent away.

In recent years, I've grown to have more respect for the relentless hard workers who win week after week. People like five-time Olympic champion Steve Redgrave, who devoted his life to rowing, pushing himself to the limit day in, day out for two decades. Or Mo Farah, who does every little thing possible in training to shave seconds off his race times, because he knows that could be the difference between winning gold and losing. There's Mo running 120 miles a week and sleeping in an oxygen tent next to his wife. In my cricketing prime, I was trying to sleep with women and then run back to the team hotel in the early hours without getting spotted by management.

In modern cricket, I'll pick out Alastair Cook, who's made himself into an all-time-great England batsman, scoring 11,000-plus runs, breaking records along the way, and he's basically only got three scoring shots – a clip, a pull and a cut. Cooky's a great example to any wannabe of how to make the most of your ability through hard work and dedication. To someone like me, who loved my cricket, but also enjoyed a night out, it seems like he's made a lot of sacrifices, but maybe they aren't sacrifices to him because he loves what he does. I couldn't have been like Cooky, but I really admire him and he's a Hall of Famer for sure.

When he's on form, Cooky will bat all day for England if that's what's required. His dig-in ability takes me back to my childhood watching Geoff Boycott on telly, although sometimes Boycs would drop anchor even if the team didn't need him to. Only joking, Geoffrey. Your record of over 8,000 runs in Test cricket, averaging 47 and losing only 20 of the 108 Tests you played shows that your single-minded approach usually paid dividends for the team.

Yes, Boycs, you can be the final inductee into the Tuffers Hall of Fame, for being one of England's greatest-ever batsmen and my babysitter.

ACKNOWLEDGEMENTS

Thanks to:

Justyn Barnes – for putting in the hard yards and spinning up a few pearlers.

Neil Robinson and Robert Curphey – for helping to dig out the gems at Lord's Library.

Andrew Samson – for the damning bowling stats from my career!

Mike Martin – for shrewd management.

My Dawnie – for your love and encouragement.

Jonathan Taylor – for Brearley-esque guidance and encouragement throughout the project.

Tom Whiting – for some deft late cuts and tweaks in the editing department.

BIBLIOGRAPHY

Agnew, Jonathan, *Over to You, Aggers* (2nd edn, Orion, 2002)

Akram, Wasim, *Wasim: The Autobiography of Wasim Akram* (Piatkus, 1998)

Aldred, Tanya, *Freddie Flintoff: England's Hero* (Carlton Books, 2005)

Ambrose, Curtly with Richard Sydenham, *Time to Talk* (Aurum Press, 2015)

Amiss, Dennis with Michael Carey, *In Search of Runs: An Autobiography* (Stanley Paul, 1976)

Anderson, James, *Jimmy: My Story* (Simon & Schuster, 2012)

Arlott, John and Mike Brearley, *Arlott in Conversation with Mike Brearley* (Hodder & Stoughton in association with Channel Four Television, 1986)

Bacher, Ali and David Williams, *Jacques Kallis and 12 Other Great South African All-Rounders* (Penguin, 2013)

Bailey, Trevor, *Sir Gary: A Biography* (Collins, 1976)

Bandara, Sampath, *Murali: The Greatest Among the Great* (Godage International Publishers, 2010)

Barnes, Justyn and Aubrey Ganguly, *The Random History of Cricket* (Carlton Books, 2015)

Baxter, Peter and Phil McNeil (eds.), *From Arlott to Aggers: 40 years of Test Match Special* (André Deutsch, 1997)

Baxter, Peter (comp.), *The Best Views from the Boundary* (Corinthian Books, 2010)

Baxter, Peter (ed.), *Test Match Special* (Queen Anne Press, 1981)

Baxter, Peter (ed.), *Test Match Special: 50 Not Out* (BBC Books, 2007)

Benaud, Richie, *Anything But . . . An Autobiography* (Hodder & Stoughton, 1998)

Benaud, Richie, *On Reflection* (Collins Willow, 1984)

Benaud, Richie, *Over But Not Out: My Life So Far* (Hodder & Stoughton, 2010)

Blofeld, Henry, *Squeezing the Orange: Life's Great Adventure and the Cricket Too!* (Blue Door, 2013)

Blofeld, Henry, *The Packer Affair* (Collins, 1978)

Booth, Dick, *Talking of Sport: The Story of Radio Commentary* (SportsBooks, 2008)

Border, Allan, *An Autobiography* (Methuen, 1986)

Botham, Ian, *The Incredible Tests 1981* (Pelham Books, 1981)

Brearley, Mike, *Phoenix from the Ashes* (Hodder & Stoughton, 1982)

Broad, Stuart, *My World In Cricket* (Simon & Schuster, 2012)

Brodribb, Gerald, *Felix on the Bat: A Memoir of Nicholas Felix* (together with the full text of the 2nd edition of *Felix on the Bat*) (Eyre & Spottiswoode, 1962)

Browning, Mark, *Richie Benaud: Cricketer, Captain, Guru* (Kangaroo Press, 1996)

Crace, John, *Wasim and Waqar: Imran's Inheritors* (Boxtree, 1992)

Chester, Frank, *How's That!* (Hutchinson, 1956)

Constant, David, *Cricket Umpiring* (Pelham Books, 1981)

Croudy, Brian, *Famous Cricketers Series No. 27: Colin Blythe* (Association of Cricket Statisticians and Historians, 1995)

Davis, Sam, *Hedley Verity: Prince with a Piece of Leather* (The Epworth Press, 1952)

Dawson, Marc, *The Bumper Book of Cricket Useless Information* (Metro Publishing, 2009)

Dawson, Marc, *Inside Edge* (Pitch Publishing, 2015)

De Villiers, AB, *AB: The Autobiography* (Pan Macmillan, 2016)

Doust, Dudley, *Ian Botham: The Great All Rounder* (Cassell, 1980)

Eason, Alan, *The A–Z of Bradman* (Alan Eason, self-published, 2002)

Edwards, Alan, *Lionel Tennyson: Regency Buck* (Robson Books, 2001)

ESPNcricinfo, *Sachin Tendulkar: The Man Cricket Loved Back* (Penguin Books India, 2014)

Fishman, Roland, *Greg Matthews: The Spirit of Modern Cricket* (Penguin, 1986)

Flintoff, Andrew, *Ashes to Ashes* (Hodder & Stoughton, 2009)

Flintoff, Andrew, *Being Freddie* (Hodder & Stoughton, 2005)

Freddi, Cris, *The Guinness Book of Cricket Blunders* (Guinness Publishing, 1996)

Gatting, Mike with Angela Patmore, *Leading from the Front: The Autobiography of Mike Gatting* (Queen Anne Press, 1988)

Gooch, Graham with Patrick Murphy, *Captaincy* (Stanley Paul, 1992)

Gough, Darren, *Dazzler: The Autobiography* (Michael Joseph, 2001)

Greenidge, Gordon with Patrick Symes, *Gordon Greenidge: The Man in the Middle* (David & Charles, 1980)

Green, Stephen, *Lord's: The Cathedral of Cricket* (Tempus, 2003)

Greig, Joyce and Mark Greig, *Tony Greig: Love, War and Cricket* (Macmillan, 2013)

Griffiths, Edward, *Jonty: Fruits of the Spirit* (CAB, 1998)

Hadlee, Richard with Tony Francis, *Richard Hadlee at the Double: The Story of Cricket's Pacemaker* (Stanley Paul, 1985)

Haigh, Gideon, *On Warne* (Simon & Schuster, 2012)

Harris, Lord, *A Few Short Runs* (John Murray, 1921)

Hignell, Andrew, *Turnbull: A Welsh Sporting Hero* (Tempus, 2001)

Hill, Alan, *Hedley Verity: A Portrait of a Cricketer* (Kingswood Press, 1986)

Holding, Michael with Tony Cozier, *Whispering Death: The Life and Times of Michael Holding* (André Deutsch, 1993)

Hopps, David, *Free as a Bird: The Life and Times of Harold 'Dickie' Bird* (Robson Books, 1996)

Johnston, Brian, *Views from the Boundary* (BBC Books, 1990)

Knight, James, *Mark Waugh: The Biography* (Collins Willow, 2002)

Knott, Alan, *Stumper's View* (Stanley Paul, 1972)

Lewis, Tony, *Double Century: The Story of MCC and Cricket* (Guild Publishing London, 1987)

Lillee, Dennis, *Menace: The Autobiography* (Headline, 2003)

Lillee, Dennis, *Lillee: My Life in Cricket* (Methuen, 1982)

Lister, Simon, *Supercat: The Authorised Biography of Clive Lloyd* (Fairfield Books, 2007)

Marks, Vic, *The Wisden Illustrated History of Cricket* (Queen Anne Press, 1989)

Marsh, Rod, *The Gloves of Irony* (Lansdowne Press, 1982)

Marsh, Rod and Ian Brayshaw, *You'll Keep* (Hutchinson, 1975)

Martin-Jenkins, Christopher, *Ball by Ball: The Story of Cricket Broadcasting* (Grafton Books, 1990)

Martin-Jenkins, Christopher, *A Cricketing Life* (Simon & Schuster, 2012)

McDonald, Trevor, *Clive Lloyd: The Authorised Biography* (Granada, 1985)

McLean, Teresa, *The Men in White Coats: Cricket Umpires Past and Present* (Stanley Paul, 1987)

Mell, George, *The Curious Game of Cricket* (George Allen & Unwin, 1982)

Midwinter, Eric, *The Lost Seasons: Cricket in Wartime 1939–45* (Methuen, 1987)

Morris, Barry, *Bradman: What They Said about Him* (ABC Books, 2001)

Murray, Peter and Ashish Shukla, *Sachin Tendulkar: Masterful* (Rupa & Co., 2002)

Narinesingh, Clifford, *Lara: The Untamed Spirit* (Royards, 2009)

Oborne, Peter, *Wounded Tiger: A History of Cricket in Pakistan* (Simon & Schuster, 2015)

Olonga, Henry with Derek Clements, *Blood, Sweat and Treason: My Story* (Vision Sports Publishing, 2010)

Pilger, Sam, *Victory! Battle for the Ashes 2005* (Carlton Books, 2005)

Procter, Mike, *Cricket Buccaneer* (Don Nelson, Cape Town, 1974)

Rayvern Allen, David, *Arlott: The Authorised Biography* (Harper Collins, 1994)

Rayvern Allen, David, *Cricket Extras* (Guinness Books, 1988)

Rayvern Allen, David, *More Cricket Extras* (Guinness Books, 1992)

Rice, Jonathan, *The Presidents of MCC* (Methuen, 2006)

Richards, Viv, *Hitting Across the Line* (Headline, 1991)

Richards, Viv, *Sir Vivian: The Definitive Autobiography* (Michael Joseph, 2000)

Sandford, Christopher, *The Final Over: The Cricketers of Summer 2014* (Spellmount, 2014)

Scoble, Christopher, *Colin Blythe: Lament for a Legend* (SportsBooks, 2005)

Shepherd, David with David Foot, *Shep: An Autobiography* (Orion, 2001)

Sobers, Garry with Tony Cozier, *Gary Sobers' Most Memorable Matches* (Stanley Paul, 1984)

Steen, Rob, *Desmond Haynes: Lion of Barbados* (Witherby, 1993)

Symonds, Andrew with Stephen Gray, *Roy: Going for Broke* (Hardie Grant, 2006)

Tarrant, Graham, *The Lord's Taverners Fifty Greatest* (Heinemann/Quixote, 1983)

Taylor, Alfred D, *Annals of Lord's and History of the MCC* (JW Arrowsmith, 1903)

Thurlow, David, *Ken Farnes: Diary of an Essex Master* (The Parrs Wood Press, 2000)

Tibballs, Geoff, *Cricket's Greatest Characters* (JR Books, 2008)

Tossell, David, *Tony Greig* (Pitch Publishing, 2011)

Various, *Flying Stumps and Metal Bats: Cricket's Greatest Moments by the People Who Were There* (Aurum Press, 2008)

Various, *Those Summers of Cricket: Richie Benaud 1930-2015* (Hardie Grant, 2015)

Vaughan, Michael with Mike Dickson, *Time to Declare: My Autobiography* (Hodder & Stoughton, 2009)

Waddell, Dan, *Field of Shadows: The Remarkable True Story of the English Cricket Tour of Nazi Germany 1937* (Bantam Press, 2014)

Walsh, Courtney with Derek Hodgson, *Courtney: Heart of a Lion* (Lancaster Publishing, 1999)

Ward, Andrew, *Cricket's Strangest Matches* (Portico, 2010)

Waugh, Steve, *Out of My Comfort Zone: The Autobiography* (Michael Joseph, 2006)

Wilde, Simon, *Shane Warne: Portrait of a Flawed Genius* (John Murray, 2007)

Other references:

Assorted MCC newsletters and back issues of the *MCC Magazine*

Assorted back issues of *Wisden Cricket Monthly*

ESPNCricinfo.com
alloutcricket.com
cricketarchive.com
cricketcountry.com
cricindex.com
theguardian.com

INDEX